The MORMON FAMILY COOK BOOK

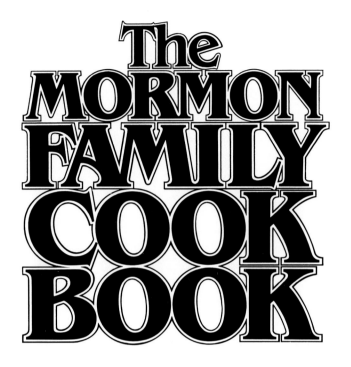

The MORMON FAMILY COOK BOOK

Helen Thackeray
Beth Nelms Brown
Maurine Hegsted

Photographs by Borge B. Andersen

Deseret Book Company
Salt Lake City, Utah

©1982 Deseret Book Company
All rights reserved
Printed in the United States of America
ISBN 0-87747-930-5
Library of Congress Catalog Card No. 82-73085
First printing September 1982
Second printing November 1982

Contents

The Mormon Family Cookbook   1

Appetizers and Beverages   5

Soups   13

Salads and Salad Dressings   19

Vegetables   33

Meat and Fish   46

Poultry and Eggs   65

Meat and Vegetable Accompaniments   81

Breads   91

Pies, Cakes, and Cookies   105

Puddings and Desserts   131

Candies   145

Canning and Preserving   151

Meet Together Often   157

Helpful Hints and Special Instructions   168

Index   173

Preface

Where do recipes come from? Very few recipes are "created"; more likely, they are "adapted." There may be only one Toll House Cookie, but there are dozens of chocolate-chip cookie favorites. We have collected a number of "perfect" pie crust recipes. The ones we use, or have tested and found "perfect" by our standards, are in this book. What is perfect for one may not be perfect for all. Ten women can make the same recipe (following the recipe "exactly," as they understand it), and each result will be different. As one author has said, "If the feeling of the art of cooking is not in your blood, the most you can expect is that what you put on the table will be *manageable*. If it is sometimes *memorable*, that will be only good luck." (Rex Stout, *The Nero Wolf Cook Book*.)

Women are, in general, pack-rats where recipes are concerned. We collect them, we use them, we add our own embellishments and simplifications, and we pass them along to friends and relatives who do the same.

The recipes in this book are either favorites of the authors, used over the years for family, entertaining, and exchanging, or are special adaptations to fit various church or other group functions. Some of the recipes bear the names of friends who contributed special favorites of their own. And, of course, some are basics—that is, they can't be that much different. A popover is a popover is a popover, even if the recipes do vary slightly.

We dare say that many people can't remember where a recipe originally came from, or just what they did to make it theirs. We claim, however, that it takes a special talent to recognize a recipe seen in print, or even in a mouth-watering photograph, that will prove to be a collector's item. We also feel proud of this collection, all good, some great, a variety of which we think you will find useful and interesting. If you find a few old favorites of your own here, be glad that you will know where to find them when you want to use them again—and that you won't have to search through a shoe box or drawer to put your hands on them.

Of the three authors of this book, Beth Brown is probably the most creative cook, and Maurine Hegsted the most scientific (after many years of teaching experimental-cooking classes at the University of Utah). Helen Thackeray frankly admits that most of her favorite recipes came right out of General Foods Test Kitchens, where she spent the largest single portion of her life and did her best cooking and tasting. All three love to cook, to experiment, and to entertain—and in *The Mormon Family Cookbook* you'll find some of our favorite recipes gathered over the years, tested by ourselves and our families and friends, and found to be special, especially for the Mormon cook.

Note: Before you use these recipes, we recommend that you check the last chapter for some special instructions and helpful hints.

◁ *Maraschino Cherries (p. 152), Graham Crackers (p. 103), Lentil Casserole (p. 37), Wheat Thins (p. 101), Fruit Ambrosia (p. 140)*

The Mormon Family Cookbook

Why a "Mormon family cookbook"? Are Mormon families different from other families? In many respects, they are very much like others; many other families will find this book valuable.

The Mormon Family Cookbook presents a collection of tested-and-proven recipes that focus on good eating for everyday family meals as well as those special occasions when the Latter-day Saints gather together. Many of the recipes fit the Mormon family especially well because of emphasis in the Church on certain aspects of everyday life and because families and family life are so important to the Saints. Recipes that are especially suited for such occasions and traditions are listed below; others may be found as you browse through the book. In most cases the emphasis is on good food that is economical (though there are some dishes that are for "strictly elegant" occasions), nutritious, and fairly simple to prepare.

"Love Thy Neighbor"

One way we show love for our neighbor is in gifts of food—a welcoming loaf of bread for the new family on the block; a casserole or salad for the family in mourning or for the family of a new mother; cookies or other treats for the elderly, the lonely, or special friends at holiday time. Whatever the dish, love is the message it carries. Here are some excellent dishes that carry well and express special concern. Pictured on page 146 are several such "gifts of love."

Cheese Balls to Go, p. 5
Pineapple Cottage Cheese Salad, p. 20
Bishop's Bread, p. 91
Apple or Zucchini Bread, p. 92
Orange Nut Bread, p. 93
Arlean's Molasses Refrigerator Muffins, p. 94
Eggnog Gems, p. 95
Viola's Sour Cream Twists, p. 99
Honey or Maple Butter, p. 103
Brownie Drops, p. 123
Noels, p. 126
Snowballs, p. 127
Caramel Corn, p. 145
Fudge Nut Crunch, p. 148
Pulled Butter Mints, p. 148
Apricot Peanut Granola, p. 149
Home-canned delicacies on pp. 151-54

Family Home Evening

Each week Mormon families gather for a special night of togetherness and fun and to study the gospel. A highlight of many family home evenings is refreshment time. In this cookbook you'll find lots of ideas for family home evening meals and treats. Children enjoy planning and serving refreshments, and waffle cookies are especially easy for them to make. Smaller children can help make punch or ice cream, while older ones will find many tempting recipes to experiment with.

Here are some suggestions to make family home evening supper or refreshment time special:

Fresh Vegetable Dip, p. 6
Gold Bricks, p. 10
Orange Julia, p. 11
Grape Juice Punch, p. 12
Tomato Bouillon, p. 12
Cream of Tomato Soup, p. 15
Layered "Masked" Salad, p. 24
Althea's Tacos, p. 52
Chicken or Turkey Enchiladas, p. 76
Company Brunch Casserole, p. 79
Banana Bread, p. 91
Delicate Dessert Pancakes, p. 97
Butterscotch Pecan Toasts, p. 101
Cheese Straws, p. 102
Cinnamon Sour Cream Coffee Cake, p. 102
Maple-Apple Flan, p. 108
Fruit in Easy Puff Shell, p. 111
Picnic Cake, p. 114
Carob Cake, p. 119
Soft Ginger Cookies, p. 125
Jumbo Raisin Cookies, p. 126
Surprise Balls, p. 127
Lemon Prune Bars, p. 128
Waffle-Iron Oatmeal Cookies, p. 130
Waffle-Iron Brownies, p. 130
Molded Ambrosia, p. 136
Favorite Fruit Ice Cream, p. 143
Easy Popcorn Balls, p. 145
Easy Chocolate Logs or Nuggets, p. 148

"Meet Together Often"

Mormons are counseled to meet together often. Gatherings of the Saints often include socializing—and good food. In this book you'll find excellent punch and cookie recipes, almost a staple in the

Mormon party diet, but you'll also find recipes tailored for Relief Society luncheons and receptions, ward dinners and picnics, and other occasions that have special meaning and follow special patterns. Suggestions are given for handling quantity recipes, planning menus, and organizing dinners for large groups, and many other helps that would apply to group feeding in almost any organization.

In addition to the section titled "Meet Together Often" (pages 157-67), the following recipes are well suited to feeding a crowd:

Tasty Egg Dip, p. 6
Mexican Platter Dip, p. 6
Ribbon Sandwiches, p. 9
Date-Nut Pinwheel Sandwiches, p. 10
Cheese Krispies, p. 10
Tropical Cooler, p. 10
Three-Fruit Slush, p. 11
Fruit Punch, p. 11
Golden Summer Punch, p. 11
Wonderful Wassail, p. 12
Layered "Masked" Salad, p. 24
Spaghetti with White Clam Sauce, p. 64

"In the Season Thereof"

The Mormons have been told in scripture, "All wholesome herbs [vegetables] God hath ordained for the constitution, nature, and use of man—every herb in the season thereof; all these to be used with prudence and thanksgiving." (Doctrine and Covenants 89:10-11.)

Church members are counseled to plant gardens. When fruits and vegetables are in season, they are more nutritious, more economical, and more flavorful. If they are fresh from your own garden or fruit trees, they taste even better. Use them to brighten every summer meal; preserve them for your year's supply to bring interest to winter meals and to keep ahead of inflation.

Floy's Green Beans, p. 34
Baked Stuffed Tomatoes, p. 41
Cottage Fried Tomatoes, p. 41
Baked Summer Squash, p. 41
Hellberg's Zucchini Goop, p. 42
Stir-Fry Dinner, p. 45
Ham, Egg, and Asparagus Casserole, p. 56
Fresh Corn Cornbread, p. 92
Summer Corn Cakes, p. 96
Rhubarb Surprise Pie, p. 108
Fresh Cherry Tart, p. 110
Afton's Fresh Peach Pie, p. 110
Fruit Shortcake, p. 116

Brown Sugar Peach Shortcake, p. 118
Home-Canned Apple Pie Filling, p. 151
Home-Canned Sour Cherry Pie Filling, p. 151
Green Tomato Mincemeat, p. 151
Raspberry Jam from Green Tomatoes, p. 152
Maraschino Cherries, p. 152
Fresh-Pack Dill Pickles, p. 152
Pickled Beets, p. 152
Fresh-Pack Dilly Beans, p. 153
Delicious Sweet Pickles, p. 153
Penny's Plum or Peach Chutney, p. 153
Garden Relish, p. 154

"Enjoy Your Year's Supply"

Mormon families are advised to store at least a year's supply of everything needed by the family in case of a disaster of one kind or another. Many cookbooks and much information have been prepared concerning the actual storage of food and how to use it. Our intention here is to include a few ideas and recipes that will help you keep your storage supply moving and your family familiar with some of your storage foods.

Split Pea Soup, p. 13
Famous Senate Bean Soup, p. 14
Tabouli (Cracked Wheat) Salad, p. 28
Easy Baked Beans, p. 33
Country-style Baked Beans, p. 33
Calico Bean Bake, p. 33
Swedish Baked Beans, p. 33
Classic Baked Beans, p. 34
Salted Beans, p. 34
Green Beans Orientale, p. 34
Dried Corn Pudding, p. 36
Lentil Burgers, p. 36
Baked Lentils, p. 37
Lentil Casserole, p. 37
"Low Energy" Cooked Wheat, p. 87
Spanish Wheat, p. 87
Armenian Pilaf, p. 87
Bulgur, p. 88
Deluxe Brown Rice, p. 88
Dried Corn Bread, p. 93
Wheat Thins, p. 101
Graham Crackers, p. 103
"Any Old Fruit" Loaves, p. 119
Jam Cookies, p. 125
Breakfast Cookies, p. 125
Canned Fruit Ambrosia, p. 140
Fruit Snack Squares, p. 140
Warm Spicy Fruit, p. 140
Peanut Butter Chews, p. 149

Pioneer Heritage

Many recipes of the Mormon pioneers are still enjoyed in Mormon households. Those found in this book have been tested to work with today's ingredients and measurements. For a real taste treat, as well as a better appreciation of the rich heritage available for all members of the Church through the early pioneers, try any or all of the following:

Potato Soup (Poor Man's Soup), p. 13
Fresh Tomato Soup, p. 14
Garden Lettuce with Cream and Sugar, p. 23
Salted Beans, p. 34
Pioneer Scalloped Potatoes, p. 39
Yorkshire Pudding, Custard Type, p. 81
Dumplings for Stew, p. 81
Milk Gravy, p. 84
Egg Noodles, p. 87
Wheat Muffins, p. 94
Suet Biscuits, p. 95
Pioneer Cake, p. 113
Old-time Poundcake, p. 116
Spanish Cake, p. 118
Raisin Cupcakes, p. 119
Grandma Grover's Cake Doughnuts, p. 120
Old-fashioned Rice Pudding, p. 131
Bread Pudding, p. 131
Pearl's Lemon Pudding, p. 131
Vanilla Pudding Sauce, p. 134
Grandma's Fruit Cobbler, p. 141
Old-fashioned Tomato Preserves, p. 154

"Hurry-up" Meals

In today's world, Mormons, like everyone else, are busy—with family and church, school and community, social activities and work. Meals to prepare quickly or ahead of time, shortcuts for "made from scratch" favorites, and quick-mix recipes are all appreciated. Among the excellent recipes for hurry-up meals in this cookbook are the following:

Quick Minestrone, p. 15
Quick Corn Chowder, p. 15
Hurry-up Clam Chowder, p. 16
Super Salmon Soup, p. 16
Savory Cabbage, p. 35
Quick Vegetable Medley, p. 44
Quick Beef Goulash, p. 48
Danish Chop Suey, p. 50
Speedy Spaghetti, p. 53
Chili Supper in a Hurry, p. 53
Mexican Skillet, p. 54
Yam and Sausage Skillet, p. 57
Chicken and Rice Casserole, p. 70
Thirty-Minute Hamburger Buns, p. 99

Crusty French Bread Pizza, p. 102
Blender Chocolate Mousse, p. 134
Heavenly Fresh Strawberry Dessert, p. 137
Easy Fruit Frappé, p. 143
Fudge Nut Crunch, p. 148

Strictly Elegant

There are times when Mormon cooks enjoy preparing elegant, gourmet-type dishes, party foods that impress guests. We all like dishes that look difficult to prepare but are really easy—but we also occasionally enjoy preparing elegant recipes even if we have to work at them. Here are some that should please the most discriminating palate.

Olive-Nut Cheese Ball, p. 5
Hot Crabmeat Appetizer, p. 9
Chilled Cucumber Cream Soup, p. 17
Creamy Borscht, Hotel Utah Style, p. 18
Avocado Strawberry Ring, p. 20
Molded Sour Cream and Cucumber Salad, p. 20
Cantaloupe Salad with French Dressing, p. 21
Creamy Romaine Salad, p. 23
Buffet Salad, p. 25
Chicken Salad Exotic, p. 25
Crab and Avocado Salad, p. 27
Super Deluxe Marinated Vegetables, p. 30
Brussels Sprouts Supreme, p. 35
Stuffed Mushrooms, p. 37
Spinach-Artichoke Heart Casserole, p. 41
Beef Fillet with Mushroom Sauce, p. 46
Cranberry Pork and Pears, p. 54
Smothered Halibut, p. 58
Swordfish Steak Meuniere, p. 58
Salmon Steaks with Mustard Dill Sauce, p. 59
Golden Salmon Bake, p. 61
Shrimp Curry, p. 62
Party Shrimp Casserole, p. 63
Coquilles Saint-Jacques, p. 64
Chicken Breasts in Caper Sauce, p. 69
Curried Baked Chicken with Coconut, p. 71
Exotic Oven Rice, p. 88
Lemon Angel Pie, p. 112
Baklava, p. 112
Linzer Cookies, p. 127
Pecan Pie Cookies, p. 128
LaRue's Sugar Plum Pudding, p. 133
Banana Split Cake Dessert, p. 133
Creme Caramel, p. 134
Rote Grutze (Fruit Soup), p. 137
Ruby (Raspberry) Sauce, p. 140
    Ruby Grapefruit, p. 140
    Ruby Sherbet, p. 140
    Peach Cardinale, p. 141

Appetizers and Beverages

Cheese Balls to Go

3 gift balls

½ pound Old English sharp cheese, shredded
2 packages (8 ounces each) cream cheese, softened
2 ounces (half of a 4-ounce square) Kraft Blue cheese
1 tablespoon Worcestershire sauce
4 green onions, finely chopped
½ cup nuts, finely chopped
½ bunch parsley, finely chopped

Combine all ingredients except nuts and parsley, and mix well. Refrigerate for at least ½ hour, or until firm (overnight, if possible). Shape into three balls. Combine nuts and parsley, and spread on bread board. Roll cheese balls in this mixture until they are evenly covered. Chill. When ready to use or deliver, wrap in clear plastic, then in gift wrap, and tie with a gay bow.

	6 Balls	9 Balls	12 Balls	15 Balls
Old English cheese	1 pound	1½ pounds	2 pounds	2½ pounds
Cream cheese, 8-ounce packages	4 packages	6 packages	8 packages	10 packages
Blue cheese	4 ounces	6 ounces	8 ounces	10 ounces
Green onions	8	12	16	20
Worcestershire sauce	2 tablespoons	3 tablespoons	¼ cup	5 tablespoons
Nuts	1 cup	1½ cups	2 cups	2½ cups
Parsley	1 bunch	1½ bunches	2 bunches	2½ bunches

Shrimp Cheese Ball

1 large or 2 small balls (30 to 40 servings)

2 packages (8 ounces each) cream cheese
1 jar (5 ounces) sharp Old English cheese spread
½ cup grated sharp Cheddar cheese
1 tablespoon lemon juice
1 teaspoon garlic salt
1 teaspoon chives, fresh, frozen, or dried
1 tablespoon salad dressing (Miracle Whip)
1 can (6½-7 ounces) small shrimp, drained
Nuts or parsley, chopped

Soften cream cheese, and combine with cheese spread. Add Cheddar cheese, lemon juice, garlic salt, chives, and salad dressing and combine well; mix shrimp in gently. Shape into 1 large or 2 small balls, and roll in chopped nuts or parsley. Chill thoroughly.

Easy Cheese Ball

1 large ball (30 to 40 servings)

1 jar (5 ounces) bacon cheese spread
1 jar (5 ounces) Old English cheese spread
1 jar (5 ounces) Roka Blue cheese spread
1 package (3 ounces) cream cheese
½ cup chopped nuts

In small bowl of electric mixer, soften and combine cheeses in the order listed; blend thoroughly. Cover bowl and chill overnight, or longer. When ready to use, scrape cheese onto chopped nuts on waxed paper. Mold into a ball, using the waxed paper, and cover the ball evenly with nuts. Use a few more nuts, if necessary.

Chopped parsley instead of nuts makes a handsome cover, but don't use it unless you expect the cheese ball to be eaten at one party. The parsley doesn't keep well; the cheese and nuts do. Chill thoroughly before serving with a variety of crackers.

Olive-Nut Cheese Ball

1 large ball
30 to 40 servings

1 package (8 ounces) cream cheese
2 packages (4 ounces each) blue cheese
¼ pound margarine
1 can (2½ ounces) chopped or sliced ripe olives
1 tablespoon chives, fresh, frozen, or dried
1 cup nuts, chopped

In large bowl of electric mixer, blend softened cheeses and margarine. Mix well. Add well-drained olives, chives, and about ¼ cup nuts. Chill thoroughly (overnight). Form cold mixture into a ball, then roll in remaining nuts. Serve as a spread for crackers. Delicious!

This cheese ball will divide nicely into two smaller balls that make great "neighbor" gifts.

Curry Vegetable Dip

1¼ cups

½ medium onion, or to taste
1 cup mayonnaise (use part yogurt, if desired)
2 tablespoons horseradish
1 scant teaspoon curry powder
Salt, pepper, and paprika to taste

Grate onion. Mix with remaining ingredients, seasoning to taste. Chill. Let stand a while to blend flavors. Serve with a variety of raw vegetables.

Green Chilies Dip

About 2 cups

½ cup onion, minced
2 tablespoons butter or margarine
1 can (4 ounces) peeled green chilies, seeded, chopped
1 cup solid pack tomatoes, drained, chopped
½ teaspoon salt
Dash of pepper
½ pound Monterey Jack cheese, cubed

Cook onion in butter over medium heat about 5 minutes, stirring often. Stir in chilies, tomatoes, salt, and pepper. Simmer until most of liquid has evaporated. Stir in cheese, and continue stirring over low heat, until cheese is melted. Serve hot with corn chips or raw vegetables.

Fresh Vegetable Dip

4 cups

1 pint sour cream
1 pint mayonnaise
1 bunch green onions, finely chopped
3 tablespoons dry parsley flakes or ½ cup fresh parsley, finely chopped
3 tablespoons Lawry's Seasoned Salt
3 tablespoons dill weed, crumbled

Mix all ingredients together. Chill. Serve with fresh vegetables, such as carrot and celery sticks, cucumber and zucchini slices or wedges, mushrooms, cauliflower and broccoli florets, and green pepper strips.

Mexican Platter Dip

3 ripe avocados
2 tablespoons lemon juice
1 teaspoon garlic salt
3 drops Tabasco
1 cup sour cream
½ cup mayonnaise
1 package (1¼ ounces) taco seasoning mix
1 can (30 ounces) refried beans
1 bunch green onion, chopped (use part of tops)
2 medium tomatoes, skinned, seeded, and chopped
1 can (2½ ounces) sliced ripe olives
4 ounces sharp Cheddar cheese, shredded (about 1 cup)
Corn or tortilla chips

Peel, pit, and mash avocados; add lemon juice, garlic salt, and Tabasco. Cover and chill.

Combine sour cream, mayonnaise, and taco seasoning mix. Cover and chill.

To assemble dip: on a large round platter or serving dish, spread beans in an even layer, leaving 1-inch space all around the edge. Top with avocado mixture, leaving bean layer exposed all around. Top with sour cream mixture, leaving avocado mixture exposed all around. Sprinkle with green onion, tomatoes, ripe olives, and Cheddar cheese. Serve as a dip with corn chips or tortilla chips, or serve onto plates in pie-shaped wedges.

Tasty Egg Dip

About 2 cups

1 package (8 ounces) cream cheese
3 tablespoons unflavored yogurt, sour cream, or buttermilk
2 tablespoons mayonnaise
1 tablespoon lemon juice
1 teaspoon Worcestershire sauce
1 teaspoon Dijon mustard
½ teaspoon seasoned salt
⅛ teaspoon red hot-pepper sauce
1 to 2 tablespoons horseradish, cream style
1 tablespoon chopped chives or green onions
2 tablespoons finely chopped celery
2 tablespoons chopped parsley
3 hard-cooked eggs, diced

Beat cheese until smooth; add yogurt, mayonnaise, lemon juice, Worcestershire sauce, mustard, salt, hot-pepper sauce, horseradish, chives, celery, and parsley, mixing well. Blend in eggs. Chill.

Serve with crisp vegetables, such as carrots and celery strips, radishes, mushrooms, cauliflower and broccoli florets, and cherry tomatoes.

Chicken Liver Paté

1 quart or 2 pint molds

    1 pound chicken livers
    1 medium onion, chopped
    2 tablespoons butter
    3 hard-cooked eggs
    2 packages (3 ounces each) cream cheese, softened
    1 tablespoon Worcestershire sauce
    1 teaspoon salt
    ½ teaspoon pepper or lemon pepper
    2 tablespoons lemon juice
    Sliced olives, pimiento strips, or minced parsley

Sauté chicken livers and chopped onion in butter until livers are lightly browned (about 5 minutes). Place livers, onion, and eggs in blender or food processor and blend until smooth. Combine one package of cream cheese with Worcestershire sauce, salt, pepper, and lemon juice. Add liver mixture and mix well. Shape into molds and chill. When ready to serve, unmold onto serving plate and "frost" with remaining cream cheese. Decorate with olives, pimiento strips, and parsley as desired. Serve spread on toast or crackers.

Mediterranean Butter

350 degrees F.
About 2 cups

    1 large eggplant
    ½ cup minced onion
    ¼ cup olive oil
    ¼ cup tomato paste
    1 tablespoon lemon juice
    Salt and pepper to taste
    1 cucumber, peeled and sliced (optional)
    1 slice lemon (optional)

Bake eggplant whole until black and soft to the touch (about 40 minutes). Peel, then chop very fine.
    In a large frying pan, sauté onion in oil until tender but not brown. Add eggplant and tomato paste. Cook, stirring often, until thick, about 15 minutes. Add lemon juice, salt, and pepper. Chill thoroughly. Pile in chilled bowl and garnish with cucumber and lemon, if desired. Serve as a help-yourself spread, delicious on crackers.

Mexican Butter

1½ cups

    2 ripe avocados
    1 large ripe tomato, peeled
    1 small clove garlic
    1 teaspoon salt
    1 teaspoon chili powder
    1 tablespoon lemon juice

Peel avocados. Chop finely. Discard juicy pulp and seeds of tomatoes, and chop remainder. Crush garlic in salt until a liquid is formed. Combine avocado, tomato, garlic mixture, chili powder, and lemon juice, mixing well. Serve at once with hot corn chips.

Pecan Spread

8-inch pie plate
350 degrees F.

    ½ cup chopped pecans
    2 tablespoons butter
    ½ teaspoon salt
    1 package (8 ounces) cream cheese
    2 tablespoons milk
    1 jar (2½ ounces) sliced dried beef, slivered
    2 tablespoons minced green pepper
    2 tablespoons dehydrated onion flakes or ½
      medium-size onion, chopped
    ½ cup sour cream

Heat pecans in butter and salt in frying pan until crisp. Blend cream cheese and milk. Add dried beef, green pepper, onion flakes, and sour cream. Spoon into pie plate. Top with nuts. Bake 20 minutes. Serve hot with crackers.

Jalapeno Jelly

About 8 cups

    ¾ cup cider vinegar
    ¾ cup apple juice
    5½ cups sugar
    4 jalapeno peppers, seeded and cored, or 1 can
      (6 ounces) canned peppers
    2 bell peppers, seeded and cored
    1 pouch liquid pectin (Certo)
    Green food coloring (optional)

Mix vinegar, apple juice, and sugar. Stir well. Add peppers and bring to a boil. Boil hard for 10 minutes, stirring often. Remove from heat; add pouch of pectin and mix well. Add 2 to 3 drops of green food coloring, if desired, and strain into sterilized jars. Seal with paraffin. To serve, dip a small amount of the jelly onto a knife and into softened cream cheese. Spread on a small snack cracker and then eat in one bite.

Hot Crab Meat Appetizer

8-inch pie plate
375 degrees F.

    1 package (8 ounces) cream cheese
    1 flat can crab meat, drained and flaked
    2 tablespoons finely chopped onion
    2 tablespoons milk
    1 teaspoon cream-style horseradish
    Dash of pepper and salt
    ¼ to ½ cup sliced almonds, toasted

Combine softened cream cheese, crab meat, onion, milk, horseradish, and seasonings, mixing until well blended. Spoon into pie pan or oven-proof dish; sprinkle with nuts. Bake 15 minutes. Serve hot as a dip or a spread with crackers, chips, or raw vegetables.
Variation: Instead of crab, use an 8-ounce can of clams and a sprinkle of dill. Omit almonds.

Hot Shrimp Rolls

350 degrees F.
24 rolls

    1 can (7 ounces) shrimp
    1 can (4 ounces) chopped ripe olives
    1 ripe avocado, chopped
    ½ cup sour cream
    ⅓ cup mayonnaise or salad dressing
    4 tablespoons lemon juice
    2 tablespoons chopped parsley
    ½ teaspoon garlic salt
    12 hard dinner rolls
    4 tablespoons butter, melted
    6 slices Swiss cheese, cut into fourths
    24 tomato slices (approximately 5 tomatoes)

Combine shrimp, ripe olives, avocado, sour cream, mayonnaise, lemon juice, parsley, and garlic salt. Cover and chill. When ready to serve, slice rolls in half and brush each half with melted butter. Place one small square of Swiss cheese on each roll and top with a heaping tablespoon of the shrimp mixture. Top with a tomato slice. Bake on a cookie sheet for 20 minutes or until lightly browned. Serve hot.

Hot Crab Rolls

In place of shrimp, use a 7-ounce can of crab, or fresh crab meat. This may also be made on a whole loaf of French bread, sliced horizontally. Arrange the cheese slices on the bread, and pile the crab mixture on top; top with tomato slices. For a whole loaf, bake about 30 minutes and slice into pieces to serve.

Ribbon Sandwiches

24 small tea sandwiches

    ½ to ¾ cup butter, room temperature
    1 loaf (24 ounces) sandwich bread, sliced
    1 pound ham, cooked, coarsely ground
    ¼ cup pickle relish (preferably red)
    2 tablespoons pimiento, chopped
    1 cup salad dressing
    9 hard-cooked eggs, chopped
    ½ teaspoon salt
    ¾ cup salad dressing or mayonnaise
    ½ cup pickle relish (green)
    ¼ cup parsley or chives, chopped

Cream butter, then spread on one side of each slice of bread. Mix ham, red pickle relish, pimiento, and 1 cup salad dressing; adjust seasonings. Spread on one-third of buttered slices of bread. Mix chopped eggs, salt, ¾ cup salad dressing or mayonnaise, green pickle relish, and parsley. Spread on another one-third of buttered slices of bread. Stack each sandwich as follows: bread with egg filling, bread with ham filling, then slice of buttered bread with buttered side against ham filling. Press evenly but lightly. Wrap well in plastic wrap or aluminum foil and refrigerate. When chilled and ready to use, with sharp knife cut off crusts on the four sides of each 3-slice sandwich. Cut each slice into thirds or fourths. Serve with cut side down, displaying layers of filling and bread. For a variation, use whole wheat bread or use both white and whole wheat loaves.

To serve at a buffet table as a whole decorated loaf, use sandwich loaf sliced lengthwise in 3, 4, or 5 slices. Spread butter and fillings the whole length, repeating or adding other fillings. Chill; cut off crusts. Frost sides and top with softened cream cheese to which is added a little milk. Decorate top with parsley, pimiento, or olive circles. Slice at the buffet table.

Date-Nut Pinwheel Sandwiches

48 sandwiches

    1 whole wheat sandwich loaf, sliced lengthwise
    1½ packages (8-ounce size) cream cheese, softened
    1½ cups chopped dates
    1½ cups crushed pineapple, drained thoroughly
    1 cup finely chopped nuts
    Butter or margarine

Unsliced sandwich bread usually must be purchased at a specialty bakery and ordered ahead. Have it sliced lengthwise into six long slices, with crusts removed. When ready to use, trim end crusts. Flatten each slice slightly with rolling pin.

Combine cream cheese, dates, pineapple, and nuts. Spread bread with butter and then with filling.

Roll slices tightly as for a jelly roll, starting with the short end. Wrap each roll in plastic wrap. Chill one hour or more. (Recipe may be made to this point a day ahead.) Cut each roll into 8 sandwiches. An electric knife does the job easily, or use a very sharp bread knife.

Cheese Krispies

350 degrees F.
About 2 dozen

    ¼ pound butter or margarine
    1 cup (4 ounces) shredded sharp Cheddar cheese
    ½ teaspoon Tabasco
    Dash of salt
    1 cup flour
    1 cup Rice Krispies

Blend softened butter and cheese. Add Tabasco, salt, and flour. Blend well. Add Rice Krispies. Form into small balls. Bake on lightly greased baking sheet about 15 minutes.

Gold Bricks

400 degrees F.
48 servings

    2 loaves unsliced sandwich bread
    1 pound butter, softened
    1 pound extra sharp cheese, grated

Cut crusts from bread. Cut bread into 1×1×2-inch pieces. Blend softened butter and cheese, and coat bread pieces on all sides. Place, not touching, on a greased baking sheet and bake for 20 minutes,

turning once. The cheese should be melted and bubbly all over and the bread slightly crusty. Cool slightly; eat with fingers as accompaniment to fruit slices, soup, or tangy vegetables. Bricks may be frozen before baking and then baked at the last minute.

Pineapple Eggnog Punch

1 gallon

    2 quarts dairy eggnog
    2 cans (18 ounces each) pineapple juice, chilled
    1 quart ginger ale, chilled
    Miniature Sherbet Cups (below)

In punch bowl combine eggnog, pineapple juice, and ginger ale. Float Miniature Sherbet Cups on top, or use a small scoop of sherbet. Serve immediately.

Miniature Sherbet Cups

12 cups

    12 maraschino cherries
    1 quart lime sherbet, softened

Cut cherries in half. In 2 miniature 12-cup muffin pans, place cherry halves, cut side down. Fill cups with sherbet; freeze. Unmold by loosening around sides. If necessary, dip pan quickly in warm water.

Tropical Cooler

5 quarts

    1 envelope raspberry-flavor instant Kool-Aid
    1 cup sugar
    3 quarts cold water
    4 fully ripe bananas (optional)
    1 can (6 ounces) frozen lemonade concentrate
    1 can (6 ounces) frozen orange juice concentrate
    1 can (1 pint 2 ounces) pineapple juice, chilled
    1 quart ginger ale, chilled

Dissolve instant Kool-Aid and sugar in water. Mash bananas or blend in electric blender. Add bananas, lemonade and orange juice concentrates, and pineapple juice to raspberry-flavored water. Stir or whip until frothy and well blended. Add ginger ale. Pour over a block of ice in punch bowl and serve.

Note: For ease in blending bananas, add a little of the sugar mixture to blender. Do not prepare bananas in advance unless you add them immediately to the fruit concentrates and juice.

Orange Julia

6 servings

    2¼ cups crushed ice
    1½ cups cold water
    1½ cups instant nonfat dry milk powder
    1 can (6 ounces) frozen orange juice concentrate
    2 tablespoons sugar
    ¼ teaspoon vanilla

Combine all ingredients in blender and whirl until frothy. Pour into chilled glasses and serve at once.

Sassy Slush

8 servings, ½ cup each

    1 cup sugar
    1 cup water
    1 can (18 ounces) grapefruit juice, or use grapefruit sections and juice
    1 cup orange juice
    2 tablespoons lemon juice

Dissolve sugar in water. Add other ingredients. Freeze to a slush in a bowl or ice-cube tray. Spoon into serving dishes and serve immediately.

Three-Fruit Slush

8 quarts (30 8-ounce servings or 60 punch cups)

    1 can (6 ounces) frozen orange juice concentrate
    1 can (6 ounces) frozen lemonade concentrate
    1 cup sugar
    2 cups water
    ½ cup fresh lemon juice
    4 to 6 bananas (about 2 cups mashed)
    3 to 4 quarts ginger ale, chilled

Reconstitute orange juice and lemonade concentrates, following directions on cans; add sugar, water, and fresh lemon juice. Whirl bananas in blender with part of fruit juice. Add to juices; mix. Freeze in freezer trays, stirring occasionally to add air into mixture. To serve, put ¼ cup of slush into a glass. Fill with ginger ale.

To store, spoon slush into container, cover, and put in freezer. Slush will remain frozen about 6 hours if taken in an ice chest to a picnic. Serve as above.

Variation 1: Add 2 to 4 packages (10 ounces each) frozen raspberries.

Variation 2: Omit bananas. Add 1 package raspberry drink mix (such as Kool-Aid) sweetened.

Golden Summer Punch

5 quarts

    1 can (12 ounces) frozen orange juice concentrate
    1 can (12 ounces) frozen lemonade concentrate
    1 can (46 ounces) unsweetened pineapple juice
    1 can (46 ounces) apricot nectar
    2 cups unsweetened grapefruit juice
    ⅔ cup sugar
    1 quart ginger ale, chilled
    Orange and lemon slices, if desired

Combine juices and sugar and stir until sugar is dissolved. Add ginger ale and serve over crushed ice, garnished with lemon and orange slices.

Banana Orange Refresher

6 to 8 servings, about 1 cup each

    3 or 4 very ripe bananas
    1 can (6 ounces) frozen orange juice concentrate
    1 to 2 quarts ginger ale or Sprite, chilled

Mash bananas thoroughly; add cold or partly frozen orange juice concentrate and mix well. Add ginger ale or Sprite. Serve over crushed ice.

To store for future use, freeze banana-orange mixture in ice-cube trays. When frozen solid, transfer to plastic bags. When ready to serve, add 2 or 3 chunks to a glass, and add carbonated drink to taste. Cubes may be whirled in a blender to form a slush.

Fruit Punch

About 6 gallons (160 5-ounce servings)

    4½ gallons cold water
    5 cans (6 ounces each) concentrate for limeade or lemonade, thawed
    2½ quarts cranberry juice cocktail
    5½ pounds (13 cups) orange-flavor Tang

Combine water, limeade or lemonade, and cranberry juice cocktail in a large container. Add Tang and stir until dissolved. Chill. Serve in punch cups or pour over crushed ice in tall glasses. Garnish with lime slices or mint leaves, if desired.

Variation: Use pineapple juice instead of cranberry juice cocktail.

Grape Juice Punch

3 quarts

    1 quart grape juice, chilled
    1 can (6 ounces) frozen lemonade concentrate
    2 to 4 cups cold water, as desired, for dilution
    1 quart ginger ale, chilled

Combine ingredients. Serve over ice. For a float, omit ice and add a scoop of vanilla ice cream.

Wonderful Wassail

18 6-ounce servings

    1 can (46 ounces) apple juice
    1 cinnamon stick
    ½ teaspoon nutmeg
    1 can (6 ounces) frozen lemonade concentrate
    1 can (6 ounces) frozen orange juice concentrate
    1 can (46 ounces) pineapple juice
    ½ cup honey or sugar
    ¼ cup lemon juice
    Orange slices (optional)

Heat apple juice, cinnamon stick, and nutmeg to boiling point. Reduce heat and simmer for 15 minutes. Add lemonade and orange juice concentrates, pineapple juice, honey, and lemon juice; simmer. Remove cinnamon stick, and serve hot. Garnish with orange slices, if desired. If beverage simmers a long time and becomes too thick or concentrated, water may be added.

Hot Tomato Zip

25 6-ounce servings

    4 cans (10½ ounces each) condensed tomato soup
    2 cans (46 ounces each) tomato juice
    2 soup cans water
    ½ cup lemon juice
    2 tablespoons sugar, or to taste
    2 tablespoons Worcestershire sauce, or to taste
    ½ teaspoon celery salt, or to taste
    Whipped cream, if desired

Combine all ingredients except whipped cream in large saucepan and heat slowly to boiling, stirring until smooth. Taste and adjust seasonings as desired. Serve hot in cups or mugs with a dab of whipped cream.

Tomato Bouillon

About 1½ quarts

    1 can (10½ ounces) beef bouillon or
      chicken soup stock*
    1 can (10½ ounces) water*
    1 can (20 ounces) tomato juice
    1 onion, sliced
    2 sticks celery, cut in several pieces
    Red pepper
    Salt

Simmer all ingredients together for 15 minutes and strain. Taste and adjust seasonings. Serve very hot, with buttered and toasted Triscuits. Put a slice of lemon that has been dipped in minced parsley in each cup of soup, if desired, or serve cold as an appetizer.

*Or use bouillon cubes or soup base and 3 cups water.

Soups

Beef Stock for Soup

8 to 10 servings

> 1 pound beef soup bone
> 1½ to 2 pounds beef short ribs
> 1 small onion, sliced
> 1 carrot, sliced
> 2 or 3 ribs of celery, sliced
> A few celery tops, if available
> ½ bay leaf
> 1 tablespoon beef soup base or 3 beef
>   bouillon cubes
> Cold water, to cover (about 3 quarts)

Combine ingredients in a 5- to 6-quart soup kettle. Bring to boil slowly and boil gently until meat is tender and begins to separate from bones. This will take about 2 hours. Remove foam as it forms on surface (a soup strainer or a piece of dampened paper towel will work fairly well).

Remove soup meat and bones to a platter and let cool. Strain soup through fine strainer or coarse cheese cloth dampened and set in strainer. (We like to prepare the stock to this point, then let it stand overnight in refrigerator; fat will rise to surface and harden so that it can all be removed. If you prefer, a fat skimmer or whisk may be used to remove what can be captured from the hot soup.)

When ready to prepare soup, return stock to the kettle and add desired ingredients. Cut the meat from the soup bones; cut away the fat, and slice the lean into bite-size pieces. Reheat in the soup with vegetables for a main meal vegetable soup. This stock and this meat make our very favorite base for hearty home-made vegetable soup. Add vegetables as desired, or use the following recipe.

Main Meal Vegetable Soup

> 3 medium potatoes, peeled and cut in chunks
> 3 carrots, peeled and sliced
> ⅓ cup pearl barley
> ½ small head cabbage, chopped or shredded
> 1 or 2 white turnips (optional)
> 1 pint or 1 can (16 ounces) tomatoes or tomato juice
> ½ package frozen green beans (optional)
> 1 or 2 small zucchini, scrubbed and cut in chunks
> Cooked meat

Prepare beef stock (above). Taste to be sure it has a hearty flavor. If not, boil down to about 2 quarts. To boiling stock, add potatoes, carrots, barley, cabbage, turnips, and tomatoes. Cook until vegetables are partially cooked. Add green beans and zucchini for last 10 to 15 minutes of cooking. Add cooked meat last 5 minutes.

Potato Soup
(Poor Man's Soup)

4 to 6 servings

> 3 to 4 slices bacon
> ½ cup onion, chopped
> 4 potatoes, sliced and cooked until just tender
> 5 cups milk
> Salt and pepper

Fry bacon until crisp; drain well and crumble. Cook onion in 2 tablespoons bacon fat until soft but not browned. Add potatoes and milk; heat. Taste to correct seasonings. Sprinkle crumbled bacon in each bowl as served.

Split Pea Soup

10 to 12 servings

> 1 pound (2⅓ cups) green or yellow split peas or
>   lentils
> 2 quarts cold water
> Meaty ham bone or 1 to 2 cups cubed ham
> ¾ cup chopped onion
> ¾ cup chopped celery
> ¾ cup diced carrots
> 1 large bay leaf
> 1 teaspoon salt
> 1 teaspoon cumin (optional)
> 1 clove garlic, pressed (optional)

Combine all ingredients in a heavy kettle. Cover and bring to boil. Simmer on low heat for about 2 hours, or until vegetables are tender. Remove ham bone; cut away all ham bits to go into the soup.

You will find this to be a very thick soup, but nicely condensed in case you wish to freeze all or part of it. Dilute for use with hot water, milk, or light cream. For lentil soup, dilute with chicken broth, diluted cream of tomato soup, or water. Remove bay leaf before freezing or serving.

If you don't have a ham bone, you may use sliced and browned-in-butter frankfurters, sliced Vienna sausage, crisp bacon bits, or seasoned croutons served atop the soup to enhance the flavor. If using lentils, 2 cups canned tomatoes plus ½ teaspoon sweet basil improves color and flavor.

Variation: Add a small can (2½ ounces) ripe olives the last minute or two of cooking.

Famous Senate Bean Soup

3 quarts (10 to 12 servings)

    1 pound dry navy beans
    1 meaty ham bone or 1½ pounds ham hocks
    1 cup chopped onion
    2 garlic cloves, minced
    1 cup chopped celery
    ⅔ cup mashed potato flakes
    ¼ cup chopped parsley
    1½ teaspoons salt
    ½ teaspoon pepper
    1 teaspoon nutmeg
    1 teaspoon oregano
    1 teaspoon basil
    1 bay leaf

In large kettle, cover beans with 6 to 8 cups water. Bring to a boil and cook 2 minutes. Remove from heat and cover; let stand one hour. Drain; add 2 quarts water and the ham bone. Bring to a boil again and simmer about 1½ hours, until beans are tender. Add remaining ingredients and simmer another 20 to 30 minutes. Remove ham bone and trim off meat. Return meat to soup and serve. Freeze leftovers, if desired.

French Onion Soup

6 servings

    ¼ cup butter or margarine
    2 cups sliced onions
    4 to 5 cups bouillon (use 2 10½-ounce cans beef
        bouillon, diluted, or make with beef soup base
        and water)
    Salt and pepper
    Worcestershire sauce
    French bread (the heavy kind is best)
    1 cup grated cheese (Gruyere, Swiss, or Parmesan)

Heat butter in a large, heavy saucepan; add onions. Stir and simmer on medium heat until onions are soft and richly browned (takes about 45 minutes). Add bouillon. Season to taste with salt, pepper, and Worcestershire sauce. Pour the hot soup into earthenware bowls or soup plates. Float a slice of toasted French bread on top, and sprinkle with grated cheese. If desired, put soup bowls on a shallow baking pan and place under the broiler until cheese melts a bit. Or sprinkle cheese on toast and broil on cookie sheet until cheese is golden before placing on soup.

Creamy French Onion Soup

When onions are browned, stir in ⅓ cup flour. Then add bouillon and salt and pepper. Simmer 20 to 30 minutes. Proceed with toast and cheese as above.

Fresh Tomato Soup

8 servings

    8 or 9 medium firm ripe tomatoes, skinned and
        coarsely chopped
    ¼ cup butter or margarine
    ½ teaspoon baking soda
    1 teaspoon salt
    1 tablespoon sugar
    ¼ cup butter or margarine
    ¼ cup flour
    2 teaspoons salt
    2 quarts rich milk (or part half-and-half)
    ⅛ teaspoon pepper, or to taste

Simmer tomatoes in a large saucepan for 10 minutes. Remove from heat and add ¼ cup butter, soda, 1 teaspoon salt, and sugar. Let cool during preparation of next step.

Melt the remaining ¼ cup butter in large kettle. Add flour and 2 teaspoons salt. Add milk; heat and stir to boiling point.

Combine the two mixtures and heat slowly. Add salt, if needed, and pepper to taste. Serve as soon as soup is piping hot.

This will be a thin soup. If you prefer, the flour could be eliminated entirely, or you could double the flour for a thicker consistency. This soup is not a smooth mixture, but the chunky tomato pieces add interest. Fresh garden tomatoes give it a delicious flavor.

Cream of Tomato Soup

About 1 quart (4 servings)

¼ cup (½ cube) margarine or butter
⅓ cup flour
2 cups water
¼ teaspoon sweet basil
¼ teaspoon onion salt
¼ teaspoon celery salt
Pinch of garlic salt
Pinch of white pepper
⅔ cup instant non-fat dry milk
2 cups tomato juice

In a 2-quart saucepan melt margarine; add flour, and blend. Add 1½ cups water; stir, on medium heat, until thickened. Reduce heat to simmer. Add seasonings; cover and cook 5 minutes. Blend non-fat dry milk with remaining water; stir into thickened mixture. Increase heat to medium; add tomato juice* slowly, stirring well. Garnish with toasted bread cubes or shredded cheese.

Reserve some of the tomato juice if soup shows indications of curdling.

Quick Minestrone

About 3½ quarts (12 servings)

5 slices bacon, cut in 1-inch pieces
1 medium onion, sliced
2 cloves garlic, pressed or minced
1 jar (15 ounces) spaghetti sauce
6 cups water
2 teaspoons beef soup base, or use 2 or 3 beef bouillon cubes
½ cup sliced celery
½ cup sliced carrots
2 cups coarsely chopped cabbage
1 teaspoon salt
¼ teaspoon pepper
2 small zucchini, cut in thick slices or chunks
1 can (16 ounces) kidney beans, drained
¼ cup macaroni (vermicelli or alphabets)
1 tablespoon chopped parsley
Parmesan cheese (optional)

In a heavy kettle, sauté bacon until slightly crisp. Add onion slices and garlic; cook until onion is transparent. Add spaghetti sauce, water, soup base, celery, carrots, cabbage, salt, and pepper. Bring to a boil, then simmer gently on low heat 30 minutes. Add zucchini and simmer another 30 minutes. Stir occasionally. Add beans, macaroni, and parsley, and simmer another 30 minutes. Serve with Parmesan cheese, if desired.

Butternut Squash Soup

4 or 5 servings

1 butternut squash (about 1 pound)
2 onions, quartered
2 carrots, sliced
3 celery stalks, chopped
½ teaspoon salt
¼ teaspoon thyme
1 cooked meaty ham bone (or ½ cup cooked cubed ham)
2 cups hot water
3 cups chicken broth
Parsley

Peel, seed, and cut up squash into 1-inch cubes. In a heavy saucepan, combine all ingredients except parsley. Cook about 30 minutes, or until vegetables are tender. Remove ham bone. Whirl soup in blender container in batches. Remove meat from bone, and add pieces to blended soup. Adjust seasonings. Garnish with parsley.

Cream of Broccoli Soup

6 servings

2 packages (10 ounces each) frozen chopped broccoli
2 cans (10½ ounces) chicken broth (or 2½ cups)
1 tablespoon chopped onion
2 cups half-and-half
Roux (mix 2 tablespoons soft butter with 2 tablespoons flour)

Cook broccoli as package directs, then add chicken broth and onion, and simmer 20 minutes longer. Remove from heat and whirl in blender until smooth. (Blend in 2 or 3 batches). Add half-and-half, then roux. Simmer until mixture thickens slightly.

Quick Corn Chowder

2 quarts (6 to 8 servings)

2 cans (16 ounces each) cream-style corn
1 medium onion, cut in pieces
1 quart milk (or part half-and-half)
Salt and pepper
Whipped cream (optional)

Whirl corn and onion in blender in batches until smooth. Combine blended mixture in saucepan with milk. Heat. Add salt and pepper to taste. Serve piping hot with a dollop of whipped cream, if desired.

Hurry-Up Clam Chowder

About 1 quart (3 or 4 servings)

> ¼ cup chopped celery
> ¼ cup chopped onion
> 2 tablespoons butter or margarine
> 1 can (about 7 ounces) clams—whole, chopped, or minced, undrained
> 1 can (10½ ounces) cream of potato soup
> 1 soup can milk
> Pepper, as desired
> Crumbled bacon (optional)
> Parsley, chopped (optional)

Cook celery and onion in butter until tender but not brown. Add clams and juice, potato soup, and milk. Season to taste with pepper. Heat. Serve with crumbled bacon and chopped parsley, if desired.

Clam Chowder

2 quarts (6 to 8 servings)

> 4 slices bacon, diced
> 1 large onion, sliced
> 2 cups potatoes, finely diced
> 2 cups celery, finely diced
> 2 cups water
> 1½ teaspoons salt
> Pinch white pepper (optional)
> 1 or 2 cans (7 ounces each) minced clams
> 2 cups half-and-half (or part milk)
> Roux (optional), see p. 85

Cook and drain bacon. Add onion, potatoes, celery, water, salt, and pepper. Simmer until vegetables are tender. Add clams with juice and half-and-half. Simmer 10 minutes. Thicken with roux.

Super Salmon Soup

6 servings

> ¾ to 1 cup sliced onions
> ¼ cup butter or margarine
> 1 can (15½ ounces) salmon
> 1 quart milk
> ½ teaspoon salt
> Pepper

Brown onions in butter in a heavy saucepan until richly colored but not burned. Stir frequently; this will take about one-half hour. Flake salmon, removing skin and large bones, if desired. Add to onion mixture. Add milk. Heat to boiling point but do not allow to boil. Add salt and pepper to taste.

This is a very simple dish to prepare, but is delicious and hearty served with saltines.

Fish Chowder

8 servings

> ¼ cup butter or margarine
> 1 medium onion, thinly sliced
> 3 carrots, thinly sliced
> 2 potatoes, cubed
> 1½ cups water
> 2 teaspoons salt
> ½ teaspoon pepper
> 1 pound fish, cut into bite-sized chunks
> 3 cups milk
> ½ teaspoon rosemary
> 1 teaspoon thyme
> 2 tablespoons flour
> 1 cup light cream

Melt butter in a large saucepan. Add onion, carrots, potatoes, water, and salt and pepper. Cover and simmer until carrot and potato are tender. Add fish, milk, rosemary, and thyme; cover. Simmer until fish is done. Blend together flour and cream, and stir into chowder to thicken it slightly.

Chicken Stock for Soup

About 4 quarts soup stock and 3 to 4 cups meat

> 1 stewing hen (4 to 4½ pounds), cut up
> 6 quarts cold water
> ¼ to ½ cup chopped onion
> ¼ to ½ cup chopped celery and leaves
> 1 or 2 carrots, chopped
> 1 teaspoon peppercorns
> ½ bay leaf
> 1 teaspoon salt or chicken soup base

Combine all ingredients in a large kettle. Bring to a boil slowly. Simmer until hen is very tender and begins to leave bone. Remove hen. Cool enough to handle, then pull meat from skin and bones, wrap in foil or plastic wrap, and refrigerate. Strain soup and chill until fat comes to the top and can be completely removed.

When ready to use, cut chicken into bite-size pieces and save for chicken noodle soup, creamed dishes, or salads. Heat soup and taste and adjust seasonings. If it seems watery, boil it hard without a cover for 5 to 10 minutes to concentrate it, then taste again. Use for chicken noodle or other types of soup or making cream sauces.

Note: Frying or roasting chickens can be used. You will need to strengthen the flavor of the soup stock by adding bouillon cubes or soup base. Add up to 4 bouillon cubes or 4 teaspoons soup base at the beginning of the simmering process. Omit the salt until broth is made. Taste and adjust seasonings.

Chicken Noodle Soup

Use 1 cup chicken broth per serving and 4 ounces noodles for each quart, more or less as desired. Cook the noodles 8 to 10 minutes, not soft but *al dente*. Add chicken bits and pieces just long enough to heat them. Serve with chopped parsley or half a lemon slice floating on the soup, if desired.

Turkey Soup

3 quarts (10 to 12 servings)

    5 to 6 cups turkey soup stock
    2 tablespoons butter or margarine
    1 to 1½ tablespoons curry powder
    ½ cup chopped onions
    ½ cup flour
    2 cups mashed potatoes
    2 cups each coarsely chopped carrots and
      celery, cooked
    2 cups each coarsely chopped broccoli, cauliflower,
      asparagus tips, zucchini. Or use an additional 5 to
      6 cups coarsely chopped cooked vegetables,
      any combination desired
    1 cup diced cooked turkey meat
    ¼ cup chopped parsley or chives

Use stock from Sweet and Sour Turkey Wings (p. 75), or see "Turkey for Many Meals" (p. 68) for instructions on preparing stock.

Melt butter in 6- to 8-quart heavy saucepan or Dutch oven. Add curry powder and cook gently for 1 minute. Add onion; blend well, then cover and cook on low heat until onion is tender but not browned (about 10 minutes). Add flour and soup stock. Stir until smooth and boiling. Whip in mashed potatoes, then add the other cooked vegetables. Taste to correct seasonings. You may wish to add salt (about ½ teaspoon). Add turkey meat and parsley or chives last. Serve piping hot.

If you are using up the leftovers from a holiday dinner, increase the mashed potatoes, if desired, and use less flour. Use whatever vegetable you have left over, including creamed onions or peas (no yams or sweet potatoes).

If you are cooking the vegetables fresh, instant mashed potatoes are easy to prepare and use. Chop the other vegetables coarsely by putting them through the coarse blade of a food grinder; a food processor with the steel blade in place is ideal for this job. Cook the hard vegetables (carrots, celery) in one pot, the softer, quicker-cooking vegetables (zucchini, cauliflower) in another. Cook in small amount of water, or steam, just until tender, then add liquid and all to the soup stock.

Chilled Cucumber Cream Soup

6 servings

    2 onions, chopped
    2 cucumbers, peeled and chopped
    2 leeks (white part), sliced
    3 tablespoons butter or margarine
    2 cups chicken broth
    Salt (½ to 1 teaspoon)
    ⅛ teaspoon white pepper
    1 tablespoon butter or margarine
    1 tablespoon flour
    ½ cup heavy cream
    1 teaspoon dill weed
    ½ teaspoon lemon juice
    Few drops hot-pepper sauce
    1 cucumber, peeled, seeded, and chopped fine

Cook onions, 2 cucumbers, and leeks in butter until soft but not brown, about 30 minutes. Add chicken broth, salt, and pepper and bring to a boil. Make a roux with 1 tablespoon butter and flour; whisk into the soup. Simmer gently for 30 minutes to develop the flavor.

Remove from heat and whirl in a blender until smooth. Strain purée into a bowl and add cream, dill weed, lemon juice, hot-pepper sauce, and chopped cucumber. Chill thoroughly. Taste to correct seasonings. Serve in soup bowls.

Creamy Borscht, Hotel Utah Style

4 to 6 servings

    1 can (16 ounces) shoe-string beets, undrained
    3 green onions, cut in pieces
    1 can (10½ ounces) beef or chicken broth,
       undiluted, or 1 cup concentrated broth made with
       soup base
    ¼ cup lemon juice
    ½ cup sour cream or plain yogurt

Add all ingredients but sour cream to blender container. Whirl to smooth. Blend in ¼ cup sour cream (yogurt makes a thinner soup but flavor is excellent and calories are reduced). Chill thoroughly. (We prefer to make the borscht to this point the day before we plan to use it; the flavor is better.)

When ready to serve, use the remaining ¼ cup sour cream as small dollops atop soup. Sprinkle with chopped chives, dill weed, or parsley, if desired.

Salads and Salad Dressings

Gelatin Salads

Whether made of fruit, vegetable, meat, or fish, gelatin salads are popular with many cooks because they can be made ahead of time and because they add a taste and color interest to even an ordinary meal. They are splendid for use on a buffet table or for a group luncheon party.

Here are some tips to remember in making gelatin salads:

1. All fruit gelatins are dessert products, so when using them in salads other than fruit salads, add salt and vinegar to enhance the flavor. Even in fruit salads, a little salt and possibly lemon juice instead of vinegar will add zest. How much is a "little"? Use 1 to 2 tablespoons vinegar and ¼ to ½ teaspoon salt in a 3-ounce package of gelatin, the larger quantity when you are using all vegetables, meat, or fish, or a combination. The smaller amount will usually be enough when part fruit is used. Taste your mixture before you pour it for chilling.

2. When you double a recipe that calls for a 3-ounce package of gelatin, double everything except the vinegar, lemon juice, and salt. Use only about 1½ times each of these ingredients.

3. Be sure the gelatin is thoroughly dissolved in the boiling liquid before adding the other ingredients. Otherwise, you will have a rubbery layer on the bottom. You should use at least one cup boiling (or very hot) liquid for each 3 ounces gelatin in order to dissolve it well.

4. If you are making a large mold, decrease the liquid by ¼ cup for each 3 ounces of gelatin so that the consistency will be firm enough to keep the salad from cracking when it is unmolded.

5. When adding ingredients to gelatin, chill the gelatin until it is very thick. Otherwise the solids will separate into a layer and will either float or sink.

6. Some fresh fruits and juices contain an enzyme that prevents gelatin from setting. Don't use fresh pineapple or pineapple juice, figs, mangoes, or papayas, or any of these fruits in combination with others, either fresh or frozen. If canned, these fruits do not cause problems.

7. To speed up the setting time, use half the liquid called for in the recipe as cold or iced, or use ice-cubes as follows: After dissolving gelatin in boiling liquid, add about one-half tray of ice cubes—7 to 10 cubes, depending on size, for a 3-ounce package; 14 to 20 cubes for a 6-ounce package. Stir about 3 minutes to melt ice or until gelatin is thickened. Remove any unmelted ice, then proceed with recipe.

8. To make unmolding easier, brush the inside surface of the molds with salad oil before filling. When ready to unmold, let them stand a few minutes to warm the oil; then turn molds onto serving plates and leave them until gelatin turns loose.

Molded Spinach–Cottage Cheese Salad

5-cup mold or 9×9×2-inch pan or 10 individual molds
5 cups (about 10 servings)

> 1 package (10 ounces) frozen chopped spinach, or
> 1 cup cooked, fresh spinach, chopped
> 1 packet (1 tablespoon) unflavored gelatin
> ¾ cup water
> 2 chicken bouillon cubes
> 2 tablespoons lemon juice
> ½ cup sour cream
> 1½ cups small-curd cottage cheese
> ½ cup chopped celery
> ½ cup chopped green pepper
> 2 tablespoons minced green onion
> Salad greens and dressing, if desired

Cook and drain spinach. Reserve drained liquid and add water to make ½ cup. Set aside. Soften gelatin in ¾ cup water in small saucepan. Add bouillon cubes and place over low heat; stir until gelatin and bouillon cubes are dissolved. Remove from heat; stir into spinach. Add reserved liquid and lemon juice. Set aside.

Blend sour cream into cottage cheese. Add the gelatin mixture. Stir in the chopped celery, green pepper, and green onion. Chill until firm.

Unmold onto chilled platter and surround with hard-cooked egg halves or deviled eggs, if desired. Or cut into squares and serve on salad greens, or unmold individual salads.

Molded Sour Cream and Cucumber Salad

9×13×2-inch pan
18 servings

2 cups boiling water
1 package (6 ounces) lime-flavored gelatin
3 cups sour cream (1½ pints)
1 large green pepper, seeded and finely chopped
2 large cucumbers, peeled, seeded, and finely chopped
½ cup minced parsley
¼ cup chopped green onion (use part of green tops)
1 teaspoon salt
¼ teaspoon pepper
2 tablespoons horseradish
2 teaspoons celery seed

Pour boiling water over gelatin, and stir to dissolve. Cool. Add sour cream and stir until smooth; add remaining ingredients. Refrigerate until set (several hours or overnight). Serve on lettuce leaf, if desired.

Pineapple Cottage Cheese Salad

Individual molds or 9×13×2-inch pan
14 to 16 servings

1 package (3 ounces) lime-flavored gelatin
1 package (3 ounces) lemon-flavored gelatin
1 cup boiling water
1 cup evaporated milk
1 cup salad dressing*
1 can (8 ounces) crushed pineapple, undrained
1 cup chopped celery
1 cup cottage cheese
1 tablespoon horseradish
1 cup chopped nuts

Combine the two flavors of gelatin, then dissolve in the boiling water (this will be a heavy syrup because there is less than the usual amount of water for dissolving the gelatin, so stir thoroughly). Add the evaporated milk to the salad dressing to make a smooth mixture, then add the dissolved gelatin gradually while stirring to blend the two mixtures well. Stir in the remaining ingredients. Pour into individual molds or into a 9×13×2-inch pan. Chill until set. Unmold individual molds onto salad greens, or cut from pan and lift squares onto salad greens.

*To use mayonnaise in place of salad dressing, add 2 tablespoons vinegar and ¼ teaspoon salt.

Orange Pecan Salad

Individual molds or 9×13×2-inch pan
12 to 15 servings

1 large package (6 ounces) orange-flavored gelatin
1½ cups boiling water
½ teaspoon salt
2 tablespoons vinegar
¾ cup mayonnaise
1 can (15½ ounces) crushed pineapple, not drained
1½ cups chopped celery
1½ cups shredded carrots
1 bunch green onions, chopped (about ¼ cup)
1 cup chopped pecans

Dissolve gelatin in boiling water. Add salt and vinegar, then blend in mayonnaise. Add remaining ingredients. Pour into molds or pan. Chill until set (2 to 4 hours). Unmold onto salad greens, or cut from pan and lift pieces onto salad greens.

Avocado Strawberry Ring

3- or 4-cup ring mold, or use individual molds
5 or 6 servings

1 cup boiling water
1 package (3 ounces) lemon-flavored gelatin
½ teaspoon salt
¾ cup ice and water
1 tablespoon lemon juice
3 tablespoons mayonnaise
2 small or medium avocados, peeled and mashed
1 pint fresh strawberries

In a small bowl, add boiling water to gelatin and salt. Stir until well dissolved. Add ice and water and stir until ice is melted. Chill until slightly thickened. Blend in lemon juice, mayonnaise, and avocado. Pour into ring mold or individual molds. Chill until firm. Unmold. Fill center of ring with strawberries.

Pineapple-Grapefruit Salad

Individual molds
6 servings

1 package (3 ounces) lemon-flavored gelatin
¼ teaspoon salt
1 cup boiling water
Juice from fruits and water to make 1 cup
1 green pepper, chopped, or ½ cup pomegranate seeds
½ cup slivered blanched almonds
1 grapefruit, freed from membrane and diced

½ cup canned crushed pineapple, drained
Salad greens
Mayonnaise (optional)

Dissolve gelatin and salt in boiling water. Add the fruit juices and water to make 1 cup. Chill until slightly thickened. Fold green pepper or pomegranate seeds, almonds, grapefruit, and pineapple into slightly thickened gelatin. Pour into 6 individual molds. Chill until firm. Unmold on crisp greens. Serve with mayonnaise, if desired.

Jellied Fruit Salad

Individual molds or square pan
10 to 12 servings

1 cup pineapple juice
1 package (3 ounces) lemon-flavored gelatin
1 cup orange juice
½ cup whipping cream
1 can (13¼ ounces) pineapple tidbits (or cut pineapple chunks in half), well drained
1 can (11 ounces) mandarin oranges, well drained
1 or 2 bananas, sliced
6 to 10 maraschino cherries, halved
½ cup slivered almonds

Heat pineapple juice to boiling point. Add to gelatin and stir until dissolved. Add orange juice. Chill. When gelatin thickens but is not set, beat with electric mixer until frothy. Whip cream until stiff; fold into gelatin. Blend in fruit and nuts. Set in individual molds or in square pan. Serve as a salad or dessert.

Molded Shrimp Salad

8 individual molds or 2-quart mold
8 servings

1 package (3 ounces) lime-flavored gelatin
¾ cup boiling water
¼ cup lemon juice
¼ teaspoon salt
1 cup sour cream
¼ cup mayonnaise
½ cup cubed avocado
½ cup chopped celery
2 tablespoons chopped green onion
2 tablespoons chopped green pepper
1 can (4 to 6 ounces) shrimp, cleaned

Add gelatin to boiling water, lemon juice, and salt; stir to dissolve gelatin well. Chill until partially set (about 20 minutes), then add remaining ingredients. Set in molds. Unmold on salad greens to serve.

Cantaloupe Salad

4 servings

2 small cantaloupe
6 peaches, sliced
2 cups honeydew melon, cubed
3 cups seeded grapes, halved
1 cup French Dressing (below)

Cut each cantaloupe lengthwise into 8 wedges; chill. Coat peaches, honeydew melon, and grapes with dressing. (Keep remaining dressing for another use.) Chill one hour. For each serving, arrange 2 cantaloupe wedges to form oval or circle and fill centers with fruit mixture.

French Dressing for Fruit Salad

1 cup sugar
3 teaspoons salt
3 teaspoons paprika
¾ cup orange juice
3 tablespoons lemon juice
3 tablespoons vinegar
3 cups salad oil
3 teaspoons onion, grated

Combine all ingredients in a bottle or jar. Cover; shake thoroughly. Use 1 cup to coat fruits in Cantaloupe Salad. Store any remaining dressing in refrigerator for use another time. Shake well before each use.

Holiday Waldorf Salad

8 servings

3 cups apples, sliced
1 cup red or black grapes, halved and seeded
1 cup celery, diced, or use cut marshmallows or miniature marshmallows
½ cup nuts
½ cup heavy cream, whipped
½ cup mayonnaise or salad dressing
½ teaspoon lemon juice or more, to taste
1 tablespoon sugar
Lettuce leaves
2 tablespoons slivered candied ginger, optional

Combine apples, grapes, celery or marshmallows, and nuts. Mix lightly. Combine whipped cream and dressing. Add lemon juice and sugar. Fold into fruit mixture. Chill. Serve on lettuce leaves topped with slivered ginger, if desired.

Garden Lettuce with Cream and Sugar

4 servings

1 quart leaf lettuce (garden lettuce, red lettuce, or very tender butter lettuce)
¼ cup whipping cream
3 tablespoons vinegar
2 tablespoons sugar

Wash, drain, and thoroughly dry lettuce leaves. Break them into a salad bowl. Mix together cream, vinegar, and sugar. Pour over salad and toss gently. Serve immediately.

Creamy Romaine Salad

8 servings

2 cloves garlic, minced and crushed
1 tablespoon mayonnaise
Black pepper, freshly ground
½ cup salad oil
⅓ cup red wine vinegar
2 heads romaine lettuce
¾ cup Romano or Parmesan cheese, freshly shredded

In a small glass bowl, combine garlic, mayonnaise, and pepper to taste. Whisk in the salad oil, then the vinegar. Rinse, pat dry, and break romaine into bite-size pieces in salad bowl. Toss with the cheese. Pour on the dressing just before serving, and toss well.

Wilted Greens

8 to 10 servings

4 slices bacon, diced
2 eggs, slightly beaten
½ cup sugar
½ cup vinegar
½ cup water
2 heads lettuce
2 or 3 hard-cooked eggs, chopped

Cook bacon until crisp. Combine eggs, sugar, vinegar, and water. Stir into bacon; cook until thickened on low heat. Break lettuce into bite-size pieces and place in a salad bowl; pour bacon mixture over greens. Garnish with chopped hard-cooked egg.

Romaine Salad Supreme

4 to 6 servings

1 clove garlic (optional)
1 large head romaine, chilled
3 green onions, finely chopped (include green tops)
1 teaspoon finely chopped fresh mint
¼ teaspoon oregano leaves
Salt and ground black pepper
1 egg
½ cup salad oil
Juice of 1 lemon
¼ teaspoon salt
½ cup grated Parmesan cheese
½ pound bacon, cooked until crisp
2 or 3 tomatoes, peeled and cut in eighths
1 cup croutons

Rub chilled wooden bowl with cut clove of garlic, if desired. Tear romaine into bite-size pieces. Add to bowl with green onions, mint, oregano, and salt and pepper to taste.

Combine egg, salad oil, lemon juice, and ¼ teaspoon salt. Beat with rotary beater until well blended, then pour over salad and toss. Sprinkle salad with Parmesan cheese; then crumble bacon over cheese. Arrange tomatoes over top, and sprinkle salad with croutons.

Spinach Salad with Mandarin Oranges

10 servings

1 package (10 ounces) spinach
1 cucumber, sliced
1 can (11 ounces) mandarin oranges, drained
1 or 2 green onions, chopped
½ pound fresh mushrooms, chopped
1 large avocado, diced
½ to 1 pound cherry tomatoes, cut in half
½ teaspoon grated orange peel
½ cup frozen orange juice concentrate
½ cup salad oil
2 tablespoons sugar
2 tablespoons wine or cider vinegar
1 tablespoon lemon juice
½ teaspoon salt

Wash, stem, and drain spinach. In large salad bowl, toss together spinach, cucumber, oranges, green onions, mushrooms, avocado, and tomatoes. Combine remaining ingredients in blender or food processor and blend thoroughly. Chill and serve over salad.

Grilled chicken breast with Texas-style Barbecue Sauce (p. 82), Swedish Baked Beans (p. 33), Picnic Potato Salad (p. 24), Golden Summer Punch (p. 11)

Old-Fashioned Cooked Potato Salad Dressing

General guide for good potato salad: Slice potatoes; while warm, toss with a seasoned oil and vinegar dressing, or even just vinegar. Add any or all of the following: chopped onions, celery, green peppers, hard-cooked eggs. Celery seed is always a tasty addition.

Old-Fashioned Cooked Dressing

2 tablespoons sugar
1 tablespoon flour
2 teaspoons dry mustard
1 tablespoon salt
1 egg, well beaten
¾ cup vinegar
¾ cup water

Combine sugar, flour, dry mustard, and salt in small saucepan; mix well. Add remaining ingredients. Cook and stir until mixture boils and is thick. Dressing will keep for about six weeks in refrigerator. If it becomes too thick, thin with water or vinegar. To use, mix about half and half with commercial mayonnaise.

Picnic Potato Salad

10 servings

8 medium potatoes
1 onion, chopped
⅓ cup bottled Italian salad dressing
3 large dill pickles, chopped
5 hard-cooked eggs, chopped
½ cup mayonnaise
½ cup salad dressing
½ cup sour cream

Wash potatoes and cook in boiling water until tender. Drain and cool slightly. Remove skins and cut potatoes into cubes. Add chopped onion. Pour Italian dressing over warm potatoes and onions. Cover tightly and refrigerate for several hours or overnight. Add chopped pickles and eggs and mix gently. Combine mayonnaise, salad dressing, and sour cream. Pour over potato salad and mix gently. Chill until serving time.

Korean Vegetable Salad

4 servings

1 small turnip, peeled
1 teaspoon salt
3 tablespoons sesame or other vegetable oil
1 small onion, finely chopped
1 cup sliced mushrooms
2 celery ribs, thinly sliced
3 green onions, sliced
1 carrot, cut in thin 2-inch strips
3 tablespoons soy sauce
1 tablespoon brown sugar
1 tablespoon vinegar
½ teaspoon ground ginger
1 tablespoon pinenuts or almonds, finely chopped

Cut turnip in thin strips. Sprinkle with salt. Set aside for 15 minutes. Heat oil in small frying pan or wok. Add turnip and onion, and stir-fry 3 to 4 minutes; transfer to paper towels to drain. Stir-fry mushrooms in oil for 4 minutes; transfer to paper towels. Stir-fry celery in oil for 3 minutes; transfer to towels. Cover stir-fried vegetables and chill. Add green onions and carrots. Combine soy sauce, brown sugar, vinegar, ginger, and nuts. Pour over vegetables. Toss lightly.

Layered "Masked" Salad

9×13×2-inch glass pan
15 to 20 servings

1 large head iceberg lettuce, chilled
1 can (8 ounces) water chestnuts, drained and sliced
1 cup thin-sliced celery
1 cup thin-sliced zucchini
1 cup coarsely shredded carrots
1 package (10 ounces) frozen peas
2 cups mayonnaise (salad dressing may be used)
1 tablespoon sugar
Parmesan cheese (½ to 1 cup)
½ pound bacon, cooked crisp and crumbled

Tear lettuce into bite-size pieces. Layer ingredients, in the order listed down through peas. Zucchini and carrots are optional, but stretch the salad nicely and add color interest. The peas should be soaked in cold water to thaw, or may be cooked a minute or two, then cooled in cold water to keep the color bright. Spread vegetables with mayonnaise, and seal well to edges of pan. Sprinkle with sugar, then Parmesan cheese, then bacon bits. Cover with foil or plastic wrap and refrigerate overnight. To serve, cut into portions with a knife. Use a broad-blade spatula to lift the entire portion onto plate; don't disturb the "frosting." This way, each guest can toss his or her own. Or salad may be layered in salad bowl; just before serving, toss to mix well with dressing. Garnish with hard-cooked eggs, tomato wedges, or parsley, if desired.

Buffet Salad

8 to 10 large servings

    ½ head lettuce
    1 small bunch curly or red lettuce
    1 head romaine
    ½ bunch watercress or spinach
    2 medium tomatoes, peeled
    1 medium avocado, peeled
    3 hard-cooked eggs
    ½ pound bacon, cooked crisp
    2 cups finely diced cooked chicken breasts*
    ½ cup crumbled blue cheese or finely grated
        American cheese
    2 tablespoons finely chopped chives or green
        onions
    1 cup Italian-type salad dressing

With a sharp knife, chop each of the greens very fine. Spread in layers in a large salad bowl, heaping up slightly in the center. Finely chop tomatoes, avocado, eggs, and bacon. Arrange these and the chicken, cheese, and chives in rows of contrasting colors over the top of the greens. For an especially attractive pattern, arrange tomato and avocado in two wide rows, side by side, across center of greens. Next to tomato, place a row of cheese, then eggs. Next to avocado, place a row of chicken, then chives. Sprinkle bacon along edges of tomato and avocado. To keep the attractive design while serving, pour part of the dressing across only one end at a time; mix lightly, and serve from that section.

Other chicken meat, canned chicken, turkey, or tuna fish may be used in place of the chicken breasts.

Sweet and Sour Salad

8 servings

    1 can (29 ounces) sauerkraut
    1 large sweet onion, sliced thinly into rings
    1 green pepper, cut in thin strips
    3 ribs celery, diced
    1 jar (2 ounces) pimientos, drained and chopped
    ¾ cup sugar, or to taste

Mix all ingredients and refrigerate overnight. Salad keeps well for several days.

Seven-Day Slaw

About 1½ quarts
10 to 12 servings

    1 quart chopped cabbage (about ½ medium head)
    ½ cup chopped green pepper
    1 cup carrots, chopped
    2 cups cold water
    2 teaspoons salt
    ½ cup finely chopped celery

Chop first three vegetables fairly fine (use a blender with water, or a food processor, or put through coarse blade of the food grinder). Soak chopped vegetables in the cold water with salt for about an hour. Drain well and add celery.

Add chilled dressing (below) to chopped vegetables. Cover and store in the refrigerator. Stir several times before serving. A 2-quart plastic container with lid makes a good storage container. This salad tastes better the second day, and will keep well for at least 7 days, or up to two weeks.

Dressing

    ½ to ¾ cup sugar
    ½ cup water
    ½ cup vinegar
    1 teaspoon dry mustard
    1 teaspoon celery seed

Combine the dressing ingredients in a small saucepan; bring to a boil, then chill.

Chicken Salad Exotic

12 servings

    8 chicken breast halves, cooked and cut into
        bite-size pieces
    1 can (15½ ounces) pineapple tidbits or chunks
    2 cans (8 ounces each) water chestnuts
    3 tablespoons vinegar
    4 tablespoons soy sauce
    1 tablespoon curry (or more, to taste)
    1⅓ cups mayonnaise
    ½ cup (4 ounces) slivered almonds, toasted
    1½ cups seedless grapes

Drain pineapple overnight. Drain water chestnuts well and pat dry on paper toweling. Combine vinegar, soy sauce, curry, and mayonnaise. Let stand several hours. About 2 hours before serving, combine all ingredients. Serve on lettuce leaves.

Chicken Fruit Salad Plate

8 to 10 servings

    ¾ cup mayonnaise
    ¼ cup sour cream
    3 tablespoons tarragon vinegar
    2 tablespoons grated onion
    ½ cup toasted almond slices
    6 stuffed olives, sliced
    Salt, pepper, and paprika to taste
    1 cup finely diced celery
    3 tablespoons capers
    1 cup water chestnuts, well drained and sliced
    1 teaspoon prepared mustard
    3 cups cooked chicken, cut in bite-size pieces

Mix together mayonnaise and sour cream; add vinegar, then all other ingredients except chicken. Let stand one hour. Combine chicken with mayonnaise mixture; let stand another hour.

Serve on salad greens with melon slices, pineapple, grapes, or grapefruit, if desired.

Cranberry and Turkey Salad Ring

1-quart ring mold
4 to 6 servings

    1 package (3 ounces) orange-flavored gelatin
    ⅛ teaspoon salt
    1 cup hot water
    ¾ cup cold water
    2 teaspoons lemon juice
    1 cup fresh cranberries, ground
    ⅓ cup sugar
    1 cup seedless white grapes, halved
    ⅓ cup walnuts, chopped (optional)
    Lettuce or other salad greens
    Turkey Salad Supreme (below)
    2 hard-cooked eggs, sieved
    Mayonnaise (optional)

Dissolve gelatin and salt in hot water. Add cold water and lemon juice. Chill until slightly thickened. Meanwhile, combine cranberries and sugar and let stand. When gelatin is slightly thickened, fold in cranberries, grapes and nuts. Pour into ring mold. Chill until firm. Unmold on crisp lettuce. Fill center of ring with Turkey Salad Supreme and garnish with sieved hard-cooked eggs. Serve with mayonnaise, if desired. If desired, 3 cups of ham or chicken salad may be used in place of turkey salad.

Turkey Salad Supreme

4 to 6 servings

    2 tablespoons lemon juice
    2 cups turkey, cooked and cut into bite-size pieces
    ½ cup diced apple
    1 cup diced celery
    ¼ cup chopped, toasted almonds
    ½ cup mayonnaise
    ¾ teaspoon salt
    Dash of pepper
    ½ teaspoon sweet basil, if desired

Sprinkle lemon juice over turkey and apple. Toss lightly. Add celery and almonds. Blend mayonnaise with seasonings. Fold into turkey mixture.

Turkey and Green Grape Salad

4 entrée-size servings

    2 cups diced cooked turkey
    1 cup sliced celery
    ½ cup seedless green grapes, halved
    ½ cup mayonnaise
    Salt and pepper as desired
    Melon halves or circles, such as cantaloupe or honeydew

Combine turkey, celery, grapes, and mayonnaise. Season to taste. Toss lightly. Serve in melon halves or circles. May be served on salad greens with melon balls or cubes for garnish.

Chicken in Gelatin

6 individual molds or 3-cup mold
6 servings

    1 envelope (1 tablespoon) unflavored gelatin
    1¼ cups chicken broth
    Grated onion (about 1 teaspoon)
    Salt and pepper
    1 cup sour cream
    1 cup cooked and cubed chicken
    ¼ cup nuts, chopped
    ¼ cup chopped ripe olives
    Salad greens
    Mayonnaise, if desired

Soften gelatin in ½ cup chicken broth. Place over low heat and stir until gelatin dissolves. Remove from heat. Stir in remaining ¾ cup chicken broth and season with grated onion, salt, and pepper. Chill until almost set. Beat in sour cream until smooth. Add chicken, nuts, and olives. Pour into lightly oiled mold or individual molds and chill until firm. Serve on crisp greens with mayonnaise.

Chicken Curry Salad with Fruit

6 servings

⅔ cup mayonnaise
2 tablespoons lemon juice
1 teaspoon salt, or to taste
1 teaspoon curry powder
2½ cups cooked chicken, cut into bite-size pieces
1 cup diced celery
Salad greens
¼ cup slivered, blanched almonds
Fruit Garnish:
    1 avocado, sliced
    ½ cantaloupe, cut into wedges
    1 cup seedless grapes
    1 cup canned pineapple chunks, drained

Blend mayonnaise, lemon juice, salt, and curry powder. Pour over the combined chicken and celery and mix lightly. Chill. Just before serving, mound salad in center of a serving platter lined with salad greens. Sprinkle with almonds. Garnish with fruits.

Salmon Salad

6 to 8 servings

1 can (15½ ounces) salmon, drained
1 cup diced cucumber
2 tablespoons grated onion
2 tablespoons lemon juice
½ teaspoon salt, or to taste
Italian dressing, mayonnaise, or salad dressing
Salad greens
12 asparagus tips, in season, or use tomato wedges or hard-cooked eggs
6 to 8 green pepper rings (optional)

Remove salmon skin and bones, if desired. Flake salmon. Toss together the salmon, cucumber, onion, lemon juice, and salt. Mix with a small amount of Italian dressing, mayonnaise, or salad dressing. Or serve on salad greens and top with mayonnaise. Garnish with asparagus, tomatoes, or hard-cooked eggs and green pepper rings.

New Orleans Shrimp Salad

5½-cup ring mold
8 servings

2 cups cooked rice
½ cup Italian dressing
½ cup mayonnaise
1 cup sliced radishes
1 medium cucumber, seeded and chopped
2 tomatoes, peeled, seeded, and chopped
1 medium green pepper, chopped
½ cup chopped celery
½ cup chopped green onion
¾ cup shredded Cheddar cheese
1 can (6 to 7 ounces) shrimp, rinsed and deveined if necessary
Leaf lettuce
Cherry tomatoes
Olives

Marinate warm rice in Italian dressing for at least 4 hours. Add mayonnaise, and stir until rice is well coated. Fold in radishes, cucumber, tomatoes, green pepper, celery, onion, cheese, and shrimp. Press into a 5½-cup ring mold; cover, and refrigerate for 2 to 3 hours. To serve, unmold onto a platter lined with leaf lettuce; fill center with cherry tomatoes and olives.

Crab and Avocado Salad

6 servings

3 large avocados, peeled, pitted, cut into cubes
2 cans (about 7 ounces each) crab meat, rinsed and picked over to remove pieces of cartilage
1 cup finely diced celery
½ cup finely sliced radishes
2 tablespoons lemon juice
2 tablespoons vinegar
4 tablespoons salad oil
2 tablespoons finely chopped green onions (use part of green tops)
Dash of cayenne pepper
Salt to taste
3 or 4 tomatoes (optional)
Louis Dressing (p. 28)

Combine all ingredients except tomatoes. For each serving, spoon out salad on a bed of lettuce on an individual serving plate. Surround with tomato wedges, peeled if desired. Serve with Louis Dressing.

Louis Dressing

1 cup mayonnaise
⅓ cup chili sauce
2 tablespoons chopped parsley
1 tablespoon finely chopped green onion
Dash of cayenne pepper
¼ cup heavy cream, whipped

Combine first 5 ingredients; fold in whipped cream. Top each salad with a dollop of dressing. Pass remainder for those who wish extra dressing.

Salad Sandwiches

6 servings

6 hard-cooked eggs
2 tablespoons sweet pickle relish
¼ cup mayonnaise
Salt and pepper to taste
6 slices sourdough bread
1 bunch red leaf lettuce
3 tomatoes, sliced thin
1 can (7 ounces) crab or shrimp
1½ cups Thousand Island salad dressing
Olives and pickled beets for garnish

Peel hard-cooked eggs and mash with a fork. Add pickle relish, mayonnaise, and salt and pepper. Chill. When ready to serve, assemble in following order: place a slice of bread on the plate and add a piece or two of lettuce. Top with a scoop of the egg salad, a tomato slice, some crab or shrimp, then a generous serving of the Thousand Island dressing. Garnish sandwich-salad with olives and pickled beets. Eat with a knife and fork.

Tabouli (Cracked Wheat) Salad

4 servings

2 cups bulgur or cooked cracked wheat, chilled
¼ cup chopped parsley
1 clove garlic, minced
1 tablespoon chopped fresh mint
⅓ cup olive or other oil
2 medium tomatoes, diced
¾ cup diced green pepper
¼ cup chopped onion
¼ cup lemon juice
Soy sauce

Soak bulgur in water 20 minutes; drain well. Or use cold cooked cracked wheat. Combine all ingredients. Toss lightly, and serve with soy sauce, as desired.

Quick Blue Cheese Dressing

About 3⅓ cups

2 cups mayonnaise
1 small onion, grated
4 tablespoons cider vinegar
Dash of garlic salt
1 cup sour cream
¾ cup chopped fresh parsley
3 ounces (or more) blue cheese, crumbled

Mix ingredients in order listed.
To make a delicious topping for baked potatoes, broccoli, asparagus, or zucchini, omit the vinegar.

Green Goddess Salad Dressing

About 1 cup

½ clove garlic, minced or pressed
1½ tablespoons finely chopped anchovies
1½ tablespoons finely chopped chives
1½ teaspoons lemon juice
1½ tablespoons Tarragon wine vinegar
¼ cup sour cream
½ cup mayonnaise
3 tablespoons finely chopped parsley
Dash of freshly ground black pepper

Combine ingredients in order given. Mix well. Chill.

Honey Dressing for Fruit Salad

2 cups

⅓ cup sugar
1 teaspoon dry mustard
1 teaspoon paprika
1 teaspoon celery seed
¼ teaspoon salt
⅓ cup honey
⅓ cup vinegar
1 tablespoon lemon juice
1 teaspoon grated onion
1 cup salad oil

Mix sugar, dry mustard, paprika, celery seed, and salt. Add honey, vinegar, lemon juice, and onion. Pour oil into mixture very slowly, beating constantly with rotary or electric mixer. Delicious on mixed fresh fruits.

Aunt Molly's Delicious French Dressing

About 2 cups

    1 clove garlic, pressed or finely minced
    ½ cup sugar
    ⅓ cup vinegar
    1 teaspoon Worcestershire sauce
    1 small onion, grated fine
    ⅔ cup catsup
    1 teaspoon salt
    1 cup salad oil

Measure ingredients into blender container. Blend well. Store in pint jar in refrigerator.

Creamy Dressing for Fruit Salad

About 1½ cups

    1 tablespoon cornstarch
    ½ cup sugar
    Dash of salt
    ½ cup pineapple juice
    ¼ cup lemon juice
    ½ cup heavy cream, whipped

Combine cornstarch, sugar, and salt in a small saucepan. Blend in pineapple and lemon juices. Cook and stir over low heat until mixture thickens and clears. Chill. Whip cream until fluffy. Using same beater, whip chilled mixture until creamy. Fold in whipped cream.

Creamy Lemon Dressing

Stir lemon yogurt, and serve with fruit for an easy, delicious dressing.

Marinated Vegetables

Marinated vegetables make delicious salads as well as add nutrition and interest to meals. Most people love them; they provide an easy way to serve a crowd; and leftovers keep for days in the refrigerator, so the vegetables can be made up ahead of time. Almost anything goes, so whatever vegetables you have from the garden, can buy economically, or have in your storage supply may be used.

The favorite three-bean salad is a prime example of marinated vegetables, but there are many variations. Make up your own, using one you find here for a pattern. Hard vegetables (such as carrots and celery) are usually better if they are partially cooked before marinating.

You will note that some of the dressings contain sugar; some do not. Some good cooks feel that this is one dish where sugar can easily be eliminated. Try the vegetables both ways and see which you like best. All are delicious!

All-Purpose Marinade

About 2 cups

    ½ cup vinegar
    ¼ cup water
    1 package Good Seasons Mild Italian Salad
        Dressing Mix
    ¾ cup salad oil

Put all ingredients into blender. Blend on high speed for one minute. Or put into a pint jar and shake hard. The blender method makes a marinade (or dressing) that doesn't separate easily, so it is ideal when feeding a crowd. To vary the taste, use part olive oil and/or part wine vinegar. Or use any flavor of dressing mix you prefer. The one listed has been found to please many guests.

In addition to vegetables, this marinade works well for tough meat, such as flank steak or London broil cuts. It helps to tenderize the meat and seasons at the same time. For this, increase vinegar to ¾ to 1 cup.

Marinated Carrot Salad

About 16 servings

    8 good-sized carrots, peeled, then cut in strips
    ½ stock celery, or use several ribs, cut in sticks
    1 large purple onion, cut in rings
    1 large green pepper, stem and veins removed,
        cut in strips
    1 can (10½ ounces) tomato soup
    ½ cup salad oil
    ¼ cup sugar
    1 teaspoon salt
    Pepper
    1 teaspoon dry mustard (optional)
    ½ cup vinegar

Prepare vegetables. Partially cook carrots and celery in boiling, salted water. Drain and combine in a bowl with onion and green pepper. Set aside. Make sauce by combining soup, oil, sugar, salt, pepper, dry mustard, and vinegar. Bring to a boil. Pour over vegetables and refrigerate, preferably overnight. Serve as a salad with greens or as a cold vegetable. Salad will keep a week or longer in the refrigerator.

Pickled Marinated Vegetables

10 to 12 servings

½ head cauliflower, cut in florets
2 carrots, pared, cut in 2-inch strips
2 ribs celery, cut in 1-inch pieces, then cut in strips
1 green pepper, cut in 2-inch strips
1 jar (3 ounces) stuffed green olives
¾ cup white wine vinegar
½ cup olive oil
1 tablespoon sugar
1 teaspoon salt
½ teaspoon oregano leaves, crushed
¼ teaspoon pepper
¼ cup water

In large frying pan, combine all ingredients with the ¼ cup water and bring to a boil. Reduce heat and simmer, stirring occasionally, covered, for 5 minutes. Cool and refrigerate 24 hours. Drain well and serve arranged attractively on tray.

Three-Bean Salad

8 to 10 servings

1 can (16 ounces) cut green beans, drained
1 can (16 ounces) wax beans, drained
1 can (16 ounces) red kidney beans, rinsed and drained
½ cup slivered green pepper
¼ cup raw onion rings
2 tablespoons sugar
⅔ cup vinegar
½ cup salad oil
1 teaspoon salt
Pepper

Combine beans, green pepper, and onion rings. Combine sugar, vinegar, oil, salt, and pepper to make dressing. Toss dressing and bean mixture together. Let stand, covered, in refrigerator overnight.

Super Deluxe Marinated Vegetables

20 to 24 servings

1 can (16 ounces) red kidney beans, drained and rinsed
1 can (16 ounces) cut green beans, drained
1 can (16 ounces) garbanzo beans
1 can (6 ounces) pitted ripe olives, halved
1 can (6 ounces) green olives, pitted and halved
1 can (12 ounces) shoe-peg corn, drained, or whole kernel niblets
1 can (4 ounces) sliced mushrooms, drained, or 1 cup sliced raw mushrooms
2 carrots, match-stick cut, blanched 3 to 5 minutes
1 cup cauliflowerets, blanched 1 or 2 minutes
¼ cup sliced green onions
2 tablespoons chopped parsley
1 clove garlic, crushed
1½ cups red wine vinegar
1 cup salad oil, or use part olive oil
¼ to ½ cup sugar (add smaller amount, then adjust for personal preference)
½ to 1 teaspoon salt

Combine vegetables in a large bowl. Combine garlic, vinegar, oil, sugar, and salt in a quart jar, and shake to blend thoroughly. Pour over vegetables and mix gently. Cover tightly and refrigerate overnight or longer.

Lima Bean Marinade

8 servings

2 packages (10 ounces each) frozen lima beans
1 large red onion, sliced ⅛-inch thick
1 cup coarsely chopped parsley
¾ cup salad oil
1 cup vinegar
2 teaspoons sugar
1 teaspoon salt
½ teaspoon pepper

Cook lima beans according to directions on package. Drain. Combine beans, onion, and parsley in a bowl. Combine salad oil, vinegar, sugar, salt, and pepper; beat or shake until well blended. Pour over vegetables. Cover; chill for 12 hours. Drain; put aside a few onion rings for top. Serve in a salad bowl lined with lettuce. Garnish with onion rings and additional parsley.

Fresh Vegetable Relish or Salad

8 servings

    2 medium tomatoes
    1 large green pepper
    ½ large cucumber, peeled
    2 large ribs celery
    1 medium onion
    1 medium zucchini
    ¼ to ½ cup sugar
    ½ cup cider vinegar
    ½ teaspoon salt (about)
    1/8 teaspoon pepper (about)

Peel and seed tomatoes and dice into small pieces. Chop vegetables. You should have about 2 cups tomato and 1 cup each of green pepper, cucumber, celery, onion, and zucchini. Shake in a jar the sugar, vinegar, salt, and pepper. Pour over vegetables and stir gently. Cover and refrigerate for 4 hours or overnight.

At serving time, remove vegetables with a slotted spoon to a serving bowl. Season with more salt and pepper, if needed. Discard liquid.

Vegetables

Easy Baked Beans

3-quart casserole
325 degrees F.
About 8 1-cup servings

  2 large cans (1 pound 12 ounces each) baked beans
    (S&W brand gives best results)
  1 can (16 ounces) stewed tomatoes
  ¼ to ½ cup molasses
  2 teaspoons dry mustard
  4 tablespoons Worcestershire sauce

Blend all ingredients in a large bowl (the mustard will blend in more easily if mixed with a small amount of liquid from the beans). Pour into greased casserole (use butter or margarine), and bake, covered, 1½ to 2 hours. If too juicy, remove lid for last of baking. This recipe multiplies very successfully to feed a crowd.

Note: Canned tomatoes may be used, but if so, they should be seasoned with a little chopped onion, green pepper, and celery sautéed in butter or margarine. Using the already seasoned stewed tomatoes is the easy way.

Country-Style Baked Beans

10 servings

  1 pound red beans
  6 cups water
  ½ pound bulk pork sausage
  1 cup chopped onion
  2 cups tart cooking apples, peeled, thinly sliced
  2 medium cloves garlic, mashed
  ¼ teaspoon pepper
  2 teaspoons salt
  1 teaspoon chili powder
  1 teaspoon dry mustard
  ¼ cup brown sugar
  1½ cups tomato juice
  Sour cream

Soak beans in water overnight. Cook in soaking water until amost tender. Flatten sausage in frying pan; brown on one side; turn. Break into medium-sized pieces; brown. Add sausage to beans with 2 tablespoons sausage fat and remaining ingredients, except sour cream. Cover and simmer 1 hour. Garnish with sour cream.

Calico Bean Bake

Large covered casserole
300 degrees F.
10 to 12 1-cup servings

  ½ pound bacon
  4 large onions, chopped, or ¼ cup dried onions
  1 can (1 pound) garbanzo beans
  2 cans (1 pound each) butter beans
  1 can (1 pound) red kidney beans
  2 cans (1 pound each) baked beans
  ½ cup cider vinegar
  ¾ cup brown sugar
  1 teaspoon salt
  ½ teaspoon garlic powder
  1 teaspoon dry mustard

Cut bacon in small pieces and fry on medium heat. Drain off all but ¼ cup bacon fat. Add onions; sauté. Drain and reserve liquid from beans. Combine all ingredients in large saucepan, and simmer 20 to 30 minutes. Add reserved liquid as needed. Bake in a covered casserole 1 to 2 hours.

Swedish Baked Beans

Frying pan with a lid
4 servings, ¾ cup each

  ½ cup onion, chopped
  2 tablespoons butter, margarine, bacon fat, or ham
    drippings
  1 apple, peeled, cored, and chopped
  2 cups cooked dry beans (about ¾ cup raw)
  ¼ cup raisins
  ¼ cup sweet pickle relish
  1 tablespoon prepared mustard
  ¾ cup catsup
  ¼ cup brown sugar
  4 slices crisp-cooked bacon, crumbled (optional)

Sauté onion in fat. Add remaining ingredients. Cover tightly and simmer 20 to 30 minutes. Bacon may be combined with other ingredients or reserved as a garnish.

Beans may be baked in a covered casserole at 350 degrees F.

Seven-day Cole Slaw (p. 25), Green and Gold Vegetable Ring (p. 44), with cauliflower, and Spaghetti Squash (p. 40), surrounded by fresh vegetables

Classic Baked Beans

3-quart casserole or bean pot
250 degrees F.
6 to 8 servings

    2 cups navy or pea beans, washed well
    1 onion, chopped
    1 bay leaf
    2 teaspoons salt
    1 can (8 ounces) tomato sauce
    ½ cup molasses
    1½ teaspoons dry mustard
    1 tablespoon vinegar
    ½ teaspoon Tabasco
    ¼ pound salt pork or thick bacon

In a large kettle, cover beans with 6 to 8 cups water. Bring to a boil and cook 2 minutes. Remove from heat; let stand, covered, one hour. Return to heat; add onion, bay leaf, and salt. Simmer, covered, about an hour, or until tender. Or soak the beans overnight in water, then cook with the additions until tender. Drain and reserve 3 cups of the cooking liquid. Combine liquid with tomato sauce, molasses, dry mustard, vinegar, and Tabasco. Put beans in pan or casserole; bury salt pork in beans, then add liquid mixture. Cover and bake 6 to 8 hours, or to desired consistency.

Pasta with Beans

4 servings, 1 cup each

    2 slices thick bacon, cut in small pieces
    ½ small onion, chopped
    1 clove garlic, peeled, chopped (optional)
    ½ stalk celery, chopped
    Pinch of basil
    Pinch of oregano or thyme
    1 fresh or canned tomato, chopped
    2 cups cooked dry beans
    2½ cups hot water
    2 ounces elbow or shell macaroni
    1 tablespoon parsley, chopped

In frying pan, cook bacon pieces on medium heat about 5 minutes, stirring occasionally. Add onion, garlic, and celery; cook 5 minutes. Add remaining ingredients; simmer until macaroni is cooked.

Salted Beans

When the green beans are at their garden best (pole beans are good for this purpose), wash well a fresh-picked supply. Snip the ends and split beans lengthwise. Layer them with ice-cream salt in a crock (beans on the bottom, then a layer of salt, then beans until your crock is about full). Add a little water—no more than about 1 cup. Cover with a plate that fits just inside the crock, and weight it down with something heavy, such as a clean rock. Store crock in a cool place. Beans prepared this way will keep all winter.

To use: Remove desired quantity from crock. Rinse well with cool water. Put beans in saucepan and cover with cold water. Bring to boil over high heat. When water comes to a boil, pour it off, and cover beans with boiling water. Boil on medium heat for about 20 minutes, or until tender. Drain. Serve buttered.

Green Beans Orientale

    1 pound fresh or frozen green beans
    2 teaspoons sesame oil
    1 tablespoon soy sauce
    ⅛ to ¼ teaspoon red pepper (cayenne)
    Dash of MSG (Accent)
    1 to 2 green onions, chopped
    1 teaspoon toasted sesame seeds
    Salt

Boil green beans until almost tender. Drain. Combine remaining ingredients and mix with beans. Chill before serving.

Variations: Substitute peas, bean sprouts, potatoes, zucchini, raw spinach, or combinations of vegetables.

Floy's Green Beans

6 servings

    6 cups fresh green beans, snapped into 1-inch pieces
    2 to 3 tablespoons bacon drippings
    15 tiny boiling onions or 1 medium-size onion,
        cut into pieces
    2 to 3 cups water
    Salt
    6 fresh mushrooms
    1 tablespoon butter or margarine

Remove string, if any, and break beans into pieces; wash thoroughly and drain. Heat bacon drippings in a large saucepan until hot but not smoking. Add beans and stir-fry for about 10 minutes, or until all beans are lightly covered in fat and have changed color from dark green to light green. Add onions and water to just cover vegetables. Cover and bring to boil. Boil gently until tender. Salt to taste. Just before serving, sauté mushrooms in butter until tender and slightly browned. Add to green beans and stir gently.

Baked Broccoli or Spinach

1- or 1½-quart casserole
350 degrees F.
6 to 8 servings

    ½ cup thick white sauce
    ½ cup mayonnaise
    3 eggs, well beaten
    1 tablespoon onion juice
    2 cups chopped broccoli or spinach, cooked, or
        2 packages (10 ounces each) frozen chopped
        broccoli or spinach, cooked per package
        directions

Make white sauce (1½ tablespoons butter, 1½ tablespoons flour, ½ cup milk). Mix with mayonnaise and add beaten eggs. Fold in vegetables (grate the onion on a plate and collect the juice). Bake in greased casserole set in pan of water about 45 minutes, or until set.

Easy Broccoli Casserole

2-quart casserole
350 degrees F.
10 servings

    2 packages (10 ounces each) frozen chopped
        broccoli, partially thawed
    1 can (5 ounces) water chestnuts, drained
        and thinly sliced
    1 can (10½ ounces) cream of chicken soup
    2 tablespoons dry bread crumbs
    ¼ cup grated Parmesan cheese
    2 tablespoons butter, melted

Break broccoli into pieces; squeeze out and discard excess liquid. Place broccoli and water chestnuts in ungreased casserole. Cover with soup. Mix bread crumbs, cheese, and melted butter. Sprinkle on top of soup. Bake, uncovered, 1 hour.

Brussels Sprouts Supreme

4 servings

    1 package (10 ounces) frozen Brussels sprouts
    1½ tablespoons flour
    ⅔ cup water
    ⅔ cup light cream
    ½ teaspoon salt
    ¼ teaspoon thyme
    ⅓ pound Italian chestnuts,* cooked and chopped
        (optional)
    2 tablespoons buttered crumbs

Cook Brussels sprouts as directed on package; drain. In a small jar with a tight lid, shake flour and water until smooth. Pour into small saucepan and add cream, salt, and thyme; bring to a boil, stirring constantly. Boil 2 minutes, or until slightly thickened. Add Brussels sprouts and chestnuts, and pour mixture into serving dish. Sprinkle buttered crumbs over top.

To cook chestnuts: Slit shells with two gashes made to form an X. Place in a heavy skillet with a little salad oil. Cover and shake over low heat until the shells loosen. Peel, removing shell and skin. Place chestnuts in salted water to cover. Boil 15 to 20 minutes, or until tender. Drain and chop coarsely.

The horse chestnuts common in many areas are poisonous and must not be eaten.

Savory Cabbage

4 to 6 servings

    1 medium head green cabbage
    Salt
    2 tablespoons butter or margarine
    2 tablespoons finely chopped onion
    ¼ cup cream
    Pepper (freshly ground or lemon pepper is best)

Shred cabbage and cook in boiling, salted water until just tender (about 10 minutes). Drain well. In the meantime, melt butter in frying pan, and sauté onion until soft and slightly browned. Add cabbage and toss well. Pour on cream and sprinkle with pepper. Heat and serve at once.

Squaw Corn

4 servings

> 4 slices bacon
> 1 medium green pepper, chopped
> 1 small onion, chopped
> 2 cups cream-style corn or fresh-cut corn
> 1 teaspoon salt
> Dash of pepper
> 4 eggs, beaten well

Fry bacon until crisp; remove from pan, and drain off all but 2 tablespoons fat. Add green pepper and onion to fat in pan, and cook until soft. Combine corn, salt, pepper, and beaten eggs. Add to pan and cook, stirring constantly, until eggs are set. Crumble in bacon. This makes a good luncheon dish served with a green salad and whole wheat muffins.

Dried Corn Pudding

1-quart casserole
325 degrees F.
6 servings

> ¾ cup dried corn
> 2 cups half-and-half, scalded
> 2 eggs, slightly beaten
> 2 tablespoons chopped green onion
> 2 tablespoons melted butter
> 1 tablespoon sugar
> 1 teaspoon salt
> ⅛ teaspoon pepper

Rinse dried corn. Add to hot half-and-half. Cover and let soak about 4 hours; then add eggs, green onion, butter, sugar, salt, and pepper. Pour into greased casserole. Bake about 35 minutes, or until knife inserted in center comes out clean.

Honeyed Carrots

	For 6	For 12
Medium carrots	6	12
Butter	1 tablespoon	2 tablespoons
Honey	2 tablespoons	4 tablespoons

Cut carrots in about 1-inch lengths, then run through the large disc of the food grinder; or use the steel blade in a food processor and chop coarsely; or slice on the bias. Cook, covered, in boiling water until just tender-crisp, about 15 minutes; drain well. Add butter and honey, and toss lightly until carrots are evenly coated. Keep warm on low heat until ready to serve.

Carrots in Onion Sauce

6 servings

> 5 to 6 carrots, peeled and bias-cut
> 1 chicken bouillon cube
> ½ cup water
> 1 small onion, sliced thin
> 2 tablespoons butter or margarine
> 1 tablespoon flour
> ¼ teaspoon salt
> Dash of pepper
> ½ cup water
> Pinch of sugar

Cook carrots with bouillon cube in ½ cup water about 10 minutes, or until just tender-crisp. While carrots are cooking, sauté onion in butter until soft and very lightly browned, stirring occasionally (about 15 minutes). Add flour, salt, and pepper to onion. Let bubble a minute or two; then add ½ cup water and stir until thickened. Add undrained carrots and a little more water to desired thickness, if needed. You want a thin glaze, not "creamed" carrots. Cook, uncovered, about 10 minutes. Add a pinch of sugar and serve.

Lentil Burgers

8 servings

> ½ pound (1¼ cups) lentils
> 3 cups water
> 1 large onion, chopped
> 1 cup chopped carrots
> 3 cups fresh bread crumbs (3 slices)
> 1 egg, slightly beaten
> 1 teaspoon garlic salt
> ½ teaspoon leaf oregano, crumbled
> ½ teaspoon salt
> 3 tablespoons butter or margarine
> Hamburger buns or toasted bread

Wash lentils; cook in 3 cups water for 15 minutes. Add onion and carrots and cook 15 minutes longer, or until lentils and carrots are tender. Remove from heat and cool slightly. Drain, if necessary. Stir in bread crumbs, egg, garlic salt, oregano, and salt. Melt butter in large frying pan. Drop lentil mixture into pan; with the back of spoon, flatten into a patty. Cook over moderate heat for about 5 minutes, or until browned on one side. Carefully turn and brown on other side. Serve in buns or on toasted bread.

Lentil Casserole

2-quart casserole or 8×4×3-inch loaf pan
325 degrees F.
6 to 8 servings

    2 cups cooked lentils (cooked according to package
        directions)
    2 carrots, sliced and cooked tender
    1 onion, chopped
    1 egg, beaten
    ¼ cup oil
    1 cup evaporated milk
    1 teaspoon salt
    ½ teaspoon sage
    1½ cups crushed corn flakes (optional)

Combine lentils, carrots, and onion in a greased casserole. Combine egg, oil, evaporated milk, salt, and sage, and mix well. Pour over lentil mixture in casserole. Top with corn flakes, if desired, and bake for 30 to 40 minutes, or until set.

Variation: Pour into greased loaf pan and bake for 1 hour. Slice and serve with gravy or sauce.

Baked Lentils

1-quart bean pot or casserole
350 degrees F.
4 to 6 servings

    1 cup lentils
    2½ cups water
    ½ cup chopped onion
    1 teaspoon salt
    2 tablespooons brown sugar
    2 tablespoons catsup
    2 tablespoons molasses
    ½ teaspoon dry mustard
    2 slices bacon, diced

Rinse lentils; drain. In saucepan, combine lentils, water, onion, and salt. Bring to boil; cover and simmer 45 minutes. Stir in brown sugar, catsup, molasses, mustard, and bacon. Pour into casserole or bean pot. Bake, uncovered, for 1 hour and 15 minutes, stirring occasionally.

Stuffed Mushrooms

350 degrees F.
About 24 mushrooms

    2 pounds fresh mushrooms, medium to large size
    ½ cup butter
    1 package (8 ounces) cream cheese, softened
    2 tablespoons cream
    ¼ cup Parmesan cheese
    ¼ cup fine bread crumbs
    ½ teaspoon garlic powder
    2 tablespoons chopped chives or green onion tops

Wash, dry, and remove stems from mushrooms. Melt butter, and dip each mushroom in butter. Combine cream cheese, cream, Parmesan cheese, bread crumbs, garlic powder, and chopped chives or onions. Fill mushrooms. Place the filled mushrooms on a baking sheet and bake for 12 minutes, or until nicely browned.

These mushrooms can be wrapped tightly and frozen or refrigerated until time of serving. They are excellent as a first course for dinner or as a main course with a salad and bread for a light luncheon. They are also good as a picnic or snack food, served cold after baking.

Noodles with Mushrooms

8-inch baking dish
6 servings

    1 package (8 ounces) egg noodles
    1 pound mushrooms
    ¼ cup (1 stick) butter
    ½ cup toast crumbs
    Salt and pepper
    Parsley

Cook noodles until tender; drain and rinse in hot water. Clean and chop mushrooms, stems and all. Sauté in butter until almost dry. Add ½ cup toast crumbs, mix well, and season with salt and pepper.

Put noodles in a shallow serving dish. Cover with hot mushroom mixture; sprinkle with parsley. Serve immediately.

Peas à la Mushrooms

4 servings

    1 cup sliced fresh mushrooms or 1 can (6 ounces)
      button mushrooms
    2 tablespoons minced onion
    2 tablespoons butter or margarine
    ½ teaspoon salt
    Dash of pepper
    ¼ teaspoon nutmeg
    Pinch of marjoram
    1 package (10 ounces) frozen peas, cooked and
      drained

In small frying pan, sauté mushrooms and onion in butter about 5 minutes, or until tender. Add salt, pepper, nutmeg, and marjoram and mix well. Pour into saucepan containing drained cooked peas. Heat and serve.

Peas with Onions and Zucchini

About 4 cups, 6 to 8 servings

    3½ cups (3 medium) zucchini, sliced ¼-inch thick
    ¼ cup butter or margarine
    1 package (10 ounces) frozen green peas and pearl
      onions, partially thawed
    ½ teaspoon salt
    ¼ teaspoon salad herbs
    Dash of pepper
    ½ cup light cream

Sauté zucchini in butter until lightly brown, about 4 or 5 minutes. Break apart the peas; add to zucchini with remaining ingredients. Cover; heat slowly just until vegetables are tender, about 4 minutes.

Low-Cal French Fries

425 degrees F.
2 servings (45 calories each)

    1 medium baking potato
    1 egg white, beaten
    Parmesan cheese
    Oregano

Cut potato lengthwise into wedges. Brush cut sides with beaten egg white; sprinkle with Parmesan cheese and oregano. Bake 25 minutes or until tender.

Farol's Golden Potato Bake

9×13×2-inch baking pan
350 degrees F.
12 to 16 servings

    7 large potatoes, boiled in skins
    1 can (10½ ounces) cream of chicken soup
    1 cup sour cream
    1 cup shredded Cheddar cheese
    ⅓ cup chopped green onion
    2 tablespoons butter or margarine, melted
    ½ cup milk
    1 cup corn flakes, crushed
    ½ cup Parmesan cheese
    2 tablespoons butter or margarine, melted

Peel cooked potatoes and shred. Spread in buttered baking dish. Mix together soup, sour cream, cheese, green onion, butter, and milk. Spread mixture evenly over potatoes; do not stir. Mix together corn flakes, Parmesan cheese, and butter. Sprinkle evenly over top of casserole. Bake about 30 minutes, or until hot and bubbly.

Cottage Potatoes

400 degrees F.
8 servings (75 calories each)

    4 medium baking potatoes
    1 cup low-fat cottage cheese
    ½ cup skim milk
    1 tablespoon minced onion
    Salt and pepper
    Paprika and parsley to garnish

Scrub and bake potatoes. Cut in half lengthwise. Scoop out center, reserving shells. Beat pulp with cottage cheese, milk, onion, and salt and pepper to taste. Spoon back into shells. Sprinkle with paprika and parsley. Bake 10 minutes, or until piping hot.

Regular or instant mashed potatoes may be substituted for the baked potatoes. Serve directly, or heat in casserole in moderate oven.

Twice-Baked Potatoes

4 to 8 servings

  4 medium to large baking potatoes, baked
  1 to 2 cups cooked vegetable,* drained thoroughly
  2 to 3 tablespoons grated onion
  1 to 2 teaspoons salt, or to taste
  ¼ teaspoon dill weed
  ⅛ teaspoon pepper
  1 egg, slightly beaten
  2 tablespoons butter or margarine (more for large
    potatoes)
  ½ cup hot milk (about)

Bake potatoes in hot oven (425 degrees F.) so they will be dry and fluffy. When they are very tender, remove from oven and cut slice from top; if potatoes are large, cut in half. Work carefully to keep shell intact. Scoop potato into ricer or food mill, or mash thoroughly. In a large bowl, place potatoes and all remaining ingredients. Whip to a light fluff. You want a moist mixture, but one that holds its shape, so it will not flatten out and run out of the shell when it is baked the second time.

You may wish to experiment with seasoning variations. For example, try curry powder in place of dill weed; use seasoned salt; crisp and add 4 to 6 slices of bacon; or add 8 ounces cream or cottage cheese. Shredded Cheddar cheese may be beaten into the potato mixture or sprinkled on top. Add milk last so you can adjust amount needed with the different ingredients.

After the potato mixture is prepared and tasted to adjust seasonings to your liking, pile it high in potato shells. Place on baking sheet and return to oven set at 375 degrees F. Bake until thoroughly heated and lightly browned, 10 to 15 minutes. This will take about 30 minutes if potatoes have been refrigerated, 45 minutes if they have been frozen. Serve immediately.

Mashed Potatoes: Use fresh cooked mashed potatoes or leftovers, reheated. Season and add vegetables as suggested for twice-baked potatoes. This is an excellent way to use up left-over mashed potatoes.

Cooked Vegetable: Use kind and amount to suit taste, varying the amount with the size of the potato. Carrots, spinach, cabbage, green beans, peas, corn, zucchini, or a mixture of your favorites may be used. One package (10 ounces) frozen peas and corn is a good combination, or try a package of frozen mixed or creamed vegetables. Small vegetables may be left whole, but mash or purée most vegetables. Cut green beans in small pieces; carrots are good mashed or shredded.

Pioneer Scalloped Potatoes

2-quart baking dish
350 degrees F.
6 servings

  4 cups peeled and thinly sliced potatoes
  1 teaspoon salt
  ⅛ teaspoon pepper
  2 tablespoons flour
  2 tablespoons onion, finely sliced or grated
  2 tablespoons butter or margarine
  ⅛ teaspoon baking soda*
  2 cups milk (about)

Layer potatoes, salt and pepper, flour, onion, and bits of butter. Add soda to milk, then pour it over the potatoes. Use enough milk so that it can just be seen between the top slices of potato. Cover and bake about 20 minutes. Remove cover and continue to bake about another 40 minutes, or until potatoes are fork tender and milk is mostly absorbed. Top will brown slightly.

Soda may be eliminated, but it keeps the cooked mixture from looking curdled.

Campfire Potatoes and Onions

4 or 5 servings

  ¼ cup margarine or bacon drippings or combination
  2 large onions, peeled and sliced in thin slices
  4 large potatoes, peeled and sliced in thin slices
  Salt and pepper

Over campfire or grill, melt margarine or bacon drippings in large, heavy frying pan. Add onions and cook until soft. Remove from pan and add potatoes. Cook until tender, turning occasionally. Add onions and continue cooking until browned.

Candied Yams 'n Apples

2-quart baking pan or casserole
375 degrees F.
6 to 8 servings

  4 medium-size yams
  2 large apples, peeled
  ¼ cup butter or margarine, melted
  ½ cup brown sugar
  ½ teaspoon cinnamon

Scrub yams; do not peel. Cook, covered, in boiling water until almost tender, 20 to 30 minutes.

Drain and cool. Remove skins and cut into quarters. Cut each apple into eighths; remove core section. Arrange yams and apples in shallow baking pan, or slice each and layer in casserole. Combine butter, brown sugar, and cinnamon. Sprinkle over yams and apples. Bake about an hour, basting often.

Yams in Orange Sauce

300 degrees F.
8 servings

    4 yams, medium size
    1 cup orange juice
    1 tablespoon grated orange rind
    ½ cup sugar
    ½ cup brown sugar
    1 tablespoon cornstarch
    2 tablespoons melted butter or margarine
    1 orange, sliced (optional)

Scrub yams and boil without peeling until tender. Drain; cool enough to handle. Remove skins and slice yams in thick slices. Place in buttered baking dish in a single layer.

Mix remaining ingredients except orange slices, and pour over yams. Bake about an hour in a slow oven. Baste several times with syrup in dish. Add slices of unpeeled orange about last 10 minutes.

Sweet Potatoes and Apples

9×13×2-inch baking dish
350 degrees F.
12 servings

    6 sweet potatoes, cooked, peeled, and cubed
      (or use yams)
    6 tart apples, peeled, cored, and sliced
    ¾ cup sugar
    3 tablespoons cornstarch
    ¾ teaspoon salt
    1½ cups water
    1 tablespoon butter or margarine
    1 tablespoon lemon juice

Place cooked potatoes and uncooked apples in baking dish. Combine sugar, cornstarch, and salt in a saucepan. Add water and cook over medium heat until mixture boils and thickens, stirring constantly. Remove from heat and stir in butter and lemon juice. Pour over sweet potatoes and apples. Bake 1 hour.

Layered Spinach and Noodle Casserole

9×13×2-inch baking dish
350 degrees F.
About 18 servings

    3 packages (10 ounces each) frozen chopped
      spinach or 3 cups chopped cooked spinach
    1 small onion, chopped
    4 tablespoons butter or margarine
    3 tablespoons flour
    1 teaspoon salt
    1 teaspoon paprika
    ⅛ teaspoon pepper
    1½ cups milk
    1 package (12 ounces) medium noodles plus
      2 tablespoons oil
    ½ pound (2 cups) coarsely shredded Swiss cheese
    Paprika (optional)

Cook spinach as package label directs; drain well. Sauté onion in 1 tablespoon butter until lightly browned. Stir into spinach.

Melt remaining 3 tablespoons butter in a small saucepan. Add flour, salt, 1 teaspoon paprika, and pepper; gradually stir in milk. Cook and stir until thickened. Stir in spinach.

Cook noodles as package label directs, except add 2 tablespoons salad oil to cooking water to prevent noodles from sticking together. Drain well.

Arrange half the noodles in a greased baking dish. Sprinkle with half the cheese. Spoon spinach mixture over the cheese. Add layer of remaining noodles. Sprinkle remaining cheese on top, then dust with paprika, if desired. Casserole may be made to this point ahead of time and refrigerated. Bake about 15 minutes if casserole ingredients are still warm, or 25 to 30 minutes if ingredients are cold, or until cheese melts and casserole is hot and bubbly.

Spaghetti Squash

6 servings

    1 spaghetti squash
    Salt and pepper
    Butter or magarine (optional)
    Spaghetti sauce (optional)

Wash squash well; cut in half lengthwise and remove seeds. Steam or cook in small amount of water until tender. With a fork, fluff up spaghetti-like threads; sprinkle with salt and pepper and melted butter. Or omit butter and serve with spaghetti sauce.

Alternate cooking method: Leave squash whole; prick a few holes to release steam. Bake on pie tin in 375-degree F. oven for about 50 minutes, or until fork tender. Squash may also be baked in halves.

Spinach-Artichoke Heart Casserole

1½-quart casserole
350 degrees F.
8 servings

    1 medium onion, chopped
    ¼ cup margarine
    2 packages (10 ounces each) frozen chopped
        spinach
    1 can (about 16 ounces) artichoke hearts, drained
    1 tablespoon flour
    1 package (8 ounces) sour cream
    ½ cup grated Parmesan cheese
    Salt and pepper to taste

Sauté onion in margarine. Cook spinach as directed on package; drain. Combine all ingredients and pour into baking dish. Bake 30 minutes.

Variation: Use cream of mushroom soup or cottage cheese in place of sour cream. Use 1½ cups Swiss or Cheddar cheese, shredded, in place of Parmesan cheese.

Baked Summer Squash

1- or 1½-quart casserole
400 degrees F.
4 to 6 servings

    4 yellow crookneck squash
    1 small onion, finely chopped
    2 tablespoons butter or margarine
    ¼ teaspoon salt
    ½ cup cream
    ¼ cup saltine cracker crumbs
    Butter
    Soft bread crumbs

Slice squash, and boil in salted water until tender. Drain well and mash. Sauté onion in butter until transparent but not brown (5 to 10 minutes). Add to squash along with salt, cream, and cracker crumbs. Pour into greased casserole. Dot with butter and soft bread crumbs. Bake for 30 minutes, or until lightly browned and firm.

Baked Stuffed Tomatoes

1-quart baking dish
350 degrees F.
4 servings

    ¼ cup butter
    1 cup dry bread crumbs
    4 medium tomatoes
    2 tablespoons finely chopped onion
    ¼ teaspoon sweet basil leaves
    ½ teaspoon salt
    Pepper

Melt butter in small skillet and blend in crumbs until evenly coated. Cut a slice from stem end of each tomato. Scoop out seeds and pulp, leaving shell intact. Combine tomato pulp and juice, onion, basil, salt and pepper. Add crumbs, enough to absorb the juice. Fill tomato shells with crumb mixture. Sprinkle remaining crumbs on top. Place tomatoes side by side in baking dish. Bake about 20 minutes.

Variations: Add bits of cooked ham, crisp bacon, broken shrimp, and/or shredded cheese to tomato mixture before adding crumbs.

Cottage-Fried Tomatoes

6 to 8 servings

    8 firm tomatoes (green ones may be used)
    Cornmeal or flour
    Salt and pepper
    4 tablespoons bacon drippings and butter
    2 tablespoons flour
    1 small to medium soft tomato, skinned and cored
    1 cup cream or milk

Slice firm tomatoes into thick slices (about ¾ inch), discarding top and bottom slices. Dip each slice into either cornmeal or flour to which salt and pepper have been added. Fry in the mixed bacon drippings and butter in a heavy pan. Brown until crust forms on one side; turn carefully and brown the other side. Add more fat if needed. Place cooked slices on an oven-proof platter and keep hot until all are fried.

Add the 2 tablespoons flour to fat remaining in pan. Remove pan from heat and smash in the soft tomato. Add the cream and blend well. Return to heat and cook, stirring, until sauce is thickened. Season to taste. Pour over tomato slices.

Zucchini and Green Chili Casserole

1½-quart casserole
350 degrees F.
4 servings

3 medium zucchini
¼ cup onion, chopped
½ teaspoon salt
Pepper
¼ cup canned green chilies, chopped
1 tablespoon butter or margarine
2 tomatoes, sliced
1 cup Monterey Jack cheese or Cheddar
   cheese, shredded

Wash and slice zucchini ½ inch thick. Place in saucepan with onion, salt, and enough water to barely cover. Cook until just tender (about 5 minutes); drain well and transfer to casserole. Sprinkle with pepper and green chilies; dot with butter. Layer tomato slices over chilies, and top with cheese. Heat in oven until cheese is melted and bubbly, 10 to 15 minutes.

Barbecued Zucchini and Onions

Grill
6 servings

4 medium zucchini, cut diagonally in ¼-inch slices
1 medium onion, sliced in thin rings
1 package dry Italian salad dressing mix
2 tablespoons wine or cider vinegar
¼ cup salad oil
2 tablespoons grated Parmesan cheese

Place zucchini and onion on a large sheet of heavy duty aluminum foil; fold up sides slightly to make a container. Combine salad dressing mix, vinegar, and oil; pour over vegetables. Sprinkle with cheese. Fold foil to make a well-sealed packet, and place on grill. Barbecue over medium heat 15-20 minutes, turning once.

Other vegetables may be added to or substituted for all or part of zucchini. Cut pieces thinner if cooking time is longer than for zucchini.

Hellberg's Zucchini Goop

1 can (46 ounces) V-8 Juice or tomato juice
2 to 3 large yellow onions, chopped
3 green peppers, chopped (or 2 green and 1 red pepper)
1 to 2 cups chopped celery (optional)
8 cups peeled, seeded, and chopped zucchini (or slice, then cut slices into quarters)
2 teaspoons salt
2 teaspoons curry powder
2 teaspoons chili powder
2 teaspoons cumin

Combine juice and vegetables in a large kettle. Bring to a boil and boil gently for 20 minutes. Turn off heat, then add salt, curry powder, chili powder, and cumin. You may wish to taste as you add the spices and vary the amounts, or leave out as you wish.

Cool mixture. Divide into 2 lots and freeze. When ready to use, to each lot add the following:

1 pound ground beef, browned lightly
1 can (15¼ ounces) red kidney beans, drained
1 can (15½ ounces) garbanzo beans, drained
1 can (15 ounces) mushroom stems and pieces, juice included
1 can (6 ounces) pitted ripe olives, juice included (halve the olives)
1 can (15 ounces) okra, drained (optional)

Heat all together. Serve over cooked rice, Chinese noodles, or serve plain with Parmesan or shredded Cheddar cheese. To complete your meal, serve with garlic bread and a green salad.

You may prefer to mix all ingredients with the original juice-vegetable mixture. If so, double second list of ingredients (meat and canned vegetables) and assemble before freezing. You will need a very large kettle, such as a preserving kettle. Freeze in containers the right size for a family meal.

Egg-Fried Zucchini Crisps

2 or 3 servings

¾ pound (3 medium) zucchini
¼ cup flour
1 egg
⅛ teaspoon salt
Butter, margarine, or bacon drippings
Soy sauce (optional)
Green onion, chopped (optional)

Wash and dry zucchini; slice off ends. Slice in 1/8-inch disks. Place flour on plate or in shallow bowl. Dip zucchini disks into flour; shake off excess. Beat egg and salt with a fork in a shallow bowl. Dip floured zucchini into beaten egg, and fry in a single layer in hot butter, turning once.

Serve plain or dipped into a mixture of soy sauce and green onions.

Zucchini Layers

2-quart casserole dish
350 degrees F.
6 servings

    3 medium zucchini, sliced thin
    1 onion, sliced thin
    2 tomatoes, sliced thin
    1 green pepper, sliced
    6 fresh mushrooms, sliced, or 1 can (4 ounces)
        sliced mushrooms
    1 tablespoon brown sugar
    ½ cup butter or margarine
    2 teaspoons prepared mustard
    1 teaspoon horseradish

Layer zucchini, onion, tomatoes, green pepper, and mushrooms in a 2-quart casserole dish. Combine brown sugar, butter, mustard, and horseradish, and dot surface with sauce. Bake 35 to 40 minutes.

Zucchini Casserole

350 degrees F.
6 servings

    2 pounds zucchini, sliced (6 cups)
    ¼ cup chopped or sliced onion
    1 can (about 10 ounces) condensed cream of chicken
        soup
    1 cup sour cream
    1 cup shredded carrots
    1 package (8 ounces) herb-seasoned stuffing mix
    ½ cup (1 stick) butter or margarine, melted

Cook zucchini and onion in boiling salted water for 5 minutes. Drain. Combine soup and sour cream. Stir in carrots; fold in drained squash and onion.

Combine stuffing mix and butter. Spread half of stuffing on bottom of baking dish. Spoon vegetable mixture on top, and sprinkle remaining stuffing over vegetables. Bake 25 to 30 minutes.

Piquant Zucchini or Summer Squash

4 servings

    4 small- to medium-size zucchini
    ¼ cup sliced onion
    2 or 3 tablespoons butter or margarine
    2 teaspoons flour
    ½ cup sour cream
    1 or 2 chilies, canned, cut in quarters (optional)
    ¼ teaspoon sweet basil (optional)
    ¼ teaspoon oregano (optional)

Slice zucchini into quarter-inch disks. Simmer in a small amount of water for about 5 minutes, leaving a bit crisp. Drain. In the meantime, brown onions lightly in butter on medium heat. Add flour and stir over heat 2 to 3 minutes. Blend in sour cream. Add zucchini, chilies, and seasonings; mix lightly. Reheat if necessary, but avoid boiling.

Vegetable Medleys

6 servings

    2 tablespoons butter, margarine, bacon fat, or
        chicken fat
    ¼ cup coarsely chopped onion
    2 or 3 cups vegetables, mixed*
    Salt, pepper, and seasonings to taste**

Melt butter; add onion and sauté 2 or 3 minutes. Prepare other vegetables appropriately, cutting or breaking into bite-size or smaller pieces. Add to onion-butter mixture and heat, stirring frequently. Add seasonings; reduce heat to very low and cook, covered, until tender. Add a small amount of water or broth if needed. Serve with any bit of cooking liquid, leaving lid off at last to reduce amount if necessary.

*Suggested combinations (a little of several vegetables adds interest in color and flavor): broccoli and cauliflower, broken into flowerets; carrot, green beans, and cauliflower; zucchini and yellow crookneck squash with green or red sweet pepper; carrot, celery, and zucchini or other summer squashes; green beans, corn, and tomato sections.

**Suggested seasonings (mix and match to suit your taste): bay leaf, sweet basil (especially with tomato), oregano, chili powder, mustard, salts (celery, garlic, seasoned), tarragon, fresh ginger root, thyme, rosemary, marjoram.

Spaghetti Primavera

About 12 servings

    2 tomatoes, skinned and coarsely chopped
    1 tablespoon oil (olive oil or a mixture of olive
        oil and cooking oil)
    1 garlic clove, pressed or finely chopped
    ¼ cup chopped parsley
    Dash of salt and pepper
    10 mushrooms, washed, trimmed, and sliced
        vertically through stems
    1 to 2 tablespoons oil
    1 cup matchstick-cut zucchini (about 1 inch long)
    2 cups broccoli florets
    1½ cups sugar snap or snow peas (optional)
    1 cup green peas
    6 asparagus spears, sliced on the diagonal (optional)
    1 pound spaghetti
    1 tablespoon oil
    ½ cup Parmesan cheese
    ⅓ cup melted butter
    1 cup whipping cream, warmed
    ⅓ cup pine nuts or slivered almonds, toasted

Sauté tomatoes in oil with garlic, parsley, salt, and pepper. In another pan lightly sauté mushrooms in oil. Blanch all other vegetables in boiling water until tender crisp. Drain well; add to mushrooms. Keep hot. Cook spaghetti as package directs, adding 1 tablespoon oil to cooking water. Drain. Lightly mix cheese, butter, and cream into spaghetti. Add salt and pepper to taste. Serve spaghetti on large platter topped with vegetables. Garnish with sautéed tomatoes and nuts. Vary vegetables with the season.

Green and Gold Vegetable Ring

12-inch ring mold or 2 8-inch ring molds or
  9×13 baking pan
350 degrees F.
12 to 16 servings

    2 pounds carrots (8 to 10 medium)
    3 packages (10 ounces each) frozen peas
    ⅓ cup butter or margarine
    6 tablespoons flour
    ½ to 1 teaspoon salt
    ¼ teaspoon onion salt
    ¼ teaspoon white pepper
    2 cups milk
    4 eggs, slightly beaten

Peel carrots and cut into small pieces. Cook carrots and peas separately until very tender. Drain and purée each.

Melt butter in a saucepan; blend in flour, salt, onion salt, and white pepper. Add milk; cook and stir until thickened. Cover and cook over very low heat 4 or 5 minutes longer. Divide sauce into 2 equal parts. Add one part to carrots and one to peas. Season to taste. Add 2 eggs to each.

Butter ring mold(s) well, including sides and center. Pour in pea mixture and smooth surface. Top with carrot mixture. Set mold(s) in pan of hot water and bake about 1½ hours, or until set. Unmold carefully onto warm platter. Serve alone or with creamed chicken, sweetbreads or fish in center. Or fill center of ring with buttered vegetables.

Orleans Rice and Vegetable Bake

1½-quart casserole
350 degrees F.
6 to 8 servings

    2 cups cooked rice
    ½ teaspoon salt
    ¼ teaspoon pepper
    2 cups chopped tomatoes
    1 package (10 ounces) frozen cut green beans,
        cooked, drained
    ¼ cup onion, chopped
    ¼ teaspoon basil
    1 jar (8 ounces) pasteurized processed cheese
        spread or 1 cup shredded cheese
    1 cup soft bread crumbs
    2 tablespoons margarine, melted

Combine rice, salt, and pepper; place in casserole. Combine tomatoes, green beans, onion, basil, and cheese spread. Pour over rice. Top with combined bread crumbs and margarine. Bake 20 minutes.

To make ahead, follow recipe directions, reserving bread crumb mixture. Cover and refrigerate. Uncover, top with bread crumb mixture, and bake 35 to 40 minutes, or until hot.

Quick Vegetable Medley

12 servings

    1 package (10 ounces) frozen peas
    1 package (10 ounces) frozen cut broccoli
    1 package (10 ounces) frozen corn
    1 package (10 ounces) frozen cut carrots
    2 tablespoons pimiento, chopped
    ⅓ cup sliced almonds

½ cup chicken broth
1 teaspoon dry minced onion
½ teaspoon dry mustard

Prepare peas, broccoli, corn, and carrots according to package directions. Drain. Place vegetables in a saucepan and add pimiento, almonds, broth, onion, and mustard. Heat to boiling and simmer for 3 minutes.

Ever-Ready Vegetable Combo

About 2 quarts

1 quart seasoned chicken broth, all fat removed
1 medium cabbage, cored and shredded
3 to 4 onions, sliced
3 to 4 carrots, bias cut
Salt and pepper

Use homemade or canned chicken broth or mixture. Let it chill until fat comes to the top; then lift fat off and discard. Bring broth to a boil. Add vegetables (use more or less of each to suit yourself), and cook until vegetables are tender-crisp, 20 to 30 minutes. Taste, and add salt and pepper as desired. At this point, you should have moist, tender vegetables, but no excess soup. Serve as a hot mixed vegetable. This "combo" will keep in the refrigerator at least a week, and may be spooned out of storage container and eaten cold or reheated, whichever you prefer.

Stir-Fry Dinner

Large frying pan or dutch oven or wok
About 6 servings

¾ pound sliced lean meat, sprinkled with garlic salt or meat tenderizer (use beef, chicken or pork or leftover meat—beef, chicken, pork, ham)
2 onions, sliced
Celery, sliced diagonally
Carrots, sliced diagonally, very thin
1 to 2 green peppers, sliced in about ¼-inch strips
Optional vegetables (use at least 5 cups of a variety):
  Jerusalem artichokes, peeled and sliced thin
  Fresh mushrooms, sliced vertically through stems
  Sugar snap peas, whole but with ends snipped
  Green onions, cut in ½-inch lengths (use some of green top)
  Cauliflowerets
  Broccoli flowers
  Zucchini, sliced
  Water chestnuts, sliced
  Bean sprouts

Tomatoes, quartered
Oriental Sauce (below)
Hot cooked rice

Heat small amount of oil in frying pan or wok (to barely cover bottom of pan). Stir-fry meat 2 minutes. Remove from pan and keep warm. Stir-fry for 2 to 3 minutes, at medium-high heat, the onions, celery, and carrots; remove and keep warm. Repeat with each of the remaining vegetables, cooking until just barely tender-crisp, and adding a small amount of oil as needed. Heat tomatoes last. Combine all the cooked vegetables and meat in frying pan or wok; add Oriental Sauce (below). Heat just to boiling point (do not boil!). Serve with hot, cooked rice.

Note: This is a good recipe for using garden vegetables or leftovers. Vary it to suit your own taste. The sauce makes the vegetables extra special.

Oriental Sauce

3 tablespoons soy sauce
2 tablespoons sugar
⅔ cup water
1½ tablespoons cornstarch, mixed with a little cold water

Mix all ingredients together in small saucepan; cook and stir until thickened.

Meat and Fish

Cinderella Roast Beef

250 degrees F.
20 servings, 3 ounces each

    5 pound chuck or arm roast of beef
      (smaller roasts dry out more)
    Salt
    Pepper

Wipe meat with damp cloth or paper towel. Rub with salt and pepper. Place on roasting rack in shallow pan. Do not cover. Roast about 36 minutes per pound, or to an internal temperature of 155 degrees F. for medium rare. (Meat is more tender if slightly on the rare side.) This slow heat method conserves meat and yields about one extra serving per pound.

Beef Fillet with Mushroom Sauce

450 degrees F.
About 12 servings

    6 tablespoons butter or margarine
    1 fillet of beef (8 to 10 pounds), well-trimmed
    Salt
    Freshly ground pepper
    Mushroom Sauce (below)

Melt 4 tablespoons butter in a shallow roasting pan. When it is just melted, turn the fillet in it until the meat is coated. Sprinkle with salt and pepper.

Bake 25 to 35 minutes for rare beef, or until desired doneness, basting frequently. Transfer the meat to a large serving dish; keep warm. Pour off most of the fat from the pan, and pour in the Mushroom Sauce (recipe below). Stir to dissolve the brown particles that cling to the bottom and sides of the pan. Swirl in the remaining two tablespoons butter.

Slice the fillet (slice only the amount to be served immediately, and leave the rest of the fillet whole to be sliced later). Spoon the sauce over the beef, or spoon part of it over the beef and serve the rest in a sauceboat.

Mushroom Sauce

About 2 cups

    2 tablespoons butter or margarine
    8 large mushrooms, sliced or halved
    Salt
    Freshly ground pepper
    2 tablespoons finely chopped shallots (green onion
      may be used)
    ¼ cup water
    2 tablespoons lemon juice
    1½ cups brown sauce or 1 can (10¾ ounces)
      beef gravy

Heat the butter in a frying pan and add mushrooms. Sprinkle with salt and pepper, and cook until mushrooms give up their liquid. Add the shallots and cook, stirring, until most of liquid evaporates. Add the water and lemon juice; cook one minute. Add the brown sauce; simmer 15 minutes.

Fresh Brisket of Beef

225 degrees F.
About 12 servings

    4 to 5 pound beef brisket, lean cut
    Seasoned salt
    Garlic salt
    Celery salt
    Meat tenderizer
    Liquid smoke
    4 teaspoons Worcestershire sauce

Season both sides of meat with seasoned salt, garlic salt, celery salt, and meat tenderizer. Put meat in glass baking dish, skin side down. Pour on about ¼ bottle of liquid smoke and 4 teaspoons Worcestershire sauce. Cover with foil and refrigerate at least 24 hours (48 hours is better). Turn the meat once or twice. When ready to cook, place in slow oven, covered, and bake about 8 hours. (A 2- to 3-pound roast will bake in about 5 hours.) Let stand about 20 minutes before carving; carve on the diagonal so as to obtain the widest slice possible. Make gravy from pan drippings, adding a bouillon cube or soup base and water, as desired. Thicken slightly with roux if needed.

Barbequed Brisket of Beef

Omit the seasonings, and pour bottled barbeque sauce over brisket. You will need at least ½ bottle; be generous. You may wish to use some of the liquid smoke and some of the meat tenderizer, although neither are necessary.

Prepared either way, this meat is good either hot or cold; it reheats very well in about ½ hour, and is moist and delicious.

Quick Sauerbraten

8 to 10 servings

    4 to 5 pounds beef brisket or chuck
    6 onions, chopped
    3 cups boiling water
    1½ teaspoons salt
    ⅓ cup lemon juice
    3 tablespoons brown sugar
    4 to 6 gingersnaps, crushed

Brown the meat in a heavy saucepan or Dutch oven over medium heat, in a little fat if necessary. Turn frequently. Add onions and brown lightly. Add water and salt. Cover, and cook over low heat for 2½ hours or until meat is tender. Remove meat and keep warm. Skim fat from pan drippings; then stir lemon juice, brown sugar, and gingersnaps into pan juices. Cook 10 minutes. Taste and adjust seasonings. Serve with dumplings, if desired.

Eye-of-Round Fillet of Beef

500 degrees F.
About 3 servings to a pound

    1 eye-of-round fillet, any size desired
    Salt, pepper, flour
    Butter or margarine

Wipe meat with a damp cloth or paper towel. Place in a shallow baking pan. Rub well with salt and pepper, and lightly with flour. Spread a thin coating of butter on spots that have no fat covering.

Place in very hot oven. Leave the temperature at 500 degrees F. for 5 minutes for each pound of meat. Then turn oven off; don't open door—leave meat cooking for 1 to 1½ hours, depending on size. Remove meat from oven and let it stand a few minutes before carving. You won't have much in the way of drippings to make gravy or to serve the

roast *au jus,* but beef soup base will take care of the lack. We like to lightly brown a few fresh mushrooms in the meat drippings; then add soup base and water for either gravy or *au jus.*

Although this is a relatively tough cut of meat, cooked this way and served at least pink (more rare if you like it that way), it is almost as good as tenderloin and much less expensive.

We sometimes rub dry onion soup mix into the meat before cooking or do the same with finely chopped carrots, onions, and celery.

Swiss Steak

325 degrees F.
8 to 10 servings

    2 pounds beef round steak (1 complete round,
        sliced about ¾ inch thick)
    ½ cup flour
    ¾ teaspoon salt
    ⅛ teaspoon pepper
    4 tablespoons cooking fat or oil

Trim excess fat from meat; cut into 8 to 10 serving-size portions. Combine flour, salt, and pepper; mix well. Pound into meat pieces with meat mallet or edge of heavy plate. Heat 2 tablespoons fat in large, heavy frying pan or Dutch oven. Brown meat pieces quickly on both sides, three or four at a time as they will fit into pan. Add more fat as needed. Proceed with one of the treatments listed below.

Treatment 1: Add 2 cups beef gravy, left-over, canned, or made from pan drippings, to meat in Dutch oven. Cover and bake for about 1 hour, or until meat is fork tender.

Treatment 2: Substitute Spanish Sauce for gravy. (See Index.)

Treatment 3: Add 2 cups sliced onions to meat in Dutch oven. Brown lightly. Cover and bake about 1 hour, or until tender. When meat is cooked, remove it to a warm serving platter. Add ¼ cup flour to drippings and onions remaining in pan, and stir to blend thoroughly. Stir in 3 cups of water and 3 beef bouillon cubes (or 3 teaspoons beef soup base). Cook and stir until gravy thickens.

Treatment 4: Remove browned meat from Dutch oven. Add 1 cup sliced onions and brown lightly (use 1 or 2 tablespoons additional fat, if necessary). Return meat to pan. Cover with cream of chicken soup (one can, 10½ ounces, diluted with one soup can water and stirred until smooth). Cover and bake at 325 degrees F. until meat is tender. Remove meat from pan. Dilute gravy, if needed, with additional water, or milk. Reheat. Taste and adjust seasonings.

Treatment 5: Crock Pot Steak. Use thinner steak, cut 3/8 to 1/2-inch thick. Cut meat into serving-size pieces. Omit flour and seasonings. Brown quickly in hot fat. (If time is at a premium, don't brown.) Arrange in crock pot. Add one can cream of chicken soup, undiluted. Cover and cook at either low or high heat as directed by pot manufacturer, according to time desired. When ready to serve, remove meat. Dilute gravy, if needed, with hot milk or water. Taste and adjust seasonings.

Treatment 6: Deluxe Swiss Steak. Proceed as for Treatment #1. While meat is baking, wash, trim, and slice about ½ pound of fresh mushrooms. Brown lightly in about 2 tablespoons butter or margarine in frying pan (5 to 10 minutes on medium heat, or until mushrooms give up their liquid). Add mushrooms and juices from the frying pan to meat the last 15 minutes of cooking.

Treatment 7: Use one large round steak. Place in crock pot or Dutch oven. Add one can (10½ ounces) cream of mushroom soup and 1 package (1 envelope) dry onion soup mix. With this method, there is no need to brown the meat first. Cover and cook as directed by pot manufacturer, or cover and bake in oven at 325 degrees F. until meat is tender, about 2 hours.

Flank Steak

6 to 8 servings

⅓ cup oil
⅓ cup Kikkoman soy sauce
1 tablespoon Italian seasoning
3 or 4 chopped green onions, including tops
1 flank steak (the thickest one you can find), scored lightly

Combine oil, soy sauce, Italian seasoning, and chopped green onions. Pour over steak in glass baking dish and let marinate several hours or overnight. Just before serving, remove meat from marinade and place on rack in broiler pan. Broil about 3 or 4 minutes on each side. Do not overcook; meat should be rare. Slice thinly at an angle and across grain.

Hickory Smoked Flank Steak

Outdoor grill
4 to 6 servings

1 flank steak (about 1½ pounds), not scored, or use bottom round steak, 1 to 1½ inches thick
Seasoned meat tenderizer
1 cup oil
¾ cup catsup
½ cup cider vinegar
3 tablespoons Worcestershire sauce
1 large onion, sliced
Hickory chips

Sprinkle steak generously on both sides with meat tenderizer; let stand ½ hour or more. In a shallow glass dish, combine oil, catsup, vinegar, and Worcestershire sauce; mix well. Place steak in marinade. Spread onion over steak. If marinade does not cover steak, turn or baste often. Let steak marinate for 3 to 4 hours or longer.

Soak a double handful of hickory chips in water while charcoal fire is heating. When fire is hot, toss the soaked hickory chips on the fire. Place meat on grill about 3 inches above fire. To keep flame down, sprinkle fire with water. (We use a sponge.) Cook about 8 minutes on each side, or until desired doneness. Use a sharp knife to carve, cutting diagonally across grain of meat into very thin slices. If hickory chips are not available, the meat will still be delicious.

Quick Beef Goulash

4 servings

2 pounds beef chuck, cut into 1½-inch squares
2 large onions
½ cup canned tomato soup
2 bouillon cubes
1½ cups water
1 tablespoon paprika
1 teaspoon vinegar
Cooked medium noodles

Brown meat in a small amount of oil in frying pan, then remove. Sauté onions in same pan until golden brown. Add meat, tomato soup, bouillon cubes, water, paprika, and vinegar, and stir to mix. Lower heat; simmer about 2 hours, or until tender. Serve with noodles. This recipe may easily be doubled or quadrupled for serving a large group.

Pepper Steak with Rice

6 servings

1 pound lean beef round steak, cut ½-inch thick
2 tablespoons butter or margarine
2 cloves garlic, minced
1½ cups beef broth
1 cup sliced green onions, including tops
2 green peppers, cut in strips
2 tablespoons cornstarch
½ cup water
¼ cup soy sauce
2 large fresh tomatoes, cut into eighths
3 cups hot cooked rice

Pound steak to ¼-inch thick. Cut into ¼-inch wide strips. Melt butter or margarine in large skillet, and brown meat until all pink is gone. Add garlic and beef broth; cover and simmer for 30 minutes. Stir in onions and green peppers. Cover and cook for 5 minutes. Blend cornstarch, water, and soy sauce, and stir into meat mixture. Cook, stirring, until clear and thickened—about 2 minutes. Add tomatoes and heat until they are hot through. Serve over rice.

Fireside Stew

8 servings

2 pounds stew meat, cut into cubes
1½ cups water
1 can (10 ounces) beef broth or consommé
1 can (8 ounces) tomato sauce
1 teaspoon salt
½ teaspoon pepper
1 tablespoon Worcestershire sauce
1 bay leaf
2 onions, quartered
6 carrots, cut in pieces
4 potatoes, peeled and quartered
1 can (16 ounces) beans (lima, pinto, kidney, Great Northern), drained
1 can (8 ounces) whole kernel corn

In heavy pan or Dutch oven, brown meat in small amount of fat. Add water and beef broth, tomato sauce, salt, pepper, Worcestershire sauce, bay leaf, and onions. Cover; cook for 1½ hours. Add carrots and potatoes; cook 30 minutes longer or until tender. Add beans and corn, and heat to boiling again.

Beef Stroganoff

About 6 servings

⅓ cup butter or margarine
½ cup onions, finely chopped
½ pound fresh mushrooms, sliced
1¼ pounds beef (top round, all fat and connective tissue removed, cut in ¼ × ¼ × 2-inch strips)
2 tablespoons flour
1 cup bouillon (or 1 to 2 bouillon cubes dissolved in 1 cup boiling water)
½ teaspoon salt
2 tablespoons tomato paste
¾ teaspoon Worcestershire sauce
¼ cup sour cream
½ cup heavy cream
Cooked rice or noodles

Melt 2 tablespoons of the butter in saucepan. Add onions, and sauté until golden; remove and set aside. Melt 2 tablespoons more of the butter. Add mushrooms, and sauté until lightly browned; remove and set aside. Melt remaining butter. Roll beef in flour, and sauté until lightly browned. Do part of the meat at a time—it's easier. Add bouillon, salt, and the onions. Cover and simmer gently until beef is tender, about ½ hour (check and add more water, if needed). Add tomato paste, Worcestershire sauce, sour cream, heavy cream, and the mushrooms. Heat thoroughly, but do not boil. Serve on rice or noodles.

Celebration Hamburger Steaks

4 servings

1 pound lean ground beef
½ teaspoon salt
Dash of pepper
4 slices bacon
4 large mushrooms

Combine beef, salt, and pepper, and shape into thick patties. Wrap with bacon strip and secure with a toothpick. Arrange on broiler pan, and place under broiler. Broil 7 to 10 minutes on each side, depending on degree of doneness desired. After turning to second side, place 1 mushroom on each patty; brush with some of the pan drippings or butter, and broil with meat. If meat appears to be too dry, add a pat of butter just before serving.

Burgoo

Soup pot, at least 8-quart capacity
16 to 18 servings

3 tablespoons oil
1 pound beef shank
1 pound pork shoulder
1 chicken, cut-up
3 quarts water
1½ tablespoons salt
3 onions, chopped
1 clove garlic, minced
2 potatoes, diced
8 ribs celery, sliced
1 can (1 pound 12 ounces) tomatoes
1 pound carrots, diced
1 package (10 ounces) frozen lima or butter beans
2 green peppers, diced
¼ teaspoon crushed red pepper
½ teaspoon black pepper
1 small onion stuck with 4 cloves
1 bay leaf
2 tablespoons brown sugar
1 package (10 ounces) frozen okra
1 cup corn, fresh from the cob or frozen
½ cup (¼ pound) butter or margarine
½ cup flour
1 tablespoon Worcestershire sauce
½ cup parsley

Heat 1 tablespoon of the oil in soup pot. Brown beef in oil; remove. Brown pork and chicken separately, adding oil as needed. Return all meats to pot. Add water and salt; cook over low heat until just tender, skimming as necessary. Cool. Remove bones and skin from meat and discard. Cut meats into bite-sized pieces and return to broth. Heat remaining oil; cook chopped onion limp. Add to broth, along with garlic, potatoes, celery, tomatoes, carrots, beans, peppers, red and black pepper, onion stuck with cloves, bay leaf, and brown sugar. Cook slowly about 1½ hours; skim and stir occasionally. Add okra and corn; cook 15 minutes longer. Before serving, knead butter and flour together until well blended, and stir into stew. Remove onion studded with cloves. Cook, stirring, until stew has thickened slightly. Add Worcestershire sauce, and adjust for seasoning. Sprinkle with parsley.

Note: A stew rich with meats and vegetables, burgoo has its origins in the 18th century. Long popular for picnics and large group gatherings, it is ideal for large family parties. If made for the ordinary family, it is ideal to serve as a leftover. The flavor improves with age!

Sweet and Sour Meatballs

350 degrees F.

	4 to 6 servings	12 servings	18 servings
Lean ground beef	1 pound	2 pounds	3 pounds
Rolled oats	½ cup	1 cup	1½ cups
Eggs, slightly beaten	1	2	3
Onion, finely chopped	⅓ cup	⅔ cup	1 cup
Salt	¾ teaspoon	1¼ teaspoons	2 teaspoons
Pepper	Few grains	Few grains	⅛ teaspoon
Worcestershire sauce	1 teaspoon	1½ teaspoons	2 teaspoons
Milk	⅓ cup	⅔ cup	1 cup

Combine all ingredients; mix well. Form into balls, each about 2 inches in diameter. Place in casserole dish in a single layer. Cover with sauce (below). Bake about 30 minutes.

Sauce

	4 to 6 servings	12 servings	18 servings
Brown sugar	½ cup	1 cup	1½ cups
Vinegar	¼ cup	½ cup	¾ cup
Prepared mustard	1 teaspoon	2 teaspoons	1 tablespoon
Barbecue sauce	¼ cup	½ cup	¾ cup
Worcestershire sauce	1 teaspoon	2 teaspoons	1 tablespoon

Combine all ingredients and blend thoroughly. Heat and pour over meatballs.

Note: We like to make up this sauce recipe the day before needed, and let it chill so that all fat can be removed. Warm in a saucepan on surface unit.

Danish Chop Suey

8 servings

4 slices bacon, chopped
1 or 2 large onions, chopped
1 pound lean ground beef
4 large ribs of celery, sliced
1 can (28 ounces) tomatoes
1 can (1 pound) kidney beans, drained

Cook bacon in frying pan. Remove from pan and drain and crumble. Add onions; sauté until soft. Add ground beef; cook until pink is gone. Add celery; cook for 3 minutes. Add tomatoes; simmer until celery is tender. Add beans; bring to a boil. Serve topped with crumbled bacon.

Middle East Pilaf with Meatballs

6 servings

Pilaf

        3 tablespoons butter or margarine
        ½ cup onion, chopped
        ¼ cup chopped celery and/or green pepper
        1 cup rice
        3 cups chicken broth
        ¼ to ½ teaspoon oregano
        1 teaspoon salt
        Few grains of black pepper
        1 cup wheat, whole or coarsely cracked, cooked

Melt butter in large skillet; add vegetables and rice. Cook about 10 minutes, stirring frequently. Add broth, oregano, salt and pepper, and cooked wheat. Cover and simmer 25 to 35 minutes, or until rice is cooked. Serve with Meatballs in Mushroom Sauce.

Meatballs in Mushroom Sauce

        2 slices bread, broken into small pieces
        ⅓ cup milk
        1 egg
        1 pound ground beef
        ½ cup finely chopped onion
        ½ teaspoon baking powder
        ¼ teaspoon cumin or sweet basil
        1 teaspoon salt
        ¼ teaspoon black pepper
        1 can (10½ ounces) cream of mushroom soup
        ½ cup milk

Beat to blend well the bread, ⅓ cup milk, and egg. Add ground beef, onion, baking powder, cumin, salt, and pepper; mix well but lightly. Shape into balls and brown in frying pan. Drain off any excess fat. Dilute soup with ½ cup milk; pour over meatballs. Cover and simmer 30 to 35 minutes.

Best-Ever Meat Loaf

375 degrees F.
6 to 8 servings

        2 slices rye or whole wheat bread
        2 slices white bread
        ¾ cup cold water
        1 pound lean ground beef

        1 medium onion, finely chopped
        Few sprigs parsley, chopped
        1 teaspoon salt
        Dash of pepper
        1 egg, slightly beaten
        3 tablespoons Parmesan cheese
        2 tablespoons margarine
        1 can (8 ounces) tomato sauce, or ½ cup bottled
           barbecue sauce
        1 teaspoon oregano (optional)

Break up the bread and soak in cold water. Squeeze out some of the water if bread seems too wet, and combine it with meat. Blend thoroughly; then add onion, parsley, salt, pepper, egg, and cheese. Shape into loaf on a greased baking pan. Spread with margarine. Bake for ½ hour. Pour on the tomato sauce and sprinkle with oregano. Bake another 20 minutes.

This meat loaf holds together and stays moist. It makes delicious cold sandwiches.

Althea's Tacos

6 servings

        1 pound lean ground beef
        1 teaspoon ground cumin
        1 teaspoon chili powder
        ½ teaspoon salt
        1 small onion, chopped
        1 small apple, chopped
        1 can (8 ounces) tomato sauce
        1 can (1 cup) water
        3 tablespoons cornmeal
        6 small taco shells, or 6 flour tortillas
        Shredded lettuce
        Chopped tomatoes
        Shredded cheese

Brown meat, breaking it up as it browns. Skim off fat. Add cumin, chili powder, salt, onion, apple, tomato sauce, and water. Combine well. Stir in cornmeal. Cook about ½ hour, or to desired thickness. Stuff taco shells. Pass shredded lettuce, chopped tomatoes, and cheese in bowls to be served with the tacos. Or warm flour tortillas gently in a dry frying pan (both sides). Spoon filling on one-half of tortilla. Fold the other half over the filling and serve, with the lettuce, tomatoes, and cheese to be added by guests.

Speedy Spaghetti

6 to 8 servings

    1 pound ground beef
    ½ onion, chopped
    ½ teaspoon salt
    ¼ teaspoon dry mustard
    ¼ teaspoon allspice
    ¼ teaspoon oregano
    ¼ teaspoon fennel seed
    ¼ teaspoon pepper
    4 ounces dry spaghetti, broken into pieces
    3 cups tomato juice
    1 can (12 ounces) tomato sauce

In a heavy frying pan or Dutch oven with a lid, brown ground beef; add onion, and cook until soft. Add salt, dry mustard, allspice, oregano, fennel seed, and pepper, and mix well. Arrange dry spaghetti in a layer over meat. Combine tomato juice and tomato sauce, and pour over spaghetti. Stir to moisten each piece of spaghetti. Cover; simmer for 30 minutes, or until spaghetti is done and moisture is absorbed.

Chili Supper in a Hurry

4 servings

    1 pound ground beef
    1 large onion, chopped
    ½ teaspoon salt
    1 tablespoon chili powder, or to taste
    1 can (16 ounces) tomatoes with juice
    1 can (15 ounces) pinto or red kidney beans, drained
    ½ small head lettuce, chopped or torn
    2 tomatoes, chopped
    2 cups corn chips
    1 cup grated sharp Cheddar cheese

Brown ground beef. Add onion and cook until soft. Add salt, chili powder, tomatoes, and beans. Bring to a boil and reduce heat. Simmer for 15 minutes. While chili is cooking, shred or break lettuce and chop tomatoes. To serve, place ½ cup corn chips in bottom of soup bowl; pour chili mixture over corn chips, and top with lettuce and tomatoes. Sprinkle with grated cheese.

To make a party dish of this or any chili, omit tomatoes and lettuce. Serve with a dollop of sour cream and a wedge of fresh lime to squeeze over it.

Pizza Burgers

8 hamburgers

    1½ pounds ground beef
    ⅓ cup Parmesan cheese
    ¼ cup finely chopped onion
    ¼ cup finely chopped ripe olives
    1 teaspoon salt
    1 teaspoon leaf oregano
    Dash of pepper
    1 can (6 ounces) tomato paste
    4 slices Mozzarella cheese, cut in half
    2 tomatoes, cut into slices
    8 buns, split and toasted or heated

Combine beef, cheese, onion, olives, salt, oregano, pepper, and tomato paste. Shape into 8 patties. Broil over grill until medium well done—about 10 minutes on first side. Turn and top with Mozzarella slice and a tomato slice. Broil an additional 5 minutes. Serve on hot buns.

Beef Enchilada Casserole

2-quart casserole dish
375 degrees F.
8 servings

    1 pound ground beef
    12 corn tortillas
    3 cups tomato juice
    ½ cup tomato sauce with peppers added (El Pato)
    2 to 3 cups grated mild Cheddar cheese
    1 head lettuce
    4 tomatoes
    Chopped onions, if desired

Brown ground beef, breaking up into small pieces. Drain off fat as meat cooks. Soften tortilla by dipping 15 to 20 seconds on each side in small amount of oil in frying pan. Drain on paper towel. Combine tomato juice and pepper-tomato sauce.

To assemble: Line bottom of casserole dish with single layer of tortillas; spread with ground beef; sprinkle with grated cheese; and pour ½ cup of sauce over all. Start next layer by completely covering previous layer with tortillas and use remaining beef, cheese, and sauce to make 3 or 4 layers. Reserve ½ cup cheese and ½ cup sauce to use as garnish and topping when casserole is served. Bake for 30 minutes, until cheese is completely melted and bubbly.

To serve, dip through layers of casserole to get some of each ingredient. Top with shredded lettuce, chopped tomatoes and onions, and some of the reserved grated cheese and sauce.

Mexican Skillet

5 servings

  1 pound sausage
  1 onion, chopped
  1 green pepper, chopped
  1 tablespoon sugar
  1 teaspoon salt
  1 tablespoon chili powder
  2 cups tomatoes
  1 cup tomato sauce
  1 cup uncooked macaroni
  ½ cup sour cream
  Parmesan cheese

Brown sausage in skillet appropriate for serving at the table. Add onion and green pepper, and cook until soft (about 5 to 10 minutes). Add sugar, salt, chili powder, tomatoes, and tomato sauce, and simmer for 30 minutes. Add macaroni; cook 20 minutes, or until macaroni is soft. Stir in sour cream gently. Sprinkle with Parmesan cheese, and serve from the skillet.

Hong Kong Pork Chops

1½-quart casserole
350 degrees F.
4 servings

  4 pork loin chops, ¾ inch thick
  4 thin slices onion
  1 can (4 ounces) sliced mushrooms, drained, or
    ½ pound fresh mushrooms, washed, trimmed, and
    sliced through stems
  ½ cup sliced water chestnuts
  1 tablespoon cornstarch
  2 tablespoons soy sauce
  ¼ cup water
  1 tablespoon lemon juice
  1 teaspoon sugar
  ½ teaspoon ground ginger
  1 clove garlic, pressed, or use ¼ teaspoon
    garlic powder

Trim excess fat from chops and brown them in fat trimmings in a hot frying pan. Remove chops to casserole. Arrange onion slices, mushrooms, and water chestnuts on chops. Combine cornstarch, soy sauce, water, lemon juice, sugar, ginger, and garlic, mixing well. Pour over chops. Cover and bake 45 to 55 minutes, or until tender. Serve sauce over chops. Good served with rice, baked in same oven with chops.

Oven-Barbecued Pork Roast

325 degrees F.
14 to 16 servings

  12 pounds (about) fresh ham or leg roast
  3½ cups barbeque sauce, any flavor

Score fat and rind of roast. Place in deep pan, fat side up. Pour on barbeque sauce. (For half ham or leg, about 6 pounds, use 1¾ cups barbecue sauce.) Bake about 4 hours, basting occasionally, or to internal temperature of 165 degrees F. Uncover and bake, basting occasionally, until well glazed—about 45 minutes, or to internal temperature of 175 degrees F. Skim fat from drippings. Serve pork hot or cold with hot drippings.

Oven-Barbecued Spareribs

375 degrees F.
4 servings

  3 to 4 pounds lean spareribs
  1¾ cups barbecue sauce, any flavor

Cut spareribs into 2-rib sections. Arrange in a single layer in shallow baking pan. Pour on barbeque sauce. Cover and bake for 45 minutes. Skim fat from pan drippings. Turn ribs and baste with drippings. Bake, uncovered, about 1 hour, or until tender, turning and basting ribs about 4 times to glaze well.

Cranberry Pork and Pears

2- to 3-quart casserole
350 degrees F.
6 servings

  6 pork chops, trimmed of fat
  Flour
  Salt and pepper
  2 cups fresh cranberries
  1 cup sugar
  1 cup water
  3 fresh winter pears

Dredge pork chops with flour; season with salt and pepper. Brown chops in fat trimmings. Remove pork chops to casserole. Add cranberries, sugar, and water. Cover and bake for 30 minutes. Halve and core pears. Place in casserole with pork chops, and baste with pan juices. Bake, uncovered, 30 minutes longer, basting occasionally.

Pork Chops over Rice

9×13×2-inch casserole
350 degrees F.
6 servings

6 pork chops
3 tablespoons oil
5 cups hot, cooked rice
1 cup sliced mushrooms
1 can (10 ounces) cream of mushroom soup
1 can (10 ounces) onion soup
1 cup sour cream

Brown pork chops in oil and drain well. Place rice in bottom of casserole dish and arrange pork chops on top. Cover with mushrooms. Combine mushroom soup, onion soup, and sour cream; blend well. Pour over pork chops. Cover and bake for 1 hour. Uncover; cook 15 minutes to brown.

Stretch the Ham

Purchase a 4- or 5-pound ham with the bone in it, and plan to use it for at least five meals for a family of five or six. Remove plastic wrapper but leave the inner paper wrapper on. Place the ham in a roasting pan and roast at 325 degrees F. for 15 minutes per pound of meat. Remove paper wrapper. Save all liquid from ham and all drippings that accumulate as the ham cooks.
Use the ham in the following ways:

Meal #1

Sunday Dinner or Company Dinner
Sliced Baked Ham
Peas à la Mushrooms
Molded Sour Cream and Cucumber Salad
Hot Rolls
Spanish Cake

Meal #2

Ham and Potato Casserole
Pineapple-Grapefruit Salad
Crispie Cornbread
Brownies

Meal #3

Ham Loaves
Scalloped Potatoes with Cheese
Swedish Fruit Salad
Chocolate Cake

Meal #4

Baked Beans with Ham Pieces
Gold Bricks
Apple, Carrot, Raisin Salad
Joan's Lemonade Cookies

Meal #5

Ham Bone with Beans (Split Peas or Lentils)
Hot Whole Wheat Bread Slices
Pineapple Cottage Cheese Salad
Grandma's Fruit Cobbler

Meal #6

Scrambled Eggs with Ground Ham
Toast
Orange Julia

It should be pointed out that these menus would not be served on consecutive days, or the family will soon grow weary of ham. Ham may be wrapped carefully and refrigerated for several days, or it may be frozen for several weeks. Bits of leftover ham may be used to add to soups, sandwich spreads, or omelets. Juices and drippings should be used to flavor the casseroles and other foods made with the ham.

Ham and Potato Casserole

2-quart casserole
350 degrees F.
6 to 8 servings

2 cups thin ham slices
3 potatoes, cooked and sliced thin
2 small dill pickles, sliced very thin
2 small onions, chopped
3 tablespoons butter or margarine
2 tablespoons flour
1 can (10½ ounces) consomme
½ cup sour cream
1 teaspoon Worcestershire sauce
3 drops Tabasco
Grated sharp Cheddar cheese

Arrange ham slices, sliced potatoes, sliced dill pickles and chopped onions in layers in casserole dish. Melt butter in frying pan. Add flour, and cook for 3 minutes, stirring constantly. Add consommé, sour cream, Worcestershire sauce, and Tabasco sauce. Cook until thick, stirring constantly. Pour over ham and potatoes in casserole, and cover with grated cheese. Bake for 30 minutes.

Ham Loaf

9×5×3-inch loaf pan
350 degrees F.
8 to 10 servings

  ¾ pound ham
  ½ pound veal or beef
  ¼ pound fresh lean pork
  2 eggs, beaten
  ¾ cup soft bread crumbs
  ¾ cup milk
  Dash of pepper
  Dash of onion salt
  Dash of seasoning salt
  2 teaspoons prepared mustard
  ¼ cup brown sugar
  ⅓ cup pineapple juice

Grind together the ham, veal or beef, and pork. Mix in eggs, bread crumbs, milk, pepper, onion salt, and seasoning salt. Pat mixture into a loaf pan. Spread top of loaf with the mustard and brown sugar, mixed together. Pour pineapple juice over the loaf. Bake for one hour.

To serve a crowd: Make up into individual loaves, using ½ cup mixture per serving. Place in large baking pans; spread with topping, and bake for ½ hour, or until done.

Ham and Asparagus Roll-Ups

9×13×2-inch baking dish
350 degrees F.
6 servings

  2 pounds asparagus, cooked and drained
  ¼ cup butter or margarine
  ¼ cup flour
  2 cups milk
  ½ teaspoon salt
  ⅛ teaspoon white pepper
  2 cups shredded sharp Cheddar cheese
  12 thin slices sandwich ham
  Paprika

While asparagus cooks, melt butter in saucepan over medium heat; stir in flour. Add milk, and stir constantly while bringing to boil. Add salt and white pepper. Remove from heat; stir in cheese and blend well. Set aside.

Roll 2 to 4 spears of asparagus in each slice of ham. Place rolls close together in baking dish, seam side down. Pour cheese sauce over all; sprinkle with paprika. Bake for 30 minutes, or until sauce is lightly browned.

Ham, Egg, and Asparagus Casserole

1-quart casserole
350 degrees F.
4 servings

  1 pound fresh asparagus (fat spears)
  2 tablespoons butter or margarine
  2 tablespoons flour
  ½ teaspoon salt (or use chicken-soup-base granules)
  1 cup milk
  1 cup shredded cheese, preferably sharp Cheddar
  2 hard-cooked eggs, peeled and sliced
  1 cup ham cubes
  Coarse, soft bread crumbs, buttered

Wash asparagus and break off tough ends. With vegetable peeler, remove scales from stocks to remove sand, if necessary. (Peeling the bottom inch or two of stock eliminates the fibrous part.) Bias-cut stocks into about 2-inch lengths. Cook in boiling water until just tender; drain. Place half of the asparagus in casserole dish.

Melt butter in small saucepan. Add flour and salt; blend well. Add milk. Cook and stir until smooth and thickened. Remove from heat. Add cheese; stir until blended.

Pour half of the sauce over the asparagus in baking dish. Add sliced eggs, ham cubes, and asparagus in layers, asparagus last. Pour on the rest of the cheese sauce. Top with buttered crumbs. Bake about 30 minutes, or until crumbs are browned and sauce is bubbly hot.

Ham and Vegetable Medley

4 servings

  1 pound fully cooked ham
  2 large tomatoes
  1 small green pepper
  1 small red pepper
  1 medium onion
  1 medium yellow crookneck squash
  1 medium zucchini
  3 tablespoons oil
  ½ cup chicken broth
  2 teaspoons basil
  ½ teaspoon salt
  ¼ teaspoon pepper

Cut ham into ¼-inch strips about 3 inches long. Cut each tomato into 8 wedges, and cut green and red peppers into ¼-inch wide strips. Cut onion and squashes into ¼-inch slices.

Heat oil in a large skillet over high heat. Add peppers, onion, squashes, and ham, and cook for about 5 minutes, stirring constantly. Reduce heat to medium; add chicken broth, basil, salt, and pepper. Cook until vegetables are crisp-tender, about 5 minutes. Add tomato wedges, and continue cooking until tomatoes are heated through.

Yam and Sausage Skillet

6 servings

    1 pound sausage links
    1 package (3 ounces) orange-flavored gelatin
    ½ cup water
    ¼ cup brown sugar
    2 tablespoons margarine
    1 teaspoon instant minced onion
    2 teaspoons dry mustard
    1 teaspoon grated lemon peel
    3 tablespoons lemon juice
    ½ teaspoon salt
    ¼ teaspoon pepper
    2 cups cooked yams (use fresh yams, cooked tender,
      or canned, drained yams)
    1 can (20 ounces) pineapple chunks, drained
    Parsley flakes or chopped green pepper for garnish

In a large skillet, brown sausages; remove from skillet. In the same skillet, combine gelatin with water, brown sugar, margarine, onion, mustard, lemon peel and juice, salt, and pepper. Heat, stirring constantly, until mixture is boiling. Add yams and pineapple. Reduce heat and simmer gently for 15 minutes. Add sausages and cook for 5 minutes. Sprinkle with parsley or chopped green pepper and serve.

Foil Dinners

For each serving, use:

    ½ onion, cut into thin slices
    ¼ pound ground beef or
      1 ham slice or
      boneless pieces of chicken meat
    ½ carrot, cut into thin slices
    2 fresh mushrooms, cut into thin slices, or use
      canned mushrooms
    Salt
    Pepper
    Cheese, pickles, olives, celery slices, as desired

Using extra-heavy-duty aluminum foil, assemble the dinner in this order: Place two slices of onion on bottom (they will steam and prevent the meat from sticking to the foil). Place meat on top of onions; then add carrot and mushroom slices and salt and pepper as desired. Top with two more onion slices. Fold and completely seal the foil. Wrap again, having the sealed edges on opposite sides to discourage leaking and burning. Place carefully on top of coals or on barbecue grill. Cook about 12 to 15 minutes on each side, turning carefully to avoid puncturing the foil. For extra vegetables: Slice potatoes, carrots, and onions, and place in extra heavy foil. Sprinkle with salt and pepper, and dot with butter or margarine. Add cheese, pickles, olives, or celery, if desired. Fold as for foil dinners and cook along with the dinners. Hot rolls or a loaf of bread may be warmed the same way for a complete hot dinner.

Fish Cooked the Canadian Method

Fish is the basic protein for many a delicious dish. It doesn't have to be all sauced up to make it tasty, but it does have to be fresh and cooked correctly. Most species commonly used at table have very delicate flesh and need little cooking. Too many cooks present fish as a most ordinary food simply because they overcook it.

The so-called Canadian method of cooking fish certainly gives the home kitchen chef a guide. A little experience helps one to develop that inner sense of timing to the exact point. We don't know where the Canadian method came from. We have seen it in print in various publications and once saw an article crediting James Beard with it. Here it is for you to adapt to your fish recipes:

Measure fish at thickest point; allow 10 minutes cooking time per inch. If fish is sauced or in foil, allow 5 minutes per pound extra. If fish is frozen, double cooking time.

Broiling or baking. Use a greased broiler and baste with butter or basting sauce. Bake at 450 degrees F., or broil 2 to 4 inches from heat. Fish should be more than ¾ inch thick for broiling.

Pan frying. Use oil or clarified butter. Dip fish in seasoned flour for crispness. Turn half-way through cooking period.

Poaching. Bring to a boil water to cover fish. Add

fish, and cover. Reduce heat; simmer gently. Begin timing when fish "shivers."

A high temperature is usually best for cooking fish by any method. Have oven, broiler pan, or frying pan hot before adding fish, so that surface is sealed and juices kept in. Fine, unsalted cracker crumbs are better for coating fish than bread crumbs, because they burn less easily.

Trout Almondine

Trout fillets (skin and bones removed)
Milk
Flour
Salt and pepper
Clarified butter
Slivered or sliced almonds (1 or 2 tablespoons for
    each serving, toasted in clarified butter)
Lemon wedges

Wash fillets in cold running water. Dry thoroughly (use paper towels). Dip each fillet in milk, then lightly in flour. Sprinkle each with salt and pepper, then brown quickly in clarified butter in a hot frying pan over medium heat. A fillet is thin, and it should brown and be cooked sufficiently in a minute or two on each side. You will need about 2 tablespoons butter in the frying pan, and more to add, depending on number of fillets to be browned. Top with almonds that have been browned in clarified butter. Serve, with lemon wedges, on hot plates.

To clarify butter: Melt amount of butter desired a little ahead of when you need it. Pour butter out of pan into a small bowl, and let it sit until the milk solids settle to the bottom. Pour off the clear fat and use for your frying. This step really is necessary in a delicate dish like this, or the fish will burn in spots.

Swordfish Steak Meuniere

Frying pan and heavy saucepan

Swordfish servings cut in about ½-inch slices,
    about 4 ounces each
Flour, paprika, salt, pepper
Cream—light, heavy, or mixture
Butter or margarine
Meuniere Sauce (below)

Dip fish in flour, seasoned with paprika, salt, and pepper. Dip fish in cream. Melt butter and let solids sink to bottom. Pour off the clear fat into a heavy frying pan. Heat and add fish slices. Brown on both sides, turning once. Cook slowly so that fish is completely cooked when it is brown enough. Spoon Meuniere Sauce over fish, and sprinkle with parsley. Fish will keep a while in a shallow baking dish with sauce spooned over it.

Meuniere Sauce

3 tablespoons butter or margarine
2 teaspoons fresh lemon juice
1 teaspoon Worcestershire sauce
Chopped parsley

Simmer butter in heavy saucepan until browned slightly (don't let it burn). Add lemon juice and whisk well. Add Worcestershire sauce. Spoon sauce over fish. Sprinkle with parsley.

Smothered Halibut

350 degrees F.
10 servings

10 halibut fillets or steaks, boned and skinned
Salt
½ cup butter
⅓ cup flour
½ teaspoon salt
1 small can (5⅓ ounces) evaporated milk
½ small green pepper, washed, seeded, and cored
Paprika

Sprinkle each side of fish lightly with salt. Melt ¼ cup butter in small saucepan. Add flour and ½ teaspoon salt, and stir until hot and bubbly. Add evaporated milk, and cook until smooth and thick. Remove sauce from heat; beat vigorously with an electric beater. Add remaining ¼ cup butter a little at a time (cut it into 4 to 6 pieces; it must be added gradually, or it will separate out of the sauce). Continue beating until cool.

Simmer green pepper in small amount of boiling water for 5 minutes; drain, then chop fine. Add to sauce. Spread a little of the sauce in a shallow baking pan, preferably one in which the fish pieces fit close together. Arrange fish over sauce, then spread remaining sauce atop the fish pieces, covering them well. Sprinkle with paprika. Bake 25 to 30 minutes, or until fish flakes easily with a fork and sauce is hot.

Sole Marinade

400 degrees F.
6 to 8 servings

    2 pounds fillet of sole (flounder, trout, or Greenland
      turbot may also be used)
    6 tablespoons melted butter
    ¼ cup lemon juice
    2 tablespoons grated onion
    2 tablespoons chopped parsley
    Salt
    Pepper

Place fillets in single layer in baking dish. Pour melted butter and lemon juice over fish, and sprinkle with onion, parsley, salt, and pepper. Marinate 20 minutes. Bake in marinade about 10 minutes, or until fish flakes easily with a fork. Be careful not to overcook.

Baked Fish with Cheese

9×9×2-inch pan
350 degrees F.
4 to 6 servings

    1½ pounds cod or haddock fillets
    Salt and pepper
    1 tablespoon finely chopped onion
    4 tablespoons butter or margarine
    ¼ teaspoon salt
    Dash of pepper
    1½ cups fine soft bread crumbs
    ¼ cup shredded American cheese
    ¼ cup milk

Sprinkle fillets with salt and pepper and arrange in greased shallow baking dish. Sauté onions in butter until delicately browned. Add ¼ teaspoon salt, dash of pepper, bread crumbs, and cheese. Toss lightly to mix. Spread over fillets, pressing firmly on fish. Pour milk around fish and bake for 30 minutes, or until fish is done and crumbs are browned.

Fish Fillets in Sour Cream

375 degrees F.
4 to 5 servings

    1 pound white fish fillets (halibut, turbot, frozen
      fillets, thawed)
    1 cup sour cream
    2 tablespoons finely chopped onion
    2 tablespoons finely chopped green pepper
    2 tablespoons finely chopped dill pickle

    1 tablespoon chopped parsley
    1 tablespoon lemon juice
    ¼ teaspoon dry mustard
    ¼ teaspoon sweet basil
    Paprika

Arrange fillets in baking dish in a single layer. Combine and mix well the rest of the ingredients, except paprika. Pour sour-cream mixture over fish. Sprinkle with paprika. Bake 15 to 20 minutes, or until fish flakes easily with a fork and sauce is hot and bubbly.

Salmon Steaks with Mustard-Dill Sauce

4 servings

    4 fresh salmon steaks or fillets, about 1 inch thick
    1 teaspoon salt
    ½ bay leaf
    1 small onion, sliced
    ½ lemon, thinly sliced
    Mustard-Dill Sauce (below)

Place salmon in a large frying pan; sprinkle with salt, then cover with bay leaf, onion, and the lemon slices. Add water to almost cover the fish; cover pan, bring water to a boil, reduce heat, and simmer about 10 minutes, or until fish flakes easily with a fork. Serve salmon on a heated platter with Mustard-Dill Sauce separately to accompany the fish.

Mustard-Dill Sauce

    3 tablespoons butter or margarine
    1½ tablespoons flour
    ½ teaspoon salt
    ½ teaspoon dill weed
    Dash of pepper
    2 teaspoons prepared mustard
    1¼ cups milk
    1 egg yolk
    2 tablespoons lemon juice

Melt butter in a medium-sized pan; stir in flour, salt, dill weed, pepper, and mustard. Add milk gradually, stirring constantly; cook until sauce is smooth and begins to bubble. Beat egg yolk; stir a little of the hot sauce into it, then return sauce to pan. Stir and cook about 1 minute longer. Blend in lemon juice.

Salmon Loaf

8×4×3-inch loaf pan
350 degrees F.
6 servings

    1 tablespoon lemon juice
    2 cups flaked red salmon (1 pound can, skin and
        bones removed)
    1 cup medium white sauce (see Index)
    ½ cup half and half
    1 egg, lightly beaten
    ½ cup finely chopped celery
    1 cup dry, finely rolled bread crumbs
    2 tablespoons butter or margarine
    Egg and Olive Sauce, if desired, or lemon wedges
        and tartar sauce

Add lemon juice to salmon. Add remaining ingredients except bread crumbs and butter. Combine well, but lightly. Pack lightly into buttered loaf pan and top with buttered crumbs. Bake about 30 minutes, or until set and lightly browned.

Serve with creamed peas; with Egg and Olive Sauce (see index); or plain with lemon wedges and tartar sauce.

Golden Salmon Bake

Shallow casserole, about 2-quart size
375 degrees F.
6 to 8 servings

    2 cups fish or chicken stock
    ½ bay leaf
    2 tablespoons grated onion
    3 whole cloves
    6 to 8 peppercorns
    6 tablespoons butter or chicken fat
    ¼ cup green pepper, cut in about 1-inch pieces
    6 tablespoons flour
    2 cups milk
    Salt and pepper
    4 egg yolks, slightly beaten
    4 cups salmon, fresh cooked or canned
    2 tablespoons lemon juice
    Buttered bread rounds, about 3 dozen

Combine stock, bay leaf, onion, cloves, and peppercorns in small saucepan and boil rapidly for about 5 minutes; strain.

Heat butter or chicken fat; add green pepper and cook until soft but not brown, about 5 minutes. Blend in flour. Add strained stock slowly, stirring to blend; then add milk. Cook while stirring until sauce

thickens. Add salt and pepper to taste. Add a little of the hot sauce to egg yolks; slowly add to remaining sauce; cook and stir for another 2 to 3 minutes.

Flake fish coarsely and arrange it in casserole. If canned salmon is used, you may wish to remove skin and big bones as you flake it. Pour lemon juice over fish; then cover with sauce. Arrange overlapping rounds of bread in a circle around edge of casserole. Bake about 25 minutes, or until bread is delicately browned and sauce is bubbly hot.

Note: To make a truly elegant casserole, use good quality red salmon. Poached fresh salmon is ideal, or a good canned red salmon will do. A 1-pound can provides about 2 cups salmon. This recipe may be easily halved or doubled.

Salmon Pie

6 to 8 servings

    Pastry for 1 9-inch pie
    1 flat can (7¾ ounces) salmon, drained and flaked
    1 package (10 ounces) frozen chopped broccoli,
        cooked, or use broccoli spears, stems chopped
        and cooked, or ⅔ cup fresh cooked and chopped
        broccoli
    3 hard-cooked eggs, sliced
    ⅓ cup finely chopped celery
    ¼ cup finely sliced green onions
    ½ teaspoon dill weed
    ⅛ teaspoon pepper
    1 cup mayonnaise
    1 cup shredded Swiss cheese

Roll pastry and fit into pie pan. Prick well, and bake at 425 degrees F. for about 10 minutes, or until very lightly browned. Remove from oven and cool slightly. Reduce oven temperature to 375 degrees F. Flake half of salmon into pie shell. Add a layer of broccoli, then of sliced egg. Combine remaining ingredients. (Save half of the cheese.) Pour half over egg layer. Top with remaining salmon, then with remaining mayonnaise mixture. Sprinkle with remaining cheese. Bake 30 minutes, or until well heated.

This pie can be made a day in advance of need, then baked when ready to serve.

Golden Salmon Bake (p. 61)

Fish Loaf with Dill Sauce

9×5×3-inch pan
350 degrees F.
8 to 10 servings

    2 cups milk
    3 cups soft bread cubes
    2 cans (about 7 ounces each) tuna or salmon,
        drained, flaked, bones removed, or use home-
        canned trout
    4 eggs, slightly beaten
    ¼ cup finely chopped onion
    1 tablespoon chopped parsley
    1 tablespoon lemon juice
    1 teaspoon salt
    1 teaspoon paprika
    Dill Sauce (below)

Combine milk and bread cubes; heat to a gentle
simmer. Remove from heat; beat until smooth.
Combine remaining ingredients in bowl; stir in milk
mixture. Pour into loaf pan. Bake for 55 minutes, or
until set. Cool in pan 10 minutes. Slice. Serve with
Dill Sauce.

Dill Sauce

    2 tablespoons butter or margarine
    2 tablespoons flour
    ½ teaspoon salt
    1 cup milk
    ⅓ cup finely chopped dill pickle
    2 tablespoons dill pickle juice
    1 tablespoon chopped pimiento

Melt butter in saucepan over low heat. Blend in
flour and salt. Add milk all at once. Cook quickly,
stirring constantly, until mixture thickens and
bubbles. Remove from heat, and add dill pickle,
pickle juice, and pimiento.

Easy Shrimp Casserole

4 to 6 servings

    ½ cup finely chopped onion
    2 tablespoons butter or margarine
    1 can (10½ ounces) cream of shrimp soup
    ½ cup milk
    1 cup shrimp, cooked and deveined
    2 tablespoons lemon juice, or to taste
    Cooked rice or patty shells

Cook onions in butter until soft but not brown.
Add soup, sour cream, and milk. Stir and heat until
smooth and piping hot, but do not let boil. Add

shrimp and lemon juice. Taste to correct seasonings.
If sauce seems too thick, add a little milk or chicken
broth to desired consistency. Serve hot on rice or in
patty shells.

Shrimp Curry

Heavy iron frying pan with tight-fitting lid
6 servings

    3 pounds fresh shrimp (the smallest you can buy
        in the shell)
    3 tablespoons powdered tumeric
    Salad oil
    4 medium-size white onions, chopped fine
    1 green pepper, cut in 1 × ¼-inch slices
    1 2-inch length fresh ginger root, chopped fine
    1 clove garlic, pressed or chopped fine
    1 teaspoon cardamom seed, freshly ground, or use
        powdered cardamom
    12 whole cloves
    12 whole peppercorns
    2 teaspoons salt
    Hot cooked rice
    Chutney (optional)
    Yogurt mixed with diced raw cucumber or zucchini
        (optional)

Wash the unshelled shrimp well, leaving droplets
of water on them, and put them in frying pan (no
oil). Sprinkle with tumeric; then cover tightly and
steam over medium heat for a minute or two.
Remove cover and stir. The shrimp should have
turned pink but not cooked. Rinse in cold water.
(The tumeric will make a mess in the sink, so be
prepared with scouring powder and sponge.) Shell
and devein the shrimp as soon as they are cool
enough to handle. Set aside until curry is made.

Cover bottom of same frying pan (if some
tumeric remains, that's fine—don't wash it out) with
oil to a depth of about ¼ inch. Heat; then add
onions. Cook and stir until onions are quite brown
but not burned. Add ingredients in the order listed
down to the cooked rice. Simmer for a few minutes.
If mixture becomes sticky, add a small quantity of
water. A few minutes before serving, add together
the salt and shrimp. Let cook gently about 5 minutes,
stirring once or twice to allow shrimp to absorb
seasonings. If the 5 minutes are up before you are
ready to serve, turn heat off and don't reheat until
ready, or shrimp will become rubbery.

Serve with hot rice and with chutney or with
diced raw zucchini or cucumber mixed into plain
yogurt.

Gourmet Shrimp* and Cheese Casserole

2-quart casserole
350 degrees F.
12 servings

3 cans (4½ ounces each) shrimp, washed, deveined, flaked
3 cups broken pieces of white bread, crusts removed
2 cups shredded sharp Cheddar cheese
9 eggs, beaten slightly
4½ cups milk
1½ teaspoons salt
¾ teaspoon dry mustard
3 teaspoons chopped onion
¼ teaspoon pepper

Layer shrimp, bread, and cheese in buttered casserole. Combine well the remaining ingredients. Pour into casserole. Bake about 1 hour, or until set. Remove from oven and let stand 10 minutes before serving.

*Crab meat may be substituted for shrimp.

Party Shrimp Casserole

2-quart casserole
350 degrees F.
6 to 8 servings

6 tablespoons finely minced onion
¼ cup butter
1 green pepper, chopped
2 cups chopped celery
2 tablespoons butter or margarine
2 tablespoons flour
1 cup milk
¼ teaspoon salt
1 cup mayonnaise
1 can (10 ounces) cream of mushroom or chicken soup
1 cup rice, cooked and cooled
1½ cups grated cheese
3 or 4 cans (4½ ounces each) medium shrimp, rinsed, drained, and deveined, or use 1½ to 2 pounds fresh shrimp, shelled, cleaned, and cooked

Sauté onion in ¼ cup butter for about 5 minutes. Add chopped pepper and celery, and cook until softened but not brown.

Make a white sauce of the 2 tablespoons butter, flour, milk, and salt. Combine with mayonnaise and mushroom soup, then add onion-pepper mixture. Stir in the rice. Add cheese, then the shrimp. Mix well and place in a casserole. Bake for 30 to 45 minutes, until hot and bubbly and lightly browned.

Crab Salad Casserole

2-quart casserole
350 degrees F.
6 servings

1 can (6½ ounces) crabmeat*, drained, boned, and flaked
1 cup soft bread crumbs
1 cup half-and-half
1½ cups mayonnaise
4 hard-cooked eggs, chopped
1 teaspoon minced onion
½ teaspoon salt
1 tablespoon chopped parsley
Buttered crumbs or crushed potato chips
Parmesan cheese (optional)

Combine all ingredients except the crumbs. Place in buttered casserole. Top with buttered crumbs or crushed potato chips. Sprinkle with Parmesan cheese, if desired. Bake about 30 minutes, or until bubbly and crumbs are lightly browned.

For a party, casserole may be baked in individual bakers or in scallop shells.

*Or use 1 cup cubed chicken meat, or 1 flat can white meat of tuna fish. With chicken or tuna, a few slices of stuffed olives (12 olives) help the flavor.

Tuna-Vegetable Casserole

9×13×2-inch pan
350 degrees F.
12 servings

1 can (10½ ounces) cream of chicken soup (or cream of mushroom soup)
1 can (10½ ounces) Cheddar cheese soup
2 cans water
2 packages (10 ounces each) frozen mixed vegetables
2 cans (6½ ounces each) chunk light tuna
1 bag (about 6 ounces) regular potato chips

Combine the creamed soup and the cheese soup with the water; heat and stir until smooth. Cook the frozen vegetables as package directs (do not salt). Drain vegetables and add to soups. Add the fish, which has been drained and flaked. Break up potato chips slightly. Reserve 1½ cups. Add the rest to the soup mixture just enough to take up any excess liquid. Taste and adjust seasoning; you may wish to salt slightly. Pour into buttered baking dish. Crush the remaining potato chips to fine crumbs, and sprinkle on top. Bake until hot and bubbly, 20 to 30 minutes.

Shrimp Pan Roast, Grand Central Oyster Bar Style

For each serving:

4 to 6 large shrimp (or more, if desired)
2 tablespoons butter
1½ cups half-and-half (part milk may be used)
1 teaspoon Worcestershire sauce
1 tablespoon thick chili sauce, drained
1 thick slice toast
1 tablespoon butter (about)

Buy fresh cooked shrimp; or buy green shrimp, then shell, devein, and cook. Combine 2 tablespoons butter, half-and-half, and shrimp. Heat. Just before serving, add Worcestershire sauce and chili sauce. Pour over toast in soup plate; add 1 tablespoon butter, and serve immediately. If desired, pass a small pitcher of lemon juice. A drop or two improves the flavor, but let the guests add their own, as the shrimp mixture curdles easily.

Note: In the photo on page 49, we use giant shrimp or scampi over toasted pumpernickel bread.

Oyster Pan Roast

Follow directions for shrimp pan roast, using about ¼ cup oysters in place of shrimp.

Coquilles Saint-Jacques

400 degrees F.
6 to 8 servings

1½ pounds (about two cups) scallops
½ pound medium green shrimp, well washed
2 sprigs fresh thyme or ½ teaspoon dried thyme
½ bay leaf
1 sprig parsley
8 peppercorns
Salt
1 cup water, or use chicken consommé
2 tablespoons lemon juice
7 tablespoons butter (no substitutes)
3 tablespoons flour
2 egg yolks
Cayenne pepper
Parmesan cheese

Combine scallops, shrimp, thyme, bay leaf, parsley, peppercorns, salt, water, and lemon juice in a small saucepan and bring to a boil. Reduce heat. Cover and simmer two minutes. Remove parsley,

bay leaf, and thyme sprigs and drain but reserve the cooking liquid. Let the scallops cool.

Melt 2 tablespoons butter and stir in the flour with a wire whisk. When blended, add the fish liquid (about 1½ cups), stirring vigorously with a whisk.

Remove the sauce from the heat and beat vigorously with an electric beater. Add the remaining butter a little at a time (it must be added very gradually). Beat in the egg yolks, and continue beating until cool. Add cayenne; taste and adjust seasoning. You may wish to add a bit more lemon juice.

Spoon a little of the mixture into 12 to 16 small scallop shells or 6 to 8 large scallop shells or ramekins. Top with equal parts of scallops and shrimps. Cover with the remaining sauce, and sprinkle with Parmesan cheese.

Bake 5 to 10 minutes, or until bubbling and golden brown. If necessary, glaze at the last minute under the broiler.

Spaghetti with White Clam Sauce

3 cups (3 to 4 servings)

1 package (8 ounces) spaghetti
2 cans (7½ ounces each) minced, chopped, or whole clams, or one tall can clams
⅓ cup oil, salad or olive or mixed
¼ cup butter or margarine
3 cloves garlic, pressed or finely chopped
2 tablespoons finely chopped parsley
1 teaspoon salt

Prepare spaghetti according to package directions, adding 1 tablespoon oil to the cooking water. Drain clams; reserve liquid. On low heat, heat ⅓ cup oil with the butter; add garlic and cook about 5 minutes. Add clam juice, parsley, and salt. Simmer, uncovered, for 10 minutes. Add clams; simmer just until they are hot. Serve over spaghetti.

This dish is nice for informal entertaining, served in a handsome soup plate, with hard rolls or crispy sour dough bread and a green salad. It makes a delightful, inexpensive, easy-to-serve company meal (just be sure your guests will eat garlic).

Poultry and Eggs

Stretch the Meat

Eggs, cheese, milk, and nuts all supply good quality protein to make any meat or fish go farther in meals that are delicious and nutritious. The purchase price of ham makes it seem expensive, but on a per-serving basis, it is very economical. Turkey can be used down to the last bone to produce good eating. Even chicken, which is in the economy class to begin with, is amazingly stretchable.

In this book we have worked with ham, turkey, and chicken to show just how far each will go. And remember, you don't have to eat these meals one after another. The meat will freeze well and long enough for you to appreciate its flavor again. Each will hold in first-class condition at three months at 0 degrees F. Don't try to freeze ham or any pork product any longer than that, for it will change flavor. Turkey and chicken will keep well up to six months.

Stretch the Chicken

One chicken (3 to 4 pounds) can be stretched to make three meals for a family of four. Simmer the breast, rib section, back, wings, heart, neck, and gizzard in 1½ quarts water until breast meat is tender, 30 to 40 minutes. (Freeze liver until enough accumulates for a meal.) Season the cooking liquid with sliced onion, sliced celery, a bay leaf, and 3 or 4 chicken bouillon cubes or chicken soup base. (Or use a 10½-ounce can concentrated chicken broth.)

Strain the broth and measure. You should have about 1 quart plus 1 cup. Taste it and fortify the seasoning, if needed, with more soup base. Chill, then remove solid fat that forms on top.

Carefully pick all meat from bones. Keep the small pieces separate from the breast meat. Refrigerate both until ready to use.

Meal #1

Chicken Noodle Soup (made with the small chicken pieces)
Tomato and hard-cooked egg salad
Cheese toast
Favorite cake or pie with fruit, ice cream, or sherbet

Make your own noodles (see Index) or use packaged noodles. Add 4 ounces noodles to the 1¼ quarts boiling broth. Boil rapidly until noodles are just tender, 8 to 12 minutes, or as package directs. Narrow, medium, or twisted noodles are all good. The last minute or two of cooking, add the chicken pieces. Serve piping hot with chopped parsley.

Since this main dish is light, the salad and dessert may need to be heavier. A hearty salad such as sliced tomatoes with sliced hard-cooked eggs would go nicely with the cheese toast. Make the cheese toast with any favorite bread (a sturdy French or sourdough or a good dark bread would be ideal). Spread it with butter or margarine and sprinkle it generously with Parmesan cheese or use shredded or sliced Cheddar or Jack cheese. Place bread slices on cookie sheet in a 400-degree F. oven until cheese melts and bread is toasted.

Complete the meal with a favorite cake or pie with ice cream or sherbet.

Meal #2

Hot Chicken Salad Casserole (use the chicken breast, cubed)
Pineapple Cottage Cheese Salad
Any favorite bread
Any hot vegetable
Fresh or home-canned fruit or cookies

To prepare chicken, pull the fillet from each side of chicken breast and cut the pieces across the grain into about ½-inch cubes. Use all the breast meat in the Chicken Salad Casserole (see Index).

Meal #3

Oven-Fried Chicken Legs (use the legs, disjointed,
  or drumstick and thigh joined)
Baked potato
1 or 2 hot vegetables
Orange Pecan Salad
Favorite bread
Apple pie with cheese slice

Use Shake and Bake or any desired coating for
chicken. If four pieces is a skimpy amount for your
family, buy a three-legged pack of chicken, or 2
extra thighs or drumsticks.

Preparing Cooked Chicken Meat

Chicken to be used in a casserole or other favorite
dishes may be cooked according to three different
methods. Choose the one that is most convenient for
you.

1. Simmered Chicken

This method is best when you also need the
broth, but some of the flavor cooks out of the meat
and into the broth. To make both meat and broth
tasty, cook with any or all of these: sliced onion,
carrot, celery and celery leaves, a bay leaf, a few
peppercorns, and possibly soup extender, such as
bouillon cubes, instant soup base, or canned broth.
Salt, pepper, and herbs may be added to taste. (Most
soup extenders are salty.)

Chicken may be cooked either whole or separated into large pieces. In an appropriate size pan,
add water to barely or not quite cover chicken.
Simmer gently until just tender, about one hour for a
young chicken, or up to three hours for an older
stewing hen.

If time permits, cool meat in stock in cooking pan,
setting the pan in a sink of cold water and changing
the water often. Remove chicken from stock; separate meat from bones and skin. Store covered in
refrigerator until time to use. With scissors or very
sharp knife, cut meat across the grain into desired-
size pieces. (Meat is easier to cut if it is cold.)

Strain broth and refrigerate. The fat will rise to
the top of the chilled broth so that it can be removed
easily. If broth lacks flavor, boil it down to concentrate it, or add chicken flavoring granules or cubes.
Broth makes a delicious base for chicken noodle
soup, a rich chicken gravy, casseroles, or any recipe
calling for chicken stock or bouillon.

Both chicken meat and broth should be frozen if
either will not be used within a few days. The meat
holds better in the freezer if a small amount of broth
is added to it.

2. Chicken Baked in Foil

Wrap chicken pieces in heavy-duty foil, folding
foil over chicken and fastening drugstore style. Fold
ends well so that no steam can escape. Place package
in shallow baking pan and cook at 425 degrees F. for
about one hour, or until pieces are fork tender.
Remove from oven; undo foil and let chicken air
until cool enough to handle.

Remove skin and bones. The small amount of
juice in the foil may be poured over the meat or
refrigerated separately. Keep chicken cold and
covered until used. With sharp knife or scissors, cut
meat into desired-size pieces.

3. Chicken Baked in Casserole

Place chicken pieces in casserole with tight-fitting
lid. Cover and proceed as for chicken baked in foil
(above), but use a 400-degree F. oven. It is better if
pieces are not more than two layers deep. If only a
few pieces are cooking, test for doneness after 45
minutes.

For use in a salad, let meat chill in a marinade of
Italian-type salad dressing or a mixture of half oil and
half vinegar, or in vinegar or lemon juice alone.

A three-pound chicken yields one pound of
cooked meat (about 1 quart cubed), exclusive of
neck and giblets.

Stretch the Turkey

A 15-pound turkey is an economical buy for a
family of five or six. It can provide meat for a hearty
Thanksgiving or special-occasion dinner as well as
leftovers for delicious meals later. Here are some
menus featuring dishes made with turkey. Recipes
for starred dishes are found in this cookbook—check
the index. Meal #1 is planned around roast turkey
and will serve up to twelve guests. About half the
turkey will be left over for later use; there should be
9 to 11 cups of turkey meat plus turkey stock. Each
of the main dishes in the other meals calls for 1 or 2
cups diced turkey meat. Thus the turkey might
stretch to give you several delicious meals.

Cheese-Spinach Soufflé Roll (p. 78)

Meal #1

Roast Turkey
Mashed Potatoes and Gravy
Dressing
Cranberry Sauce or Cranberry Ice*
Buttered Green Peas with Small Onions
Yam Rolls*
Steamed Old-time Christmas Pudding with Sauce*

Meal #2

Squash Soup* with Crackers
Turkey Salad Supreme*
Hot Rolls
Molded Ambrosia Salad*

Meal #3

Turkey Biscuit Roll*
Fresh Spinach and Mandarin Orange Salad*
Buttered Carrots
Apple Cake*

Meal #4

Enchilada Casserole*
Buttered Corn and Green Beans or Peas
Tossed Salad
Almond Baked Peaches*

Meal #5

Turkey and Ham Tetrazzini*
  (use ¾ of the recipe)
Rice
Lettuce and Tomato Salad
Pineapple Carrot Cake*

Meal #6

Scalloped Turkey and Dressing*
Baked Yams
Waldorf Salad
Favorite Fruit Ice Cream*
Crisp Cookies

Meal #7

Turkey Vegetable Soup (see Beef Vegetable Soup*)
Elegant Bran Bread*
Butterscotch Pie*

Turkey for Many Meals

When the turkey goes into the oven for roasting, put the neck, heart, and gizzard into saucepan, cover with water, add a little salt and/or other seasoning, and simmer until tender, about 1 hour. The broth can be added to gravy, used for liquid in the dressing, or stored in the refrigerator or freezer for later use. Debone the neck and store for later use. The gizzard and heart may be chopped and added to gravy or dressing. Do not include liver in this pot—it is a delicacy to be floured and fried. It can be eaten now or frozen or refrigerated for later.

Make enough dressing for three meals and cook it in a baking pan rather than in the turkey, so that you will have enough left over for later meals. You might also wish to double the quantity of potatoes prepared.

When dinner is over:

1. Debone the turkey, separating large pieces from small and perhaps light pieces from dark. Break the carcass just below the ribs, and put carcass and bones in a large kettle. For a richer broth, add a beef shank and seasoning vegetables, such as sliced onion, carrot, celery and celery leaves, and seasonings, such as a bay leaf, salt, pepper, and herbs. A soup extender, such as bouillon cubes, instant soup base, or canned chicken broth, may also be added.

Cover, or almost cover, with water, and simmer 1 to 2 hours. Strain. Cool quickly by putting kettle in a sink of cold water or outside if it is a cold day; then refrigerate. When cool, lift off fat and pour broth into storage containers. Pick off bits of meat remaining on carcass or shank and add to broth. Discard bones. Refrigerate broth to be used within 4 days; freeze any excess in convenient amounts.

2. Slices or pieces of meat can be frozen plain or with a small amount of broth added. Use in many ways, but use within a few weeks.

3. Refrigerate turkey, left-over dressing, and gravy (also mashed potatoes, if double quantity was cooked on first day). Arrange in sections in baking dish; cover with foil, and reheat in oven in a day or two.

4. Refrigerate part of breast meat to use for turkey salad within a few days. Refrigerate or freeze small parts of meat for turkey tacos or enchiladas or other favorite dishes.

5. Put part of the remaining dressing in a freezer-to-oven dish (or use heavy aluminum foil for a package). Place slices or larger bits of turkey on top of dressing and pour part of left-over gravy over all. Cover tightly and freeze for use a few days or weeks later (do not store long). Menu for this meal might include the turkey and dressing, baked yams, vegetable, Waldorf salad, and dessert.

6. Place slices of turkey meat in a freezer bag with some of the left-over gravy. Freeze in amounts for a family meal or for individual meals if this fits your life-style. These can be quickly heated in a microwave oven or in a boiling water bath if the bag is boil-proof, or by emptying into a saucepan and heating directly. Make as many packages as the meat and your ingenuity allow.

7. Make turkey sandwiches. Wrap properly and freeze. These can be put in lunch bag while still frozen and will be thawed by lunch time. If used at home, they can be heated in the oven (if wrapped in foil); toasted under the broiler, turning once; toasted on a buttered grill or fry pan, turning once; or dipped in a mixture of 1 beaten egg to 2 tablespoons milk, then cooked on buttered grill or fry pan like French toast.

Note: Cooked turkey meat may be used in place of cooked chicken meat in most recipes. It can sometimes be used to replace pork or beef. Try it in croquettes, vegetable-meat pies, meat pin-wheels (rolled in baking powder biscuit dough), salads, casseroles, creamed or à la king dishes (serve over rice, noodles, baking powder biscuits, corn bread, or toast), or in tacos, enchiladas, or tamales.

Chicken Supreme

2-quart casserole
350 degrees F.
6 to 8 servings

1 or 2 chicken(s) (about 4 pounds)
1 pound precooked ham
1 can (8 ounces) water chestnuts, or use 1 cup slivered almonds, browned in butter
Supreme Sauce (below)

Cook chicken. (See page 66.) Cool. Discard skin and bones, and slice chicken meat very thin. Slice the ham and chestnuts thin. Layer chicken, ham, chestnuts, and Supreme Sauce (below) in casserole. Place in oven until hot and bubbly, about 30 minutes.

Supreme Sauce

2 cloves garlic
2 teaspoons butter or margarine
3 cups chicken broth
2 cups milk, or part half-and-half
2 tablespoons catsup
¼ teaspoon saffron (optional)
1 teaspoon Accent
⅛ teaspoon sugar
⅛ teaspoon cayenne
½ teaspoon salt
4 tomatoes, skinned, seeds removed, and coarsely chopped
¼ cup cornstarch
¼ cup milk

Mince or press garlic, and brown in butter. Add chicken broth, milk, catsup, saffron, Accent, sugar, cayenne, and salt. When boiling, add tomatoes, seeds and pulp removed and chopped coarsely. Mix cornstarch with milk, and add to sauce gradually, cooking to desired thickness, and stirring constantly. Taste and adjust seasoning.

Chicken Breasts in Caper Sauce

9×13×2-inch pan
350 degrees F.
8 servings

8 chicken breast halves
1 can (10½ ounces) cream of mushroom soup
½ cup sour cream
½ cup nippy Cheddar cheese, shredded
1 tablespoon (or more) capers and juice
Worcestershire sauce and Tabasco to taste
Dash of garlic salt
½ cup mayonnaise

Wash and salt halved chicken breasts. Make single layer in pan. Cover with foil, and bake until tender, about 1 hour. Cool chicken; debone, and remove skin. Return chicken to broth in pan, and cover again. Keep warm until ready to serve.

Combine soup, sour cream, cheese, capers, Worcestershire sauce, Tabasco, and garlic salt. Heat in double boiler or heavy saucepan. Add mayonnaise just before serving. Taste and adjust seasonings.

Place chicken breast on nest of rice. Pour sauce over all, or just over chicken breasts, as desired.

Chicken Breasts in Vegetable Creme

13×9×2-inch casserole
350 degrees F.
8 to 10 servings

      10 chicken breast halves, about 3½ pounds
      2 cans (13¾ ounces each) chicken broth
      ½ cup chopped onion
      ½ cup chopped celery
      1 cup chopped carrots
      2 teaspoons salt
      Vegetable Creme (below)

Place chicken breasts in a large pot. Add chicken broth, vegetables, and salt. Cover, and simmer gently until breasts are tender, about 1 hour. Remove breasts, cool slightly, and remove skin and bones, keeping meat in one piece. Cover well to prevent chicken from drying while you purée the broth: Increase heat; boil broth about 20 minutes, uncovered, to reduce. Put broth and vegetables through food mill, or whirl in a blender. Measure 1½ cups broth-purée. Make Vegetable Creme.

Vegetable Creme

      ¼ cup chopped green pepper
      3 tablespoons butter or margarine
      3 tablespoons flour
      1½ cups broth-purée
      2 cups light cream
      ½ teaspoon salt
      Dash of pepper
      ¼ teaspoon powdered savory (optional)
      2 tablespoons diced pimiento
      1 to 2 tablespoons lemon juice (optional)

Sauté green pepper in melted butter a few minutes. Blend in flour, broth-purée, and cream, cooking and stirring until smooth and thickened. Add seasonings and pimiento. Taste. Add lemon juice if desired.

Arrange chicken breasts, not overlapping, in casserole. Cover with Vegetable Creme Sauce. Place in oven, and cook until hot and bubbly, about 30 minutes. Serve with freshly cooked, seasoned rice. Buttered broccoli makes an excellent vegetable accompaniment.

Creamed Chicken and Mushrooms

6 servings

      1 to 2 tablespoons butter or margarine
      1 to 2 cups sliced mushrooms (¼ to ½ pound), washed well and thoroughly dried
      2 cups medium white sauce (see Index)
      ¼ cup light cream, if desired
      2 cups cooked chicken, cubed into bite-size pieces
      Salt and pepper

Melt butter in medium frying pan. Slice mushrooms from cap through stem into melted butter. Cook and stir for 5 minutes, or until mushrooms give up their juice. To white sauce in a medium saucepan, add cream, chicken, and mushrooms. Taste and adjust seasonings; add a little salt and pepper, if desired. Serve hot in patty shells or over hot biscuits or squares of hot cornbread.

This recipe may easily be doubled. Use one whole chicken, 3 to 3½ pounds.

For more chicken flavor, use part (up to one half) chicken stock for milk in the white sauce recipe.

Chicken à la King

Sauté 1 teaspoon chopped onions and ¼ cup chopped green pepper with the mushrooms. Proceed as above. To the sauce add ¼ cup chopped pimiento or 1 jar (2 ounces). Taste and adjust seasoning.

Chicken and Rice Casserole

2-quart casserole
350 degrees F.
4 to 6 servings

      1 frying chicken, cut in pieces
      1¼ cups cooked rice
      1 can (10½ ounces) cream of chicken soup
      ¼ cup finely chopped onion
      1 tablespoon chopped parsley
      1 teaspoon salt
      ⅛ teaspoon thyme
      1⅓ cans water
      Paprika (optional)

Flour the chicken pieces and brown in a small amount of fat in frying pan or Dutch oven. Remove browned pieces to casserole. Add rice. Combine soup with remaining ingredients except paprika, and stir until well blended. Pour over chicken and rice. Sprinkle with paprika, if desired. Bake about 30 minutes, or until chicken is fork tender.

Tangy Garlic and Sour Cream Marinated Chicken

4 to 6 servings

1 cup sour cream
1 tablespoon lemon juice
2 cloves garlic, crushed
¾ teaspoon lemon pepper
¾ teaspoon celery salt
½ teaspoon salt
½ teaspoon paprika
1 tablespoon Worcestershire sauce
1 fryer, cut up, or 6 chicken breasts

Combine all ingredients but chicken. Pour over chicken pieces, covering all surfaces. Cover tightly, and refrigerate overnight or for several hours. Remove chicken from marinade, and broil on grill or bake in oven set at 350 degrees F. until tender.

Baked Almond Chicken Casserole

10×6×2-inch baking or casserole dish
350 degrees F.
4 to 6 servings

3 cups chopped cooked chicken
4 ribs celery, sliced
1 cup salad dressing (Miracle Whip)
½ cup slivered almonds, toasted
1 cup grated Swiss cheese
¼ cup chopped onion
2 tablespoons chopped pimiento
1 teaspoon salt
Dash of pepper
1 tomato, cut in wedges

Combine chicken, celery, salad dressing, ¼ cup almonds, cheese, onion, pimiento, salt, and pepper. Mix lightly. Place in buttered baking dish or casserole. Sprinkle with remaining almonds. Bake for 25 minutes. Top with tomato wedges and return to oven for 5 minutes, or until tomatoes are hot.

Curried Baked Chicken with Coconut

500 degrees F., then 350 degrees F.
4 servings

1 frying chicken (2 to 2½ pounds), cut up
¼ cup flour
1 teaspoon salt
¼ teaspoon pepper
2 tablespoons butter or margarine
2⅓ cups Curry Sauce (below)
1 cup coconut

Wash and dry pieces of chicken. Mix flour, salt, and pepper together. Dust chicken with flour mixture, and place pieces in shallow roasting pan. Dot with butter. Bake at 500 degrees F. for 20 minutes, then at 350 degrees F. for 15 minutes longer. Remove from oven. Pour Curry Sauce over chicken; sprinkle with coconut. Return to oven, and continue to bake 20 to 30 minutes longer, or until tender.

Curry Sauce

2⅓ cups

½ cup onion, chopped
1 tablespoon curry powder
1 tablespoon applesauce
¼ pound bacon, finely chopped
1 tablespoon tomato paste
1 teaspoon sugar
¼ cup lemon juice
1 tablespoon flour
1 cup consommé
1 tablespoon flaked coconut
1 tablespoon heavy cream
1 clove garlic, crushed

Mix ingredients together and cook over low heat for 10 to 15 minutes.
Note: Cook chicken giblets and use the stock in place of consommé. Chop giblets and add to sauce.

Orange Chicken Delicious

6 servings

   3 pounds frying chicken parts, or use 6 chicken
      breast halves
   ½ teaspoon salt or seasoned salt
   ⅛ teaspoon pepper
   Fat for frying (half butter or margarine, half
      shortening)
   3 tablespoons brown sugar
   1 tablespoon cornstarch
   ¼ teaspoon salt
   ⅛ teaspoon ground ginger
   ⅓ cup orange marmalade
   ⅔ cup orange juice (or use half chicken broth)
   1 tablespoon lemon juice
   1 whole orange, thinly sliced, with slices cut in half
   Almond Rice (below)

Rub chicken pieces with salt and pepper. Brown in hot fat (start with about 2 tablespoons and add more as needed). Pour excess fat from pan. Combine remaining ingredients except orange slices and rice, and add to chicken. Cover and simmer for about one-half hour, or until chicken is fork tender. Add orange slices; simmer 10 minutes longer. Serve with Almond Rice.

Almond Rice

   2 cups Minute Rice
   2 tablespoons butter or margarine
   ¼ teaspoon salt
   ¼ cup dry roasted almonds
   ¼ cup dry currants or raisins

Prepare rice according to package directions, adding butter and salt. Just before serving, stir in almonds and currants. (One-fourth cup chopped almonds browned in butter may be used.)

Curried Chicken with Dumplings

4 servings

   2 tablespoons oil
   1 broiler-fryer (2½ to 3 pounds), cut up
   1 pound small white onions (or use 2 to 3 medium
      yellow onions, quartered)
   1 tablespoon curry powder
   ⅓ cup raisins
   1 teaspoon salt
   1 teaspoon brown sugar
   2 cups water

   2 tablespoons flour in ¼ cup water
   ½ cup plain yogurt, or use buttermilk
   1 large red cooking apple, cored, quartered,
      and sliced
   1 cup biscuit mix
   ⅓ cup milk (about)

In large frying pan, in hot oil, cook chicken pieces until browned on all sides. Remove chicken. In drippings remaining in pan, cook onions until browned. Stir in curry powder; cook 1 minute. Return chicken pieces to pan; add raisins, salt, brown sugar, and water; heat mixture to boiling. Reduce heat to low; cover and simmer 25 minutes. Skim off fat. Remove chicken pieces from pan.

Stir flour with ¼ cup water; stir into liquid in frying pan, and cook over medium heat until slightly thickened, stirring constantly. Stir in yogurt until smooth. Add chicken pieces and apple slices. Stir milk into biscuit mix just until blended. (You want a soft dough.) Drop dough by tablespoonfuls into simmering liquid in frying pan. Reduce heat to low; cover and cook 15 minutes until chicken and apple slices are fork-tender and dumplings are set.

Spanish Chicken Casserole

A deep casserole, about 3 quarts
350 degrees F.
8 to 10 servings

   8 chicken breast halves
   1 can (10½ ounces) cream of celery soup
   1 can (10½ ounces) cream of mushroom soup
   1½ cups milk
   1 small onion, chopped fine
   7 to 8 small taco shells (dry corn tacos)
   1 can (4 ounces) diced green chilies
   3 cups (about ¾ pound) sharp Cheddar cheese,
      shredded

The day before, cook chicken breasts. Remove skin and bones, and cut meat into bite-size pieces. Mix soups, milk, and onion. Break taco shells into pieces. Make two layers of ingredients in a deep casserole: soup mixture, taco shells, chicken, chilies, cheese. Repeat. Refrigerate overnight.

Bake about 1 hour. Everything is already cooked in this casserole, so when it looks done, it is done. Don't let it dry out. Liquid will be absorbed by taco shells.

This recipe may be halved for 5 servings. Use only one kind of soup, your favorite of the two.

Chicken Custard Casserole

9×13×2-inch casserole
350 degrees F.
15 to 20 servings

    1 chicken (about 3 pounds), cut in pieces
    1 onion, chopped
    1 celery rib and leaves, chopped
    1 bay leaf
    4 chicken bouillon cubes
    1 can (10½ ounces) cream of mushroom soup
    4 to 6 slices cracked wheat bread, cubed
    4 eggs, well beaten
    ¾ teaspoon sage
    Roux (see Index)
    Parsley, if desired

Simmer chicken pieces in water just to cover, with onion, celery, bay leaf, and bouillon cubes (or use 4 teaspoons chicken soup base). Cook until chicken is very tender. Remove chicken from broth and pick the meat from the bones. Discard bones and skin. Cover chicken so it won't dry out, and place in refrigerator until needed.

In the meantime, strain the broth and taste. If it seems watery and lacking in flavor, boil it hard about 5 minutes, then taste and add salt and pepper, if needed. Refrigerate until ready to put casserole together.

Cut cooled chicken into bite-size pieces. In a large bowl, combine mushroom soup and 1 cup of the chicken broth. Blend until smooth. Add bread cubes, eggs, sage, and chicken. Pour into casserole dish; cover and place in refrigerator and let stand overnight (a must). Bake about 45 minutes, or until custard is set. Cut in squares and serve topped with chicken gravy made from remaining broth thickened with roux (see Index). Garnish with parsley.

Crescent Chicken Rolls

350 degrees F.
8 servings

    1 package (3 ounces) cream cheese, softened
    2 tablespoons butter or margarine, melted
    2 cups cooked, cubed chicken or 2 cans (5 ounces each) boned chicken
    ¼ teaspoon salt
    ⅛ teaspoon pepper
    2 to 3 tablespoons milk
    1 tablespoon chopped chives or onion
    1 tablespoon chopped pimiento (optional)
    1 can (8 ounces) refrigerated crescent rolls
    1 tablespoon melted butter or margarine
    ¾ cup seasoned croutons, crushed, or your favorite dressing mix

Blend cream cheese and 2 tablespoons melted butter. Add chicken, salt, pepper, milk, chives, and pimiento. Mix well.

Separate crescent dough into 8 triangles, as marked. Spoon ¼ cup of meat mixture near base of triangle and roll up, crescent style. Brush each roll with melted butter; then dip in crouton or dressing crumbs. Place on an ungreased baking sheet and bake 20 to 25 minutes, or until golden brown. Serve hot with any favorite cream sauce. Good with hot cream of chicken or mushroom soup, diluted with about ½ can of milk. Or use a good mushroom sauce (see Index).

Variation: To make 4 servings, like sealed sandwiches, separate crescent dough into 4 rectangles. Press perforations together firmly, to seal. Spoon about ½ cup of meat mixture on one side of center. Fold other side over mixture and seal edge of dough, top, bottom and side. Finish and cook as for crescent roll above.

This recipe, in either form, may be increased to any desired number for a crowd. The oblong sandwiches go great as finger food at back yard parties, and look great piled on a handsome platter.

Chicken Salad Casserole

2-quart casserole
325 degrees F.
4 to 6 servings

    2 cups diced cooked chicken breast
    1 cup diced celery
    1 cup saltine cracker crumbs (about 8 square crackers)
    2 hard-cooked eggs, chopped
    1 cup mayonnaise
    1 can (10½ ounces) cream of chicken soup
    1 teaspoon minced onion

Combine all ingredients, and spoon into buttered casserole. If desired, sprinkle with buttered bread crumbs. Bake for 30 minutes, or until bubbling hot.

Rock Cornish Hens

About 9×13×2-inch pan
300 degrees F.
8 servings

4 Rock Cornish hens, split in half lengthwise
⅓ cup fresh lemon juice
½ cup (¼ pound) butter or margarine, melted
Stuffing

Have butcher split the frozen hens. Remove plastic wrap, and rub each half with lemon juice. Let stand in refrigerator about half an hour; remove, and dip each half in melted butter. Place hens on broiler rack, skin side down, and broil until golden. Turn hens, and broil skin side until golden.

Place hens on stuffing in a shallow roasting pan, skin side up. Cover pan tightly with foil; bake one hour, or until hens are tender.

Stuffing: Use any favorite recipe, or a packaged product, prepared as directed. Or use this delicious Apple-Rice Stuffing:

Apple-Rice Stuffing

Combine one package long-grain wild rice mix, prepared according to package directions, with 1 cup chopped apple, 1 cup finely chopped celery, and ½ teaspoon poultry seasoning.

Broiled Rock Cornish Hen

450 degees F.
2 servings

1 frozen Rock Cornish hen, thawed
¾ teaspoon salt
⅛ teaspoon pepper
2 tablespoons butter or margarine
1 tablespoon lemon juice
1 can (8 ounces) pineapple slices, drained
1 tablespoon brown sugar
Hot cooked rice, for 2 servings
1 tablespoon chopped parsley

Remove giblets and neck from cavity of hen. Refrigerate for later use. Rinse hen in running water; pat dry with paper towels. With kitchen shears, cut hen in half or have butcher saw frozen hen in half, lengthwise. Sprinkle with salt and pepper. Place halves, skin side down, in broiling pan. Place 1 tablespoon butter in each cavity; pour lemon juice over chicken. Broil hen 5 minutes, then brush with melted butter from cavity. Broil 15 minutes longer. Turn hen, and broil another 15 to 20 minutes, or until drumstick moves easily up and down, brushing with pan drippings once or twice.

During last 5 minutes of cooking, arrange pineapple slices around hen. Sprinkle fruit with brown sugar, and broil until golden. Combine rice and parsley. Serve hen on plate with parsley rice and broiled pineapple slices. Spoon pan drippings over hen.

This recipe may easily be doubled, tripled, or enlarged to fit a large broiler pan, or more, if desired, since portion size is controlled.

Oven-Barbecued Turkey

325 degrees F.
8 to 10 servings

1 small (about 9 pounds) oven-ready turkey or boneless turkey roast
1¾ cups barbecue sauce, any flavor

Tie turkey drumsticks together to tail. Twist wings over back. Place turkey breast side up on rack in deep roasting pan. Pour on half the sauce; cover, and bake for 30 minutes. Pour on remaining sauce; cover, and bake 3 hours. If boneless roast is used, time the baking as package directs. Pour off pan drippings; skim off fat. Then bake uncovered, basting frequently with drippings, about 1 hour, or to internal temperature of 190 degrees F. Serve hot or cold with hot drippings as sauce.

Scalloped Turkey and Dressing

In a casserole dish or baking dish, place slices of leftover turkey on a bed of leftover dressing (or prepare dressing using a favorite package mix). Top with leftover gravy. Heat in 350-degree F. oven 30 to 45 minutes.

Sweet and Sour Turkey Wings

8 servings

3 turkey wings
1 can (20 ounces) pineapple chunks
½ cup brown sugar
¼ cup cornstarch
½ teaspoon ground ginger
½ cup vinegar
2 to 3 tablespoons soy sauce (or to taste)
1½ cups bias-sliced carrots
1 cup sliced onion
2 cups green pepper strips, about 2 large
   green peppers
Cooked rice for 8 servings

Simmer turkey wings in water to cover. (Use celery ribs and leaves, chopped onion, and bay leaf to season the cooking water.) Cook until meat is tender, about an hour. Let cool in broth, then remove the skin and bones from the meat. Cut meat in bite-size pieces. Strain broth and chill. Remove fat that comes to the surface of broth.

Drain pineapple. Measure the juice; add defatted turkey broth to make 3 cups of liquid. (Water or chicken broth may replace turkey broth if leftover cooked turkey is used.)

Combine brown sugar, cornstarch, and ginger in a 3- to 4-quart saucepan. Stir in the 3 cups liquid, vinegar, and soy sauce. Bring mixture to boil, stirring constantly until thickened. Add carrots and onion. Cover and simmer 10 to 15 minutes, until vegetables are tender-crisp. Cut green pepper into ¼-inch strips; add green pepper and turkey to sweet-sour sauce and heat for another 5 minutes. Serve on hot cooked rice.

This recipe may be doubled. It may also be made with already cooked, left-over turkey. All of it keeps well, though the green pepper loses its color if held too long in the mixture.

Leftover turkey stock may be used for a turkey soup (see Index) or for enriching gravy.

Turkey Creole

4 servings

½ cup finely diced onions
2 tablespoons diced green pepper
⅔ cup sliced celery
3 tablespoons butter or margarine
1½ cups canned tomatoes
1 bay leaf
½ teaspoon celery salt
⅛ teaspoon cayenne pepper (optional)
½ teaspoon sugar
¼ teaspoon sweet basil
1 cup chopped cooked turkey
½ cup cooked peas (optional)
1¼ cups cooked rice
Salt and pepper

Sauté onions, green pepper, and celery in butter in a skillet until tender. Add remaining ingredients. Season to taste with salt and pepper. Heat thoroughly before serving.

Turkey and Ham Tetrazzini

8 servings

¼ cup butter or margarine
¼ cup flour
1 teaspoon salt
¼ teaspoon white pepper
¼ teaspoon nutmeg
1 cup turkey or chicken broth
1 cup milk or more if needed
3 cups cooked cut-up turkey
½ cup cooked cut-up ham
¼ cup green pepper, chopped
1 cup ripe olives, pitted, cut in half lengthwise
½ pound fresh mushrooms
½ cup slivered almonds
Parmesan cheese
Paprika

Melt butter in saucepan; add flour, salt, pepper, and nutmeg, and blend. Add broth and milk, stirring while cooking until thickened. Add remaining ingredients except Parmesan cheese and paprika. Simmer a few minutes. Serve over rice or noodles. Garnish with cheese and paprika.

Variation: Pour sauce over layers of remaining ingredients; top with Parmesan cheese and paprika. Cover and bake in 325- or 350-degree oven until hot, about 20 minutes. Serve with rice or noodles.

Basic Turkey or Chicken Sandwich Filling

1¼ to 1¾ cups, 5 to 7 sandwiches

    1 cup diced cooked turkey or chicken
    1 cup finely chopped celery
    ⅛ to ¼ teaspoon salt
    Pepper
    ¼ cup mayonnaise or salad dressing

Combine ingredients and mix well.

Variations

1. Add 3 tablespoons pickle relish and 1 hard-cooked egg, chopped.
2. Add ¾ cup chopped cucumber (omit celery).
3. Add ⅓ cup chopped stuffed green olives.
4. Add 1 teaspoon horseradish.
5. Add ⅓ cup chopped green onions and 1 teaspoon Worcestershire sauce.
6. Add ¼ cup cottage cheese and ½ cup drained, canned crushed pineapple. Reduce celery to ½ cup.

Omit mayonnaise or salad dressing, or add as needed to moisten.

Turkey Biscuit Roll

425 degrees F.
6 servings

    3 cups gravy or white sauce
    1 egg, slightly beaten
    1 tablespoon minced onion
    2 cups cooked and diced turkey
    3 cups biscuit mix
    1 cup milk

Heat 1 cup gravy or sauce; pour over egg and mix well. Add onion and turkey. Season to taste. Prepare biscuit dough with milk, as for biscuits. Roll dough into rectangle about ¼-inch thick. Spread turkey mixture on dough, leaving 1 inch clear at far long side. Roll gently toward far side. Place seam side down on ungreased cookie sheet, and bake 25 minutes or until golden and cooked. Heat remaining gravy to serve with roll slices.

Good-Bye Turkey

2-quart casserole or baking pan
400 degrees F.
6 servings

    ½ cup chopped onion
    2 tablespoons butter or margarine
    3 tablespoons flour
    ½ teaspoon salt
    ¼ teaspoon pepper
    ½ pound fresh mushrooms or ⅔ cup canned
        mushrooms, undrained
    1 cup light cream
    2 cups cubed cooked turkey
    1 cup cubed cooked ham
    1 can (8 ounces) water chestnuts, sliced
    1 to 2 tablespoons lemon juice (optional)
    ½ cup shredded Swiss cheese
    1½ cups soft bread crumbs
    3 tablespoons butter or margarine, melted

Cook onion in 2 tablespoons butter until softened but not brown. Add flour, salt, pepper, mushrooms, and cream. Cook and stir until thickened. Add turkey, ham, and water chestnuts. Adjust seasoning and add lemon juice if desired. Place in 2-quart casserole or baking pan.

Mix Swiss cheese, bread crumbs, and melted butter. Sprinkle around edge of casserole. Bake about 25 minutes, or until lightly browned and bubbly hot.

Chicken or Turkey Enchilada

9×13 pan
350 degrees F.
8 servings

    1½ dozen corn tortillas
    3 cups cubed, cooked chicken or turkey
    2 cups chicken broth
    1 can (10½ ounces) cream of celery soup
    1 can (10½ ounces) cream of mushroom soup
    1 green pepper, chopped
    1 medium onion, chopped
    1 can (16 ounces) tomatoes
    1 can (4 ounces) green chili salsa
    2 teaspoons salt
    1½ pounds shredded mild cheese

Layer bottom of pan with 6 tortillas torn into 8 pieces each. Layer with one-third of the chicken. Combine broth, soups, green pepper, onion, tomatoes, green chili salsa, and salt; cook 5 minutes. Pour one-third of the sauce over chicken layer, then one-third of the cheese. Repeat layering two more times, ending with cheese. Bake one hour.

Enchilada Casserole

7-inch casserole
350 degrees F.
6 servings

  2 tablespoons butter or margarine
  ½ cup onion, chopped
  ½ cup celery or green pepper, or a mixture of both
  1 can (16 ounces) tomato sauce
  ½ to 1 teaspoon chili powder
  ¼ teaspoon sweet basil
  ¼ teaspoon oregano
  1 package (7-inch size) corn tortillas
  1 cup cooked meat, diced (turkey, beef pot roast, or chicken)
  1 cup shredded cheese

Melt butter; add onion, celery, and green pepper, and cook about 5 minutes, occasionally stirring. Add tomato sauce, chili powder, sweet basil, and oregano. Place a tortilla in bottom of buttered casserole; add a thin layer of turkey and cheese, then sauce. Repeat for all. Bake 20 to 30 minutes or until hot.

Turkey Turnovers

Baking sheet
425 degrees F.
4 servings

  2 tablespoons finely chopped onion
  3 tablespoons butter or margarine
  ¼ cup flour
  ¼ teaspoon celery salt
  ⅔ cup turkey or chicken broth, or ⅔ cup hot water and 1 chicken bouillon cube
  ⅔ cup milk
  1 cup finely chopped cooked turkey
  Salt and pepper
  Pastry for one-crust 9-inch pie
  1 teaspoon chopped parsley

Sauté onion in butter or margarine until tender. Add flour and celery salt and blend. Gradually add stock and milk, stirring constantly. Continue to cook and stir until thickened. Add ½ cup of sauce to turkey; mix well. Season to taste with salt and pepper. Reserve remaining sauce.
Roll pastry 1/8-inch thick into rectangle about 10×8 inches. Then cut in 4 rectangles about 4×5 inches. If necessary, roll out each small rectangle to correct size. Place turkey mixture across half of each rectangle, spreading to within ¼ inch of edges.

Moisten edges with cold water. Fold uncovered half of pastry over mixture. Press edges together with fork. Prick tops. Bake on baking sheet 25 minutes or until done.
Add 3 tablespoons milk or stock to remaining sauce, and heat. Add parsley. Serve over hot turnovers.

Fluffy Omelet

10-inch frying pan
350 degrees F.
4 servings

  2 tablespoons Minute Tapioca
  ¾ teaspoon salt
  ⅛ teaspoon pepper
  ¾ cup milk
  1 tablespoon butter or margarine
  4 egg whites
  4 egg yolks

Combine tapioca, salt, and pepper in saucepan; add milk. Cook and stir over medium heat until mixture comes to a boil. Stir in butter. Remove from heat and cool slightly.
Meanwhile, beat egg whites until stiff. Beat egg yolks until thick and lemon colored. Gradually blend tapioca mixture into egg yolks; fold into egg whites. Pour into hot buttered frying pan. Cook over low heat for 3 minutes. Then place in oven and bake for 15 minutes, or until a knife inserted in center comes out clean. Cut across omelet at right angle to handle of pan, being careful not to cut all the way through. Carefully fold omelet over, from handle of pan to opposite side, and turn out onto serving platter. Fill and top with Spanish Sauce (see Index), or a tasty cream sauce, if desired.

Cheese Omelet

Prepare Fluffy Omelet as directed, adding ½ cup grated American cheese with the butter. Remove from heat and stir until cheese is melted.

Blender Quiche

8- or 9-inch pie pan, or 4 individual shallow bakers
350 degrees F.
6 servings

    ½ cup biscuit mix
    3 eggs
    2 cups milk
    ½ teaspoon salt
    Dash of cayenne pepper
    ½ teaspoon prepared mustard
    6 to 8 slices bacon, cooked crisp and crumbled
    ¾ to 1 cup shredded Cheddar cheese, or use part
        Swiss, part Cheddar

In blender container, put biscuit mix, eggs, milk, salt, pepper, and mustard. Blend on high speed (or "blend" button) for 2 minutes. Pour into greased pan or individual bakers. Sprinkle with bacon, then cheese. Press cheese down slightly. Bake 30 to 40 minutes, or until custard is set (pie pan will take longer than individual bakers).

Note: This is a standard blender quiche, lending itself to many variations. Instead of bacon, use about 1 cup cubed cooked ham, chicken, or turkey. Place meat in pie pan. Layer atop meat favorite ingredients, such as mushrooms, sliced green pepper, pimiento, or stuffed green olives. Pour egg mixture over all. Top with cheese.

Quiche Lorraine

350 degrees F.
6 servings

    ¾ cup onion, sliced
    2 tablespoons butter or margarine
    1 9-inch pie shell, unbaked
    8 ounces cheese, shredded—2 parts Swiss, 1 part
        Cheddar
    1 cup light cream or milk or mixture
    3 eggs, beaten lightly
    1 tablespoon flour
    ½ teaspoon salt
    ¼ teaspoon dry mustard
    ⅛ teaspoon pepper
    1 teaspoon Worcestershire sauce
    4 to 6 slices bacon, cooked and crumbled, or
        1 cup ground ham

Sauté onion in butter until tender but not brown (5 to 10 minutes). Spread in pie shell. Top with cheese. Add cream to eggs. Add combined flour, salt, dry mustard, and pepper; add Worcestershire

sauce. Pour over ingredients in pie shell. Top with crumbled bacon or ground ham. Bake 50 to 60 minutes, or until set. Serve hot.

This quiche may be baked in a regular quiche pan (1 large or 2 small). You will get a thinner product that can be cut in smaller wedges (12 to 16) for party appetizers.

Sausage Fondue

9 × 13-inch baking pan
350 degrees F.
8 servings

    8 slices bread, cubed
    2 cups grated medium or sharp cheese
    1½ pounds link sausage, cut in thirds,
        browned and drained
    4 eggs
    2¼ cups milk
    ¾ teaspoon dry mustard
    1 can (10½ ounces) cream of mushroom soup
    ½ cup milk

Arrange bread cubes in bottom of greased pan. Top with cheese and sausage. Beat eggs; add milk and mustard. Pour over bread, cheese, and sausage. Refrigerate several hours or overnight.

When ready to bake, dilute mushroom soup with milk, and pour over mixture. Bake 1 hour or until set. Baking temperature may be 300 or 325 degrees F. with increased baking time.

Cheese-Spinach Soufflé Roll

10 × 15 × 1-inch baking pan
350 degrees F.
8 servings

    ⅓ cup butter or margarine
    6 tablespoons flour
    1¼ cups milk
    6 eggs, separated
    Dash of cayenne pepper or ⅛ teaspoon white pepper
    ¾ teaspoon salt
    ¼ cup grated Parmesan cheese
    ½ cup medium or sharp shredded Cheddar cheese
    ¼ teaspoon cream of tartar
    ¼ pound sliced cheese (optional)

Fit waxed paper into a jelly roll pan, letting it extend up sides and ends. Grease well, including sides.

Melt butter in saucepan on medium heat. Add flour, and stir until smooth. Add milk all at once;

heat and stir until smooth and very thick. Remove from heat. Add slightly beaten egg yolks, pepper, and salt, and blend well. Stir in Parmesan and Cheddar cheeses.

Using a very clean bowl, beat egg whites with cream of tartar until stiff peaks form when beater is lifted straight up. Add one-fourth of the beaten egg whites to sauce. Mix well. Gently fold in remaining whites.

Spread mixture into prepared pan. Bake 15 minutes, or until puffed and lightly browned. Cool slightly; turn onto waxed paper dusted lightly with grated Parmesan cheese. Spread filling (below) on soufflé, leaving one-half inch uncovered on both long sides. Using waxed paper as a helper, roll up soufflé and place seam side down on a warm, heat-proof serving platter.

Garnish with slices of cheese, and return to oven to soften cheese. Serve at the table.

Filling

2 packages (10 ounces each) frozen chopped spinach
2 tablespoons butter or margarine
¼ teaspoon salt
¼ cup chopped onion
¼ cup shredded medium or sharp cheese
½ cup sour cream

Cook spinach as directed on package. Drain into collander and press with back of large spoon to remove excess liquid. Melt butter in saucepan; add salt and chopped onion. Cook until onion is golden. Remove from heat; fold in well-drained spinach, grated cheese, and sour cream.

Baked Chilies Relleno

7×11-inch baking dish
325 degrees F.
4 to 6 servings

2 cans (4 ounces each) whole green chilies
6 eggs, separated
1 tablespoons flour
¼ teaspoon salt
¼ teaspoon pepper
½ pound Monterey Jack cheese, thinly sliced
Chilies Relleno Sauce (below)

Carefully wash chilies; remove seeds, and drain. Beat egg whites until stiff, but not dry. Beat egg yolks until thick and creamy. Blend in flour, salt, and pepper. Fold in beaten egg whites. Gently spread half of the egg mixture in greased baking dish. Place all of chilies opened flat over egg mixture. Cover with cheese slices. Top with remaining egg mixture. Bake 25 minutes. Serve hot with Chilies Relleno Sauce.

Chilies Relleno Sauce

1 can (16 ounces) stewed tomatoes
2 teaspoons minced onions (fresh or dried)
Pepper
¼ teaspoon salt
¼ teaspoon oregano or basil
Garlic powder

In a medium saucepan combine all ingredients. Simmer uncovered for 10 minutes. Serve hot.

Cheese Puff or Strata

2-quart casserole
350 degrees F.
6 servings

8 slices white bread
3 tablespoons butter or margarine, softened
2 cups shredded medium or sharp Cheddar cheese
4 eggs
2½ cups milk
1 tablespoon prepared mustard
1 teaspoon Worcestershire sauce
1 teaspoon salt
⅛ teaspoon paprika

Spread bread with butter; cut into large cubes. Place one-third in a buttered baking dish. Sprinkle with one-third cheese. Repeat with remaining bread and cheese to make two more layers of each. Beat eggs with remaining ingredients; pour over bread-cheese layers; cover. Refrigerate at least 3 hours or overnight. Bake, uncovered, 1 hour, or until puffed and golden and sharp knife inserted in center comes out clean (not milky).

Company Brunch Casserole

9×9×2-inch casserole
350 degrees F.
9 to 12 servings, 1 egg each

    2 cans (10½ ounces each) cream of chicken soup
    1 soup can milk
    2 teaspoons grated onion
    1 teaspoon prepared mustard
    1 cup (¼ pound) Swiss cheese, shredded
    9 to 12 eggs
    1 loaf French bread, small diameter, sliced thin
      and buttered

Combine soup, milk, onion, mustard, and cheese. Heat and stir until cheese melts and mixture is smooth. Put about one inch of sauce in bottom of baking dish. Carefully break eggs, so that yolk remains intact, onto sauce. Spoon remaining sauce around and over eggs. Place bread slices around edge of casserole, overlapping slightly. Bake about 20 minutes, or until eggs are done to your liking (touch them lightly with a finger; they should wiggle a little). Serve with ham, bacon, or sausage, if desired.

Meat and Vegetable Accompaniments

Yorkshire Pudding

9×9×2-inch pan or 12 muffin cups
425 degrees F.
6 to 8 servings

  2 eggs
  1 cup milk
  1 cup flour
  ¼ teaspoon salt
  ¼ cup fat or pan drippings from beef roast

Beat eggs; add milk, flour, and salt. Beat until smooth. Heat fat or drippings in pan; pour batter over hot fat. Bake 20 to 30 minutes, or until puffed and light brown on tips. Cut into squares and serve at once.

For muffin tins: Spoon 1 teaspoon fat in each cup. Divide batter evenly among cups. Bake 15 to 20 minutes, or until puffed and light brown.

LaRue's Yorkshire Pudding

1-quart casserole
450 degrees F.
About 9 servings

  2 eggs, separated
  ½ cup flour
  ½ teaspoon salt
  1 teaspoon baking powder
  ½ cup milk

Beat egg whites until stiff. Beat yolks until thick and creamy. Sift flour, salt, and baking powder; add to yolks with milk. Mix well. Fold whites lightly into batter. After removing roast beef from pan, measure about ¼ cup drippings into a one-quart casserole or pan. Pour batter quickly into hot grease; return to oven and cook 20 to 25 minutes. Make gravy with drippings remaining in roasting pan. Serve pudding in squares.

LaRue's family calls this "Mom's Special Yorkshire Pudding." She says it is not actually Yorkshire pudding because it has baking powder in it. That way it holds up for a long time. Her family prefers it to the actual dish.

Yorkshire Pudding, Custard Type

9×9×2-inch pan
400 degrees F.
4 to 6 servings

  ¼ cup flour
  2 cups milk
  2 eggs, beaten
  ¼ teaspoon salt

Combine ingredients and beat until smooth. Pour into well-buttered pan, or preferably into a pan containing meat drippings (about ¼ cup drippings from a beef roast is ideal). Bake about 40 minutes, or until puffy and brown. Cut in squares; serve with beef gravy.

Dumplings for Stew

6 medium dumplings

  1 cup flour
  1¼ teaspoons baking powder
  ½ teaspoon salt
  1 tablespoon melted butter or margarine
  ½ cup milk (about)

Sift flour, baking powder, and salt together. Combine butter and milk, and add to flour mixture, stirring lightly just until all flour is dampened (add a little more milk, if necessary, to form a soft but not runny dough). Drop small amounts from spoon onto simmering stew in deep kettle, resting dumplings on meat or vegetables. Simmer 10 minutes, uncovered. Then cover tightly and cook 10 minutes longer without removing cover.

Biscuit mix may be used, adding milk only. It makes a richer dough that sometimes falls apart as it cooks.

Baked Pineapple Dressing

1-quart casserole
350 degrees F.

¼ cup butter or margarine, melted
½ cup brown sugar (or white sugar)
4 eggs, lightly beaten
1 large can (20 ounces) crushed pineapple, undrained
5 slices stale bread, cubed
¼ teaspoon salt

Combine all ingredients in a large bowl. Pour into casserole and bake uncovered about 30 minutes, or until set and lightly browned. Serve with ham or roast pork.

Mushroom Bread Stuffing

2-quart casserole
350 degrees F.
12 servings

1 cup chopped onion (1 large)
½ pound fresh mushrooms (3 cups), cleaned and sliced through stems
¼ cup butter or margarine
1 can (10½ ounces) cream of mushroom soup
1 soup can of milk
12 cups soft bread cubes (stale)
⅓ cup minced parsley
1 teaspoon rubbed sage
⅛ teaspoon pepper
¼ cup butter or margarine, melted

Sauté onions and mushrooms in ¼ cup butter in large frying pan until soft but not browned, 10 to 15 minutes. Add soup and milk, and stir until hot and creamy. Toss together bread cubes, parsley, sage, pepper, and melted butter. Add the mushroom mixture. Toss together lightly; spoon into buttered casserole. Bake, uncovered, about 35 minutes, or until lightly browned.

Lemon Barbecue Sauce

2 cups sauce

1 cup butter
1 clove garlic, minced
1 tablespoon flour
⅔ cup water
1 tablespoon sugar
1 teaspoon salt
½ teaspoon pepper

6 tablespoons frozen, fresh, or bottled lemon juice
¼ teaspoon Tabasco
½ teaspoon thyme

Melt butter. Cook garlic in butter until clear; stir in flour. Add remaining ingredients and cook until slightly thick. Excellent as a basting sauce for broiling or grilling chicken or seafood.

Texas-style Barbecue Sauce

2 cups sauce

¼ cup (½ stick) butter or margarine
1 large onion, chopped fine
½ cup vinegar (we like red wine vinegar)
2 cloves garlic, minced
½ cup lemon juice
1 tablespoon grated lemon peel
½ cup catsup
2 tablespoons Worcestershire sauce
4 drops Tabasco sauce
½ teaspoon chili powder
½ teaspoon powdered sage
1 tablespoon flour

Melt butter. Add onion, and cook until soft. Add remaining ingredients and cook for 30 minutes, until slightly thick and flavors have blended. Use as a basting sauce for meats on the grill. Heat remaining sauce and serve with meat.

This tangy barbecue sauce is especially good on chicken and is delicious with beef or pork.

Firehouse Barbecue Sauce

2 cups catsup
2 cups water
¼ cup Worcestershire sauce
1 tablespoon chili powder
1 large onion, sliced and separated into rings
Meat: chicken, ribs, hamburger, or pot roast

Combine catsup, water, Worcestershire sauce, and chili powder. Prepare meat and place in shallow baking pan. Cover with onion rings, and pour on sauce. Roast until meat is done.

Note: This is a simple and delicious barbecue sauce, made quickly with ingredients usually on hand. It is popular in many fire stations because it is easy and can cook a long time without any attention.

West Coast Marinade for Beef

1 cup salad oil
½ cup soy sauce
½ cup lemon juice
¼ cup Worcestershire sauce
½ cup prepared mustard
1 tablespoon coarsely cracked black pepper
2 cloves garlic, minced
Beef cubes or steaks

Combine all marinade ingredients and mix thoroughly. Cut beef into 1-inch cubes and place in marinade. Turn or stir occasionally. The meat can stay in this marinade up to 48 hours. When ready to cook beef, remove from marinade and place on skewers or on grill and cook to desired doneness, basting often with marinade.

Mustard Sauce for Ham

About 1 pint

½ can (10-ounce size) tomato soup
½ cup prepared mustard
½ cup vinegar
½ cup sugar
¼ cup butter or margarine
3 egg yolks

Combine ingredients, and cook on low heat or in double boiler until thick, stirring to keep smooth. Strain. Serve hot on ham loaf, or serve chilled.

Mustard Ring

¾ cup sugar
½ teaspoon salt
2 tablespoons dry mustard
½ cup vinegar
½ cup water
4 eggs, well beaten
1 envelope gelatin in 1 tablespoon cold water
½ teaspoon horseradish
1½ cups whipping cream, whipped

Combine sugar, salt, and dry mustard. Add vinegar, water, and eggs. Soak gelatin in 1 tablespoon cold water. Add to egg mixture and cook on low heat or over hot water, stirring constantly, until creamy. Add horseradish; cool. Fold in whipped cream. Pour into a 4-cup ring mold and chill until set. Serve with baked ham or roast beef.

Whipped Cream Mustard Sauce

About 1½ cups

1 tablespoon sugar
3 tablespoons prepared mustard
2 tablespoons vinegar
1 tablespoon water
½ teaspoon salt
2 egg yolks, slightly beaten
1 tablespoon margarine
1 tablespoon horseradish
½ cup whipping cream

Combine sugar, mustard, vinegar, water, salt, and egg yolks in a small saucepan. Cook on medium heat, stirring constantly, until mixture thickens. Remove from heat; stir in margarine and horseradish. Cool.

Whip cream to soft peaks. Fold into the cooled, cooked mixture. Refrigerate until serving time. Leftovers will keep several weeks in the refrigerator.

Spanish Sauce

About 1 quart

½ cup chopped onion
¼ to ½ cup chopped green pepper
2 to 3 tablespoons butter or margarine (as needed)
1 cup chopped celery (optional)
1 can (4 ounces) sliced mushrooms
1 can (28 ounces) or 1 quart tomatoes
2 teaspoons sugar (if desired)
½ to 1 teaspoon salt
Dash of cayenne pepper

Sauté onion and green pepper in butter until softened but not brown. Add remaining ingredients. (Use either celery or mushrooms, or both.) Simmer until vegetables are tender (10 to 15 minutes). Adjust seasonings to taste.

Serve with meat, fish, or cheese dishes. If desired, thicken slightly with about 1 tablespoon roux (see Index) to use in making Spanish Omelet.

Milk Gravy

2 cups

3 tablespoons meat drippings (bacon, beef,
  poultry, or ham)
3 tablespoons flour
2 cups milk
Salt and pepper

Leave 3 tablespoons fat drippings in frying pan in which meat was cooked. Add flour and brown slightly while stirring. Remove from heat and add milk, stirring well to blend. Return to heat; cook and stir until mixture is thick and smooth. Season to taste. Serve with potatoes, biscuits, or cornbread.

Note: This gravy is usually made from fried beef drippings, but other meat drippings are commonly used. If the meat is ham, this gravy is called "red-eye" gravy in New England; it is served over the ham slice.

Seafood Sauce

About 1½ cups

1 cup mayonnaise
2 tablespoons catsup
1 tablespoon chili sauce
1 teaspoon finely minced green pepper
1 tablespoon tarragon vinegar
1 teaspoon grated horseradish
Dash of cayenne pepper

Combine all ingredients, and mix well. Serve with shrimp, crab, or mixed seafood cocktails or as a dip for seafood.

Snappy Sauce

About ½ cup

½ cup mayonnaise or ¼ cup mayonnaise
  and ¼ cup sour cream
1 teaspoon lemon juice
½ teaspoon prepared mustard
1 tablespoon horseradish (optional)

Blend ingredients. Serve on fish or vegetables (especially good with broccoli).

Egg and Olive Sauce

About 3 cups sauce
9 to 12 servings

2 tablespoons butter or margarine
¼ cup flour
2½ cups milk
1 teaspoon salt
Dash of pepper
½ teaspoon Worcestershire sauce
2 to 3 hard-cooked eggs, chopped
½ cup sliced stuffed olives

Melt butter over medium heat. Add flour, stirring well to blend. Gradually stir in milk. Add salt, pepper, and Worcestershire sauce. Cook and stir until mixture is thick and creamy. Stir in chopped eggs and sliced olives. Taste and add more salt and pepper, if desired. Serve with fish loaves or wherever a tasty cream sauce is desired.

Glazed Apples

Large frying pan
16 servings

8 medium-size red cooking apples
  (tart apples are best)
Butter or margarine
¼ cup light brown sugar
¼ cup light corn syrup
1 tablespoon lemon juice

Core but do not peel apples; cut into ½-inch thick rings. Or cut in half, then into ½-inch wedges. Melt ¼ cup butter in frying pan. Add apples, one-third at a time, and cook about 2 minutes or until just tender, turning once with pancake turner. Remove apples to platter.

In same pan over medium heat, melt ¼ cup more butter; add brown sugar, corn syrup, and lemon juice. Cook, stirring until brown sugar is dissolved and mixture is slightly thickened. Return apples to frying pan with rubber spatula; stir gently to coat apples well with brown-sugar mixture.

Blender Hollandaise Sauce

1 scant cup

½ cup butter or margarine
3 egg yolks
2 tablespoons lemon juice
Dash of cayenne pepper

Warm blender by leaving very hot water in it for a few minutes. Heat butter until almost boiling. Pour hot water from blender; put in yolks, lemon juice, and cayenne. Cover; quickly turn on and then off. With blender on high, and using only small opening in cover, slowly pour in hot butter. Blend until thick and somewhat fluffy, about 30 seconds, with occasional scraping down of sides.

Serve warm on vegetables or fish. To warm, heat over warm water. Keeps well in covered dish in refrigerator.

Mock Hollandaise Sauce

1 cup

¾ cup mayonnaise
¼ cup butter or margarine
¼ teaspoon salt
Dash of pepper
1 tablespoon lemon juice
1 teaspoon grated lemon rind (optional)

Blend mayonnaise, butter, salt, and pepper; heat, stirring constantly, until butter melts and mixture is hot and smooth. Stir in lemon juice and rind. Makes about 1 cup.

White Sauce

1 cup

Ingredients	Thin	Medium	Thick
Flour (tablespoons)	1	2	3 to 4
Butter or margarine (tablespoons)	1	2	3
Milk (cups)	1	1	1
Salt (teaspoons)	¼	¼	¼

Method I — Roux

Cream flour and butter until well mixed. Add to hot milk; heat while stirring until thickened. Reduce heat to simmer (turn heat off, if using electric range); cover tightly and cook a few minutes longer. Add salt to taste. Or instead of creaming, melt butter in pan, then add flour and blend. The creamed butter-flour mixture may be made in quantity and refrigerated for quick use.

Method II — Paste

Mix flour with ¼ cup of the milk until smooth. Heat remaining milk; stir in flour paste, and continue cooking and stirring until thickened. Reduce heat to simmer (turn off, if using electric range); cover tightly and cook a few minutes longer. Add butter and salt to taste.

Variations

1. Tomato sauce. Omit milk and add 1 cup tomato juice or V-8 Juice. Season to taste with celery salt, onion salt, garlic salt, or sweet basil leaves.

2. To make gravy, substitute all or part of milk with chicken, turkey, or beef stock.

3. Add cooked, chopped vegetables (onions, celery, green pepper, or mushrooms) to sauce or sauté fresh chopped vegetables in butter before adding flour.

Quick Peach Chutney

About 8 servings

⅓ cup chopped onion
½ cup raisins (golden raisins are nice, if available)
¼ cup brown sugar
⅓ cup vinegar
1 teaspoon curry powder
½ teaspoon ginger
¼ teaspoon salt
1 stick cinnamon
1 can (29 ounces) sliced cling peaches, well drained*

Combine all ingredients except peaches in small saucepan. Bring to a boil and simmer on low heat for 10 to 15 minutes. Pour over peaches in refrigerator dish; cover. Let stand overnight or longer. Chutney will keep several weeks; it is delicious served with pork, poultry, or ham.

*Use the drained juice for another purpose, such as in punch.

Mock Sour Cream

8 servings, 2 tablespoons each (10 calories per tablespoon)

    1 cup cottage cheese
    1 tablespoon lemon juice
    Salt
    Pepper
    1 tablespoon chives, chopped

In a blender, whirl cottage cheese and lemon juice until smooth. Add salt, pepper, and chives to taste. Serve on baked potatoes.

Curried Fruit

2-quart casserole
325 degrees F.
14 to 16 servings

    1 can (29 ounces) peach halves
    1 can (16 ounces) apricot halves
    2 cans (20 ounces each) pineapple chunks
    1 can (29 ounces) pear halves
    ⅓ cup margarine or butter
    1 cup brown sugar
    4 teaspoons curry powder

Drain fruit. Melt butter or margarine; add sugar and curry powder. Arrange fruit in baking pan. Pour butter-curry mixture over fruit. Bake for 1 hour.

Raw Cranberry Relish

About 1 quart

    2½ cups ground cranberries (12-ounce package)
    ¾ cup sugar
    1 orange, including peel and pulp
    1 can (13½ ounces) crushed pineapple, or 2 apples

Combine cranberries and sugar and let stand while preparing orange. Score orange so you can remove the peel in sections. Cut away as much as possible of the white part just under the skin. Remove seeds from fruit and grind, along with the thin skin. Save the juice, and add with skin and pulp to cranberry-sugar mixture. Blend in pineapple and juice. Or use apples, cored and ground, and peeled if desired.

Store in refrigerator in fruit jars. Let stand overnight before using. Will keep up to two weeks in refrigerator. Also freezes well.

Quick Spiced Peaches

8 servings

    1 can (29 ounces) cling peach halves with juice
    1 stick cinnamon
    1 teaspoon whole cloves
    2 tablespoons vinegar

Drain peach juice into a saucepan. Add cinnamon, cloves, and vinegar; simmer 10 minutes. Remove from heat. Add peaches. Cover and let stand overnight. Serve the peach halves to enhance any ham, pork, or poultry dish.

Confetti Corn Relish

2 cups relish

    1 can (12 ounces) whole kernel corn, drained
    ¾ cup chopped celery
    ¼ cup French dressing
    ½ teaspoon salt
    2 tablespoons chopped onion
    2 tablespoons diced green pepper
    1 tablespoon diced pimiento
    1 tablespoon vinegar

Combine all ingredients and cover. Refrigerate for several hours. Serve with hamburgers, steaks, and sandwiches.

Gingered Cucumber Slices

4 to 6 servings

    1 or 2 large cucumbers (see instructions)
    ⅓ cup white wine vinegar or white vinegar
    1 tablespoon sugar
    1 teaspoon salt
    1 teaspoon grated fresh ginger (or ½ teaspoon ground ginger)

For this recipe use the long, thin English or Armenian (sometimes called Syrian or Chinese) cucumbers, if available; peel them only if you prefer. Or you can use regular cucumbers and peel them. If they are fully mature, cut them in half and scrape out any large seeds.

Slice cucumbers very thin to make about 2 cups; combine the cucumbers in a bowl with the vinegar, sugar, salt, and ginger. Cover and refrigerate for at least 1 hour or overnight, stirring several times. Lift cucumbers out of marinade, and serve in small individual dishes. Spoon a little of the marinade over top to moisten.

Egg Noodles

The equivalent of one 8-ounce package

- 1 cup flour
- ¼ teaspoon salt
- 1 egg yolk (or use the whole egg and reduce liquid a bit)
- 2 tablespoons (about) water, or cream

Mix salt with flour. Combine slightly beaten egg with water (we like cream if we have it on hand, because the noodles are more tender). Stir into flour mixture to make a very hard dough. If it is too dry to handle, add water a few drops at a time, but keep it hard; don't let it get sticky.

Knead dough on a lightly floured board until smooth (about 5 minutes). Cover and let stand for 20 to 30 minutes. Divide it into 2 or 3 parts, and roll each part paper thin. (This is the only difficult part—to roll very hard dough very thin.) Roll each piece of dough jelly-roll fashion, or fold into several layers and slice evenly into narrow strips. Separate and straighten strips, and let dry thoroughly. Store in a jar in refrigerator until ready to use. When ready to cook, drop into rapidly boiling liquid and boil for 10 to 15 minutes, or until tender but not mushy.

Exotic Oven Rice

2-quart casserole
350 degrees F.
6 to 8 servings

- ½ cup butter
- 1 cup regular or converted rice
- 3 cups boiling water
- 3 chicken bouillon cubes

Melt butter in frying pan. Add rice. Cook for 10 minutes (rice will still be white). Stir.

Put in casserole and add boiling water in which bouillon cubes have been dissolved. Stir. Place in oven for 1 hour. Stir once.

To double recipe: Double everything except butter; use ¾ cup or 1½ sticks.

Cheese Grits

2-quart casserole
350 degrees F.

- 1 cup grits, cooked according to package directions
- ½ cup (¼ pound) butter or margarine
- 1 jar (5 ounces) bacon cheese
- 3 eggs, well beaten
- ⅔ cup milk
- ½ cup sharp Cheddar cheese, shredded

Cook grits. Add butter and cheese, and stir to melt the cheese. Combine eggs and milk; mix well. Add to grits mixture. Pour into well-greased casserole and cover with shredded cheese. Bake for 45 minutes or until set.

Serve as a side dish for a ham dinner or a main dish for a family lunch or supper.

"Low-Energy" Cooked Wheat

In a heavy saucepan, combine 2 cups water with each cup of wheat to be cooked. Add ½ teaspoon salt per cup of wheat. Bring to boil and cook for 5 minutes. Remove from heat; cover tightly and place in 350-degree F. oven. Turn off oven immediately. Leave wheat undisturbed for 8 to 10 hours.

Spanish Wheat

8 servings

- 3 strips bacon
- 1 medium onion, chopped
- 1 green pepper, chopped
- 3 cups cooked whole wheat
- 1 quart tomatoes (4 cups) and juice
- Salt and pepper to taste

Brown bacon in frying pan; remove to cool, then crumble. In bacon drippings, cook onion and green pepper until soft. Add wheat and tomatoes; cover and simmer for 5 to 6 hours. (The longer the wheat cooks, the more of the flavors it absorbs.) To serve, add crumbled bacon and season to taste with salt and pepper.

Bulgur

In a heavy saucepan, combine 1 cup wheat with 1 cup water. Cover pan, bring to boil, then turn heat down and simmer for 1 hour. Drain off any remaining liquid.

Spread wheat in a thin layer on large baking sheet and bake at 200 degrees F. for 2 hours or until completely dried out. Crack with heavy rolling pin or grind coarsely in wheat grinder.

Armenian Pilaf

4 to 6 servings

    2 tablespoons butter or margarine
    3 tablespoons minced onion
    1 cup bulgur
    2 cups chicken stock or broth (canned may be used)
    ½ teaspoon salt
    ½ teaspoon pepper

Melt butter; add onion, and cook until soft. Add remaining ingredients and cover. Simmer over low heat for 20 minutes, or until all liquid is absorbed, stirring occasionally. Turn off heat and allow to stand for 15 to 20 minutes. Reheat to serve, if necessary.

Variations: For Beef Pilaf, use beef stock in place of chicken stock, and add ½ teaspoon Worcestershire sauce.

Parmesan Pilaf: Increase onion to ¼ cup, and add ½ teaspoon garlic salt. When cooking is complete, stir in ⅓ cup Parmesan cheese and 1 tablespoon minced parsley.

Deluxe Brown Rice

6 to 8 servings

    1 cup sliced carrots
    3 tablespoons oil
    ½ cup sliced green onions
    2 apples, peeled, cored, sliced
    3 cups cooked brown rice
    1 teaspoon salt, or to taste
    ½ cup seedless raisins
    1 tablespoon sesame seeds

Sauté carrots in oil about 10 minutes. Add onions and apples. Cook 10 minutes longer. Stir in rice, salt, and raisins. Cook, stirring gently until rice is heated through. Add sesame seeds; toss lightly.

Far East Rice

4 cups, about 8 servings

    1 cup Minute Rice
    ¾ cup thin carrot strips
    ½ cup chopped onion
    ½ bunch green onions, cut in 1-inch lengths
    ¼ cup raisins
    2 tablespoons butter or margarine
    1 cup water
    ½ package (5 ounces) frozen peas or green beans
    1 teaspoon salt
    ½ cup cashew nuts, or use pecans
    1½ teaspoons butter or margarine

Sauté rice, carrots, onion, green onions, and raisins in 2 tablespoons butter in large frying pan until vegetables just begin to brown (about 5 minutes), stirring frequently. Add water, peas or green beans, and salt. Bring to a boil, breaking up peas with a fork, if necessary. Cover, reduce heat, and simmer 5 minutes. Lightly sauté nuts in 1½ teaspoons butter. Stir into rice mixture. Serve immediately.

Green and Yellow Rice

2-quart casserole
350 degrees F.
6 to 8 servings

    3 cups hot cooked rice
    ¼ cup butter or margarine
    4 beaten eggs
    2 cups shredded sharp Cheddar cheese
    1 cup milk
    1 package (10 ounces) frozen spinach, cooked
      and drained well
    1 tablespoon chopped onion
    1 teaspoon Worcestershire sauce
    ½ teaspoon marjoram
    ½ teaspoon thyme
    ½ teaspoon rosemary
    ½ teaspoon salt, or to taste

Combine rice and butter. Combine eggs, cheese, and milk, and gently stir into rice. Stir in spinach, onion, Worcestershire sauce, herbs, and salt. Set casserole, uncovered, in a pan of water in oven; bake for 45 minutes.

Green Rice

Covered 10-inch frying pan
5 servings, ½ cup each

    1 green pepper, cored, seeded, and chopped
    ⅓ cup coarsely chopped parsley
    3 tablespoons chopped onion
    3 cups chicken broth
    3 tablespoons oil
    1 cup raw rice
    ½ teaspoon salt
    ¼ teaspoon garlic salt, optional

Whirl green pepper, parsley, and onion in blender with part of chicken broth. Heat oil in frying pan. Add rice and salt, and stir to coat and heat rice. Add blended mixture and remaining chicken broth. Cover and simmer until rice is tender, about 20 to 30 minutes.

All-Purpose Sauce for Vegetables

1 pint

    1 cup sour cream
    1 cup mayonnaise
    1 tablespoon chopped onion
    1 tablespoon chopped green pepper

Blend all ingredients well. Serve hot or cold. Sauce keeps well refrigerated. Serve on baked potatoes, mashed potatoes, broccoli, asparagus, zucchini, sliced tomatoes, sandwiches, etc. Use in place of butter.

Breads

Bishop's Bread

9×5×3-inch loaf pan
350 degrees F.

3 eggs, beaten
1 cup sugar
¼ cup butter or margarine
1½ cups flour
1½ teaspoons baking powder
½ cup walnut halves
½ cup Brazil nuts, whole
½ cup dates, cut in halves
1 bottle (4 ounces) maraschino cherries, undrained
2 ounces sweet or semisweet chocolate, cut in large pieces

Combine eggs, sugar, butter, flour, and baking powder and beat until smooth. Add to batter the walnuts, Brazil nuts, dates, cherries and juice, and chocolate. Mix only enough to distribute the ingredients. Bake in loaf pan, lined with greased and floured waxed paper, for at least 1 hour, or until toothpick inserted in center comes out clean and loaf is well browned. (Bread may be baked in small cans or miniature loaf pans for gift-giving.)

Elegant Bran Bread

375 degrees F.

8 5×2½×2-inch, or 3 9×5×3-inch loaf pans

3 packages (3 tablespoons) active dry yeast
2 cups warm water
1 teaspoon sugar
2 cups All-Bran cereal
⅓ cup sugar
1 tablespoon salt
¾ cup shortening
2 cups boiling water
4 eggs
5 to 5½ cups flour (may be part whole wheat)
¼ cup sunflower seed kernels (optional)
½ cup All-Bran cereal

Soften yeast in warm water to which 1 teaspoon sugar has been added. Combine 2 cups cereal, sugar, salt, and shortening in large bowl of electric mixer. Add boiling water and stir until shortening is melted. Cool to lukewarm. Add yeast mixture. Beat in eggs and 3 cups flour. Using a wooden spoon stir in addi-

tional flour as needed to make a soft dough. Add seeds and remaining cereal. Knead slightly. Divide dough and shape into loaves; place in well-greased pans. Let rise until double. Bake 40 to 50 minutes if using large pans, 20 to 30 minutes for small pans, until browned and crusty.

Wrap extra loaves in foil and freeze.

To use, remove foil from loaves and thaw. Slice and butter; rewrap in foil and heat at 400 degrees F. about 20 minutes. Serve piping hot from foil in a basket.

Banana Bread

1 9×5×4-inch loaf pan
350 degrees F.

½ cup margarine
1 cup brown sugar or ½ cup each white and brown sugar
2 eggs
2 cups flour
1 teaspoon cinnamon
1 teaspoon baking soda
¼ teaspoon salt
¼ teaspoon allspice
¼ teaspoon nutmeg
1 cup mashed banana, very ripe
1 tablespoon liquid (sour milk, buttermilk, or fruit juice)

Cream margarine and sugar; add eggs and beat well. Sift dry ingredients together; add to egg mixture with banana and liquid; mix thoroughly. Bake in greased or wax-paper-lined loaf pan for 1 hour or until bread tests done. Cool on cake rack.

Variations

1. Use 1 cup whole wheat flour plus 1 cup white in place of white flour.
2. Change spices to suit your taste or even leave them out.
3. Use applesauce in place of part or all of banana.
4. Use old jam to replace banana; reduce sugar to ½ cup. If jam is very thick, add a bit of liquid.
5. Add ½ to 1 cup chopped walnuts or pecans.

Clockwise, from top left: Golden Yam Rolls (p. 99), Bishop's Bread (p. 91), Arlean's Molasses Refrigerator Muffins (p. 94), Irish Soda Bread (p. 93), Phyllis's Whole Wheat Bread (p. 97), Easy Brioche (p. 100), Orange Nut Bread (p. 93), Bran Muffins (p. 94), Elegant Bran Bread (p. 91)

Apple or Zucchini Bread

2 9×5×4-inch or 3 7×3×2-inch pans
350 degrees F.

3 eggs
1 cup oil
1 cup sugar
⅓ cup molasses
2 teaspoons vanilla
2 cups flour
½ cup whole wheat flour
1 teaspoon salt
1 teaspoon baking soda
½ teaspoon baking powder
2 teaspoon cinnamon
2 cups shredded apple or 2 cups shredded zucchini
1 cup nuts, chopped

Beat eggs. Add oil, sugar, molasses, and vanilla; beat mixture until thick and foamy. Combine flours, salt, soda, baking powder, and cinnamon, and add to egg mixture. Stir just until blended. Add apples and nuts. Combine well.

Divide batter between greased and floured loaf pans. Bake for 1 hour or until bread tests done, or use three smaller pans and bake for 45 minutes. Leave bread in the pan for about 10 minutes to cool; then turn out on rack and cool thoroughly.

Danish Nut Loaf

3 7×3×2-inch loaf pans
350 degrees F.

2 eggs, beaten
1¾ cups sugar
2 cups buttermilk
4 cups flour
2 teaspoons baking powder
1½ teaspoons baking soda
1 teaspoon salt
1 to 1½ cups walnuts, chopped
1 to 1½ cups raisins

Mix eggs, sugar, and buttermilk. Sift together flour, baking powder, soda, and salt. Add to egg-sugar-buttermilk mixture. Add nuts and raisins. Pour into 3 well-greased loaf pans. Bake 60 minutes, or until bread tests done.

Note: The fat hasn't been forgotten. This is a chewy, delicious bread with no fat in it. It slices beautifully and stays moist for sandwiches.

Bonanza Bread

8×4×3-inch loaf pans
325 degrees F.
2 loaves or 1 loaf and 18 muffins

1 cup flour
1 cup whole wheat flour
½ teaspoon salt
½ teaspoon baking soda
2 teaspoons baking powder
⅔ cup nonfat dry milk powder
⅓ cup wheat germ
½ cup firmly packed brown sugar
¼ cup chopped nuts
½ cup unsalted dry roasted peanuts, chopped
½ cup raisins
3 eggs
½ cup oil
½ cup molasses
¾ cup orange juice
2 medium bananas, mashed (about 1 cup)
⅓ cup dried apricots, chopped

Combine flours, salt, soda, baking powder, dry milk, wheat germ, brown sugar, nuts, peanuts, and raisins in a large bowl; blend thoroughly with fork. Beat eggs; add oil, molasses, orange juice, bananas, and apricots, and beat thoroughly. Add mixture to dry ingredients and stir just until all dry ingredients are moistened. Pour into pans and bake for 1 hour, or until center is firm when pressed lightly. Cool slightly in pan; then remove from pan and cool completely. When cool, wrap tightly and store in a cool place.

Variations

1. Add ½ small orange, ground or chopped very finely, to the liquid ingredients before adding liquids to dry ingredients.

2. Use raw chopped apple, grated carrot, applesauce, fresh ground apricots, peaches, pears, or zucchini instead of bananas.

Irish Soda Bread

8-inch round pan or a baking sheet
375 degrees F.

    3 cups flour
    3 teaspoons baking powder
    ½ teaspoon baking soda
    1 tablespoon sugar
    ½ teaspoon salt
    1½ cups buttermilk (or use 1½ cups milk soured
        with 1½ tablespoons white vinegar)
    1 tablespoon butter or margarine, melted

Sift dry ingredients together into a bowl. Add buttermilk all at once, and mix with a fork just until blended. Turn dough onto a lightly floured board and knead lightly until smooth. Shape into a ball, and place in a well-greased pan or on a well-greased baking sheet. Use your hands to flatten dough into a 7-inch circle. With a sharp knife, score top, cutting about ¼ inch deep and in about 2-inch squares. Bake about 30 minutes, or until lightly browned and loaf sounds hollow when flipped. Turn out onto cooking rack; brush with melted butter. Cool completely before cutting.

Irish Bannock

Increase sugar to ¼ cup. Add to dry ingredients ½ to 1 teaspoon caraway seeds and ⅓ to ½ cup raisins. A mixture of light and dark raisins is nice.

Orange Nut Bread

9×5×3-inch loaf pan, or 2 7×5×3-inch loaf pans
350 degrees F.

    2¼ cups flour
    2 teaspoons baking powder
    ½ teaspoon soda
    ¾ teaspoon salt
    ¾ cup plus 1 tablespoon sugar
    ¾ cup nuts, chopped
    ½ cup raisins
    ¼ cup ground orange rind
    1 egg, well beaten
    ½ cup milk
    ½ cup orange juice
    2 tablespoons shortening, melted

Sift flour, baking powder, soda, salt, and sugar together. Add nuts, raisins, and orange rind. Combine egg, milk, and orange juice. Add to flour mixture with shortening; mix only until flour is damp-

ened and fruit and nuts are well distributed. Spoon batter into greased pan. Bake for 1 hour, or until it tests done. (Bake small loaves about 45 minutes.) Let cool in pan 10 minutes; turn out and let stand until cold. Wrap in waxed paper or aluminum foil; let stand overnight before slicing.

Fresh Corn Cornbread

1½-quart casserole
325 degrees F.
8 servings

    2 cups fresh corn cut from the cob
    ½ cup yellow cornmeal
    2 tablespoons sugar
    3 tablespoons flour
    2 eggs, beaten
    1½ cups milk
    1 teaspoon salt
    1 tablespoon minced onion
    ¼ cup oil

Combine all ingredients and mix thoroughly. Pour into well-greased casserole and bake for 1 hour, or until set and knife comes out clean when inserted in center. This is a "spoon bread" that is delicious served instead of traditional bread as an accompaniment to a meal.

Dried Corn Bread

8×8×2-inch pan or muffin tins
400 degrees F.
9 servings

    1 cup whole wheat flour
    4 teaspoons baking powder
    ¾ teaspoon salt
    ¼ cup sugar
    1 cup dried corn, coarsely ground
    2 eggs, beaten
    1 cup reconstituted dry milk
    ¼ cup oil or melted shortening

Combine whole wheat flour, baking powder, salt, sugar, and dried corn. Beat eggs with milk and oil; add to dry ingredients. Mix lightly. Bake in greased pan or muffin tins 20 minutes, or until done.

Crispy Cornbread

9×13×2-inch pan
400 degrees F.
8 to 10 servings

  1 cup flour
  3½ teaspoons baking powder
  1 teaspoon salt
  3 tablespoons sugar
  1 cup yellow cornmeal
  1 cup milk
  1 egg, beaten
  ¼ cup melted shortening
  2 tablespoons butter or margarine, softened

Sift flour, baking powder, salt, sugar, and corn-meal together into a bowl. Combine milk, egg, and melted shortening. Pour into flour mixture and stir just enough to moisten dry ingredients. Do not mix or beat.

Bake in a well-greased pan for about 20 minutes. Brush with soft butter immediately after removing from oven. Bread will be thin and crusty. Cut into 20 to 24 pieces. Serve hot.

Variation 1: Add ½ to ¾ cup crisp cooked, chopped bacon to sifted flour mixture. This makes a good breakfast bread, or a base for creamed meat or fish, such as chicken, turkey, or tuna.

Variation 2: For a standard cornbread, make as above except bake in an 8×8×2-inch pan at 425 degrees F. for 40 minutes.

Wheat Muffins

12 muffin cups
400 degrees F.
12 muffins

  ¼ cup sugar, honey, or molasses
  2 tablespoons butter, margarine, or shortening
  1 egg, well beaten
  1 cup cooked whole wheat
  ¾ cup milk
  1 cup flour (white, whole wheat, or combination)
  2½ teaspoons baking powder
  ½ teaspoon salt

Combine sugar and butter; add egg and mix well. Whirl cooked whole wheat and milk in blender until smooth. Add to sugar-butter mixture. Combine dry ingredients; stir into wheat mixture. Fill greased muffin tins two-thirds full. Bake 25 to 30 minutes.

Variations: Add ½ cup nuts, or 1 cup dried fruit, chopped, or ½ cup whole cooked wheat.

Bran Muffins

400 degrees F.
12 2½-inch muffins

  1½ cups ready-to-eat bran cereal
  1¼ cups milk
  1 egg
  ¼ to ⅓ cup oil
  1¼ cup flour
  3 teaspoons baking powder
  ½ teaspoon salt
  ¼ to ½ cup sugar

In large mixing bowl, add milk to bran. Let stand 2 minutes. Add egg and oil, and beat to blend. Sift together flour, baking powder, salt, and sugar. Add to bran mixture, and mix gently to just barely dampen flour (batter will be lumpy). Spoon gently into well-greased muffin tins. Bake 25 minutes, or until lightly browned. Remove from tins while warm.

Variations: Add with the flour mixture ½ cup chopped nuts or raisins or softened small pieces of dried apricots or prunes.

Arlean's Molasses Refrigerator Muffins

375 degrees F.
3 dozen muffins

  4 cups flour
  ½ teaspoon ginger
  ½ teaspoon cinnamon
  1¼ cups margarine
  1 cup sugar
  4 eggs
  1 cup molasses
  1 cup buttermilk
  2 teaspoons baking soda
  ½ cup nuts, chopped
  ½ cup raisins

Sift together the flour, ginger, and cinnamon. Cream together margarine and sugar. Add eggs and beat well. Combine molasses, buttermilk, and soda; mix well. Work quickly, as it foams up. Beat into the creamed mixture. Stir flour mixture gently into creamed mixture. Add nuts and raisins; mix lightly.

Refrigerate in a covered container. When ready to bake, dip, without stirring, into well-greased muffin pan or fluted paper cups in muffin pans. Bake about 15 minutes, or until well browned.

Batter keeps about 3 weeks in refrigerator.

Eggnog Gems

Muffin tin or Bundtlette pans
325 degrees F.
24 muffins

½ cup butter or margarine
1½ cups sugar
2 eggs
3 cups flour
3 teaspoons baking powder
2 cups commercial eggnog (or use recipe below)
1 cup chopped candied cherries
Frosting (below)
Candied cherry halves

Cream butter and sugar. Beat in eggs. Combine flour and baking powder and add alternately with eggnog. Fold in candied cherries. Pour into well-greased muffin or Bundtlette pans. Bake for 30 minutes or until browned. Cool. Frost. Top each with a candied cherry half.

Frosting

1½ cups powdered sugar
¼ teaspoon nutmeg
¼ teaspoon cinnamon
Eggnog (below)

Mix powdered sugar, nutmeg, and cinnamon together. Add eggnog to make spreading consistency. Drizzle over each cupcake.

Eggnog

4 cups milk
⅓ cup sugar
1 package instant vanilla pudding
2 egg yolks
1 teaspoon vanilla
2 egg whites

Beat milk, sugar, vanilla pudding, and egg yolks together. Stir in vanilla. Beat egg whites until stiff, and fold into mixture. This may be served as a delicious holiday drink or as a substitute for commercial eggnog in recipes. If desired, add ½ teaspoon nutmeg to achieve the commercial flavor.

Suet Biscuits

8×8×2-inch pan, or pie pan
425 degrees F.
12 large biscuits

1 cup very finely chopped or ground suet
2 cups flour
4 teaspoons baking powder
¼ teaspoon salt
Milk, to make a soft dough, about 1 cup

Blend suet into sifted dry ingredients. Add milk. Mix until you have a sticky dough that drops from a spoon. Drop biscuits onto a greased baking sheet or close together in pan; bake 12 to 15 minutes. They will bake crusty if separated, or into a light, fluffy mass that will separate into soft biscuits if placed close together. Serve piping hot.

Note: These biscuits are delicious cooked in the drippings from a roast, as you would Yorkshire Pudding.

Butter Fingers (Baking Powder)

425 degrees F.
16 rolls

½ cup milk (about)
2 cups biscuit mix
¼ cup (½ stick) butter or margarine, melted

Add milk to biscuit mix in a bowl and mix to form a soft dough. Roll dough on lightly floured board into a ½- to ¾-inch-thick rectangle. Cut lengthwise into 3-inch strips. Then cut each strip crosswise into ¾-inch fingers. Dip each into melted butter and place on ungreased baking sheets. (For crusty rolls, place ½ inch apart; for crust on tops only, place close together.) Bake for 15 minutes or until golden brown.

For 4 dozen rolls, use 1¼ cups milk, 5 cups biscuit mix, and ½ to ¾ cup melted butter; roll half the dough at a time.

Butter Fingers (Yeast)

400 degrees F.
16 fingers

    1 loaf frozen bread dough
    ½ cup butter or margarine
    Parmesan cheese (optional)

Thaw dough until soft enough to be malleable, 2 to 4 hours. Cut loaf lengthwise into 16 strips (half, then each half into 8 strips). With hands, roll each strip between palms to form an even rope, pencil thin. Roll each rope in butter melted in shallow baking pan. Place strips about 1 inch apart; let rise ½ to ¾ hour. Sprinkle with Parmesan cheese, if desired, and bake until nicely brown. Serve hot or cold.

Scotch Scones

425 degrees F.

    1 pound (4 cups) biscuit mix
    ½ cup sugar
    1½ teaspoons grated lemon or orange rind
    1 cup raisins
    2 eggs, beaten
    ⅔ cup milk (about)

Combine biscuit mix, sugar, orange rind, and raisins. Combine eggs and milk and add to dry mixture. Knead lightly. Roll into rectangle. Cut into squares, then cut squares in half from corners. If desired, brush with slightly beaten egg whites. Bake on baking sheet about 10 to 12 minutes.

Popovers

6 5- or 6-ounce custard cups

    1 cup flour
    ¼ teaspoon salt
    2 eggs, lightly beaten
    1 cup milk
    1 teaspoon melted butter

Sift flour with salt. Beat remaining ingredients lightly; then combine with flour. Stir until well blended and smooth. Place custard cups on a baking sheet. Fill cups about half full of batter (a little more than half full if using 5-ounce cups). Place in cold oven. Immediately turn heat to 425 degrees F. Bake until well browned and well "popped," about 35 minutes. Popovers may also be baked in a preheated oven.

Summer Corn Cakes

About 12 small pancakes, or 4 servings

    1 egg
    ⅓ cup milk
    1 cup fresh corn cut from the cob*
    2 tablespoons butter or margarine, melted
    3 tablespoons flour
    ¾ teaspoon baking powder
    2 teaspoons sugar
    ½ teaspoon salt

Beat egg and milk together; mix in uncooked corn kernels. Add butter, then dry ingredients sifted together. Drop by tablespoons on lightly oiled griddle. Fry until bubbles appear on the surface and underside is browned. Turn and brown the other side. Serve with maple syrup or honey or maple butter. These pancakes go well with ham or sausage for a lunch or supper.

*Canned whole kernel corn may be used, but it should be chopped or ground.

Cottage Cheese Pancakes

8 large pancakes, 4 servings

    3 eggs, separated
    1 cup cottage cheese
    ¼ cup flour
    Pinch of salt
    Frozen raspberry jam or maple or honey butter

Beat egg yolks. Add cottage cheese. Stir in flour and salt. Beat egg whites until stiff. Fold whites into yolk mixture. Grease griddle with butter. Fry each cake until browned; turn and brown the other side. Serve with frozen raspberry jam or maple or honey butter.

Blender Pancakes

400 degrees F.
About 10 large pancakes

    1 cup milk
    ¾ to 1 cup whole wheat flour
    2 tablespoons sugar
    ¼ teaspoon salt
    1 teaspoon baking soda
    2 teaspoons baking powder
    2 eggs
    ½ cup oil

Put milk into blender; add flour. Blend for 2 minutes, starting at lowest speed and increasing gradually to highest. Add sugar, salt, soda, and baking powder, then eggs, then oil, blending until smooth after each addition. Cook on hot griddle. Serve with syrup or preserves, as desired.

Delicate Dessert Pancakes

6 dessert portions, 3 pancakes each

2 eggs
1 teaspoon salt
1 tablespoon sugar
1 cup cold water
½ cup light cream
¾ cup sifted flour

Beat eggs with electric beater or blender until very light and frothy. Beat in salt and sugar. Combine water and cream and add alternately with the flour, a small amount at a time, beating well after each addition. Pour batter onto a hot, oiled griddle, making 3½-inch circles. Bake to a golden brown on each side. Place 1 tablespoon Maple Butter (see Index) on rough side of each pancake, and roll up. Serve as dessert with fruit (sliced fresh strawberries are delicious) or for a party breakfast with bacon, with or without fruit.

Farol's Butterflake Rolls

Muffin pans
400 degrees F.
30 rolls

1 package (1 tablespoon) dry yeast
2 tablespoons lukewarm water
2 eggs, slightly beaten
3 tablespoons sugar
½ tablespoon salt
½ cup evaporated milk
½ cup hot water
4 cups flour (about)
½ cup (1 stick) softened butter
2 tablespoons melted butter (about)

Soften yeast in 2 tablespoons lukewarm water. Combine with eggs, sugar, salt, milk, and hot water. Add flour (use electric mixer, if available). Beat, then knead until smooth and elastic. Let rest 10 minutes.

Roll out about ¼ inch thick. Spread with soft butter. Fold in half and roll again; spread with butter. Repeat five times. Roll ½ inch thick. Cut with cookie cutter to fit greased muffin pans. Brush top with melted butter. Let rise 2 to 4 hours (until tripled in bulk). Bake 8 to 10 minutes.

Phyllis's Whole Wheat Bread

5 7×5×2-inch loaf pans
350 degrees F.

6 tablespoons warm water
1 tablespoon sugar
3 packages (3 tablespoons) dry yeast
4 cups very hot water*
6 tablespoons oil
3 tablespoons sugar, honey, or molasses
5 teaspoons salt
12 cups whole wheat flour

Combine warm water and sugar; gently stir in yeast. Set aside. In a large container or bread mixer, combine hot water, oil, sugar, salt, and 6 cups flour. Beat with a wooden spoon. Mix in yeast mixture and remaining flour. Knead in bread mixer 10 minutes, or by hand until smooth and elastic. Cover and let rise in warm place until double in bulk, about 1 hour. Punch down. Let stand 30 minutes.

Divide dough into 5 equal parts; shape and place in greased loaf pans. Cover with waxed paper and let stand for another 30 minutes. Remove to oven and bake about 30 minutes or until browned and crusty. Turn onto cooling racks; brush tops with melted butter, if a soft crust is desired.

This dough makes delicious hot rolls. Use any quantity desired and shape into pan rolls, Parker House, crescent, or as desired.

*For extra nutrition, add 1⅓ cups instant nonfat dry milk to hot water.

Easy Pan Rolls

Buy frozen dinner rolls (white or whole wheat) in the amount needed. About 4 to 5 hours before baking time, remove still frozen rolls from package and arrange on buttered baking pan. Set to rise as directed on the package.

When the dough has thawed enough to be slightly softened, stretch each roll to a slightly elongated or round and flattened shape. Brush well with melted butter or margarine. Let continue to rise for a total time of about 4 to 5 hours, or until about triple in size.

Bake according to package directions. Remove from baking pan to wire racks to cool. When ready to use, reheat in 400 degrees F. oven in heavy paper bags or on baking pans, uncovered, for about 5 minutes. Any extra rolls can be frozen.

Dilly Bread

2-quart casserole dish
400 degrees F.

½ package (½ tablespoon) dry yeast
¾ cup warm water
1 teaspoon sugar
1 tablespoon margarine, butter, or oil
¼ cup nonfat dry milk powder
1 teaspoon salt
1½ teaspoons dill weed*
1¾ to 2 teaspoons minced dry onion
2 to 3 cups flour

Sprinkle yeast on warm water in large warm mixing bowl. When yeast has softened, add remaining ingredients, reserving part of flour. Beat well with wooden spoon. Add remaining flour as needed to make soft dough too sticky to knead. Beat well. Cover and let rise until doubled. Stir down; place in greased casserole dish. Cover and let rise until doubled. Bake 30 minutes, or until bread is lightly browned and sounds hollow when tapped on top.

For a regular loaf of bread, increase flour to make a soft, kneadable dough. Knead well, let rise, punch down, shape into loaf, and bake in bread pan.

From spice shelf, not the dried dill used for making pickles.

Quick Italian Hot Rolls

13×9×2-inch baking pan or 2 8-inch round baking pans
375 degrees F.
16 rolls

3½ to 4 cups flour
2 packages (2 tablespoons) dry yeast
2 tablespoons sugar
2 teaspoons garlic salt
1 teaspoon Italian seasoning
1 cup milk
½ cup water
2 tablespoons butter or margarine
1 egg
½ cup grated Parmesan cheese
2 tablespoons butter or margarine, melted
¼ cup grated Parmesan cheese

In large mixer bowl, combine 1½ cups flour, yeast, sugar, garlic salt, and Italian seasoning; mix well. In saucepan, heat milk, water, and butter until warm (butter does not need to melt). Add to flour mixture. Add egg. Blend at low speed until moistened. Beat 3 minutes at medium speed. By hand, gradually stir in ½ cup Parmesan cheese and enough

flour to make a firm dough. Knead on well-floured surface until smooth and elastic, about 3 to 5 minutes. Place in greased bowl, turning to grease top. Cover; let rise in warm place for 15 minutes.

Punch down dough and divide into 16 pieces. Form into balls. Dip tops into melted butter and ¼ cup cheese. Place in well-greased pans. Cover and let rise in warm oven about 10 minutes. Bake 20 to 25 minutes, or until golden brown. Remove from pan to cool.

Cornmeal Refrigerator Rolls

400 degrees F.
4 to 5 dozen rolls

2 packages (2 tablespoons) dry yeast
½ cup lukewarm water
1 cup milk, scalded
½ cup shortening
½ cup sugar
1 tablespoon salt
½ cup cold water
3 eggs, beaten
5 to 6 cups flour
1 cup cornmeal

Soften yeast in lukewarm water. Set aside. Pour scalded milk over shortening, sugar, and salt; stir occasionally until shortening melts. Add cold water; cool to lukewarm. Stir in eggs and 2 cups of the flour. Add softened yeast and cornmeal. Beat until smooth and well mixed. Stir in enough additional flour to make a soft dough.

Turn out on lightly floured board or canvas; knead until satiny, about 10 minutes. Round dough into ball. Place in greased bowl and brush lightly with melted shortening. Refrigerate overnight.

Remove dough from refrigerator three hours before baking. Shape into rolls. Place on greased cookie sheet. Brush with melted shortening. Cover and let rise. Bake for 15 to 20 minutes, or until nicely browned.

Marj's Hot Rolls

375 degrees F.
5 dozen rolls

½ cup (1 stick) butter or margarine
1 cup milk
2 packages (2 tablespoons) dry yeast
½ cup warm water
3 eggs, beaten

½ cup sugar
1 teaspoon salt
4 cups flour

Melt butter in small saucepan. Pour in milk and remove from heat. Soften yeast in warm water. Add beaten eggs, sugar, salt, and yeast mixture. Beat well to blend. Add flour and beat thoroughly to develop a very soft dough. Allow to stand 1 hour. If dough appears to be too soft to work with, stir in flour to make dough of desired consistency. Roll out and shape into rolls; then place in well-buttered pan to rise. Allow to rise in warm place for at least 1 hour, until dough has doubled in bulk. Bake for 8 to 12 minutes or until golden brown.

Note: To keep Parker House rolls from popping open, stretch out rounds, then fold over so that top laps slightly over bottom.

Golden Yam Rolls

Baking sheet
400 degrees F.
48 rolls

1 package (1 tablespoon) dry yeast
1½ cups warm water
⅓ cup sugar
2 teaspoons salt
⅔ cup melted butter or margarine
2 eggs, slightly beaten
¾ cup mashed yams
5 to 5½ cups flour

Dissolve yeast in warm water. Stir in sugar, salt, butter, eggs, yams, and enough flour to make a soft dough. Turn dough onto a lightly floured board and knead for 5 minutes, or until smooth and elastic. Place in greased bowl; then cover and refrigerate until about 2 hours before serving time. (If using immediately, continue on to next step.)

When ready to shape dough, divide it into 4 parts. Roll each part into a 12-inch circle. Spread each circle with melted butter; cut into 12 pie-shaped pieces. Roll loosely, starting with large end. Place on greased baking sheet and allow to rise until double in bulk. Bake for 15 to 18 minutes, or until lightly browned.

Thirty-minute Hamburger Buns

Cookie sheet(s)
425 degrees F.

	30 buns	10 buns
Warm water	3½ cups	1 cup + 3 tablespoons
Oil	1 cup	⅓ cup
Sugar or	¾ cup	¼ cup
honey	½ cup	2 tablespoons
Yeast*	6 tablespoons	2 tablespoons
Salt	1 tablespoon	1 teaspoon
Eggs, beaten	3	1
Whole wheat flour	10½ cups	3⅓ cups

Combine warm water, oil, sugar, and yeast. Mix, then let rest 15 minutes. Add remaining ingredients and combine thoroughly. Roll dough to about ¾-inch thickness. Cut into rounds about 4 inches in diameter. (A clean, empty can may be used.) Place buns on cookie sheet. Brush tops with melted butter or margarine. Let rise at room temperature, out of a draft, for about 10 minutes. Bake for ten minutes, or until lightly browned and done. Buns freeze well for later use.

One-half the amount of yeast may be used if you double the time for rising.

Viola's Sour Cream Twists

400 degrees F.
About 30

3 cups flour
1 cup butter or margarine
¾ cup sour cream
1 package (1 tablespoon) dry yeast
¼ cup warm water
1 egg plus 2 egg yolks
Sugar, sprinkled on bread board

Mix flour and butter together as for pie crust. Scald sour cream and cool to lukewarm. Mix yeast with warm water to soften. Beat eggs slightly and mix in sour cream; add yeast. Add to flour-and-butter mixture. Blend well.

Refrigerate for at least 2 hours. Roll in sugar into rectangle. Fold both ends to center; repeat 3 times. Roll into an oblong about 4 inches wide. Cut into 1-inch strips and twist twice. Place on ungreased cookie sheets and bake until slightly brown. (Do not let rise.)

Basic Sweet Dough

375 degrees F.
About 2 dozen rolls

>   1 package (1 tablespoon) dry yeast
>   ¼ cup warm water
>   ½ cup milk
>   ¼ cup sugar
>   1 teaspoon salt
>   3 tablespoons softened butter or margarine
>   2½ to 3 cups flour
>   1 egg

Dissolve yeast in warm water. Add milk, sugar, salt, and butter. Stir in about 1 cup of flour to make a batter. Add egg and beat for 1 minute. Stir in 1 more cup flour and beat to form a soft dough. Turn out on floured board and knead until smooth and elastic, adding flour, if necessary. Shape into a ball and place in greased bowl. Turn dough over and cover loosely. Allow to rise until doubled in bulk, about 1 hour. Shape as desired for sweet or cinnamon rolls.

Easy Brioche

Fluted tart pans, or paper baking cups in muffin tins
375 degrees F.
2½ dozen

>   1 package (1 tablespoon) active dry yeast
>   ¾ cup milk, scalded
>   ½ cup cold water
>   ¼ cup sugar
>   1 teaspoon salt
>   4 egg yolks
>   ½ cup (1 stick) soft butter or margarine
>   4½ cups flour (about)
>   1 egg white

Measure yeast into large mixing bowl. Cool scalded milk slightly, add cold water, then add to yeast and sugar. Add salt, egg yolks, and butter, then add half the flour; beat until smooth. Add remaining flour a little at a time until you have a soft dough that can be handled. Turn onto floured board and knead a little. Leave dough in a warm place, free from drafts, until doubled. Shape into a long roll about 2 inches in diameter, and cut off pieces to half fill tart shell. Or cut chunks of dough and work smooth with your hands to half fill the shells. With your finger, make a dent in the center; moisten this hole with a little egg white (to make it stick), and press in a small round ball of dough. Let rise until very light, then brush with beaten egg white. Bake until well browned, about 20 minutes.

Mary Lou's Easy Sticky Ring

Angel food or Bundt pan
Cold to 375 degrees F.
About 16 servings

>   16 to 18 frozen uncooked rolls (Rhodes)
>   ½ cup pecan halves (more, if desired)
>   1 package (3⅝ ounces) butterscotch pie filling (not instant)
>   ¾ cup brown sugar
>   1 teaspoon cinnamon
>   ½ cup (1 stick) butter, melted

Butter pan well. Spread pecan halves in butter so that rounded side is down. (Chopped nuts may be used.) Drop rolls in pan to form a single layer.

Blend together pudding mix, brown sugar, and cinnamon. Sprinkle over rolls, covering each one. Use all the mixture. Pour melted butter over all. Cover pan with plastic wrap and refrigerate overnight. Next morning, remove cover from pan and place in cold oven set at 375 degrees F. Bake about 30 minutes, or until sugar is well dissolved and bubbly. Turn out onto a cake plate, one that will catch the dripping syrup.

Bubble Wreath

10-inch tube pan
400 degrees F.

>   1 recipe sweet roll dough or 24 frozen-roll dough, thawed and each cut in half
>   2 tablespoons butter or margarine
>   2 tablespoons light corn syrup
>   ½ cup brown sugar, packed
>   8 candied cherries, cut in half
>   Blanched slivered almonds or toasted pecan halves
>   ½ cup sugar
>   1 teaspoon cinnamon
>   ½ cup melted butter

Prepare sweet roll dough or frozen rolls, shaping into 48 small balls. In the bottom of pan melt the butter or margarine. Add corn syrup and brown sugar and mix well. Carefully place the candied cherry halves in a circle in the brown sugar mixture. Sprinkle with nuts. Combine sugar and cinnamon; dip each ball into the melted butter, then into the cinnamon-sugar. Place the balls in the pan, arranging lightly in layers. Cover and let rise till double. Bake for 35 to 45 minutes, or until well done and golden brown. Loosen bread from pan and turn out quickly.

Beaten Batter Coffee Cake or Rolls

12 to 15 muffin cups or
2 baking pans 8 inches diameter
375 degrees F.

    1 package (1 tablespoon) dry yeast
    1¼ cups warm water
    ¼ cup sugar
    ⅓ cup nonfat dry milk powder
    1 teaspoon salt
    ⅓ cup oil, melted butter, or margarine
    1 egg, lightly beaten
    2½ to 3 cups flour

Sprinkle yeast on warm water in prewarmed large bowl. Add remaining ingredients, using enough flour to make a thick batter. Cover and let rise until double and bubbly. Stir down gently and drop by spoonfuls into greased muffin tins or baking pans, filling not more than ⅔ full. Let rise in pans until doubled. Bake 20 to 30 minutes, or until golden.

Variations

1. Fruit-nut bread: To batter before first rising, add any or a combination of chopped nuts or dates, raisins, candied fruits.
2. Cinnamon bread: To batter, while adding flour, add ½ to 1 teaspoon cinnamon and ⅛ teaspoon nutmeg.
3. Herb bread: Reduce sugar to 2 tablespoons; add to batter, while adding flour, ½ teaspoon minced dry onion and/or ¼ teaspoon of any or all of oregano, celery seed, thyme, marjoram. This is delightful with vegetable or meat salads.
4. Orange bread: Mix ¼ cup grated orange peel with ¾ cup sugar. Sprinkle in greased pans before adding batter or on top of batter in baking pans.
5. Fruit-topped bread: Arrange halved and pitted fresh fruit, such as plums or apricots, on top of batter in pans. Combine ¼ cup butter, ¼ cup flour, ¼ cup sugar, 1 teaspoon cinnamon. Sprinkle over fruit. Let dough rise; bake.

Garlic Bread

    1 loaf French bread
    ½ cup (¼ pound) butter or margarine, softened
    ½ to ⅔ cup mayonnaise
    Garlic salt, to taste
    Parmesan cheese

Slice bread on the diagonal, to desired thickness. Arrange slices on baking sheet. Combine butter, mayonnaise, and garlic salt; blend well. Spread generously on sliced bread. Sprinkle with cheese. Place under broiler for a minute or two, until golden brown.

Butterscotch Pecan Toasts

4 servings

    2 tablespoons butter or margarine
    ½ cup brown sugar
    4 slices toasted bread
    ½ cup chopped pecans

Combine butter and brown sugar and spread on toasted bread. Sprinkle with pecans, and broil until brown sugar is bubbly all over and pecans are toasted.

Wheat Thins

350 degrees F.

    1¾ cups whole wheat flour
    1½ cups white flour
    6 tablespoons oil, emulsified in blender with ¾ teaspoon salt and 1 cup water
    Salt and/or seasoned salt

Mix flours. Combine oil, water, and salt; add dry ingredients. Make smooth dough, then roll as thin as possible on ungreased cookie sheet (not more than ⅛-inch thick). Mark with knife to size of crackers desired. (Mark well but do not cut through.) Prick each cracker a few times with fork. Sprinkle lightly with salt or seasoned salt as desired. Bake 30 to 35 minutes, until crisp and light brown. Remove from sheet and cut through marking.

Cinnamon Sour Cream Coffee Cake

9-inch Bundt or tube pan or 9×9×2-inch square
  baking pan
375 degrees F.

    ¾ cup butter or margarine
    1 cup plus 2 tablespoons sugar
    2 eggs
    1 cup sour cream*
    1 teaspoon vanilla
    2 cups flour
    ½ teaspoon baking soda
    1 teaspoon baking powder
    ½ teaspoon salt, if desired
    ½ cup finely chopped nuts
    ¼ cup brown sugar
    ½ teaspoon cinnamon
    ¼ teaspoon nutmeg

Cream together butter and sugar; add eggs and
beat well. Add sour cream and vanilla. Sift together
flour, soda, baking powder, and salt. Add about half
of the dry ingredients to creamed mixture; blend
well. Add remaining dry ingredients and blend well.

Mix together nuts, brown sugar, cinnamon, and
nutmeg. Sprinkle part of this mixture in a buttered
baking pan to make a light coating. Spoon half of
batter into pan; sprinkle evenly with remaining nut
mixture; spoon remaining batter on top. Zig-zag a
knife through batter once. Bake about 45 minutes, or
until cake tests done. Remove from oven and cool in
pan for 10 minutes. Invert pan on rack to release
cake. Cake is best served warm, but it reheats very
well. It may be served cold, and it's good the next
day, too.

Note: This recipe has been adjusted for altitudes
near 5,000 feet. At altitudes under 3,000 feet, use
1¼ cups sugar and bake at 350 degrees F. At altitudes near 7,000 feet, use 1 cup of sugar.

**Sour cream is best, but a substitute is 1 tablespoon vinegar plus 1 cup whole
milk for liquid, with an increase in butter to 1 cup.*

Crusty French Bread Pizza

400 degrees F.
12 to 14 servings

    1 long loaf French bread
    1 jar (14 ounces) prepared pizza sauce
    1 pound sausage
    1 onion, chopped
    1 can (8 ounces) sliced mushrooms

    1 can (2½ ounces) chopped ripe olives
    1 pound mozzarella or Monterey Jack cheese,
      shredded
    1 tablespoon dried Italian seasoning

Split bread lengthwise. Spread with pizza sauce.
Brown sausage and crumble over both halves of
bread. Sprinkle onion, mushrooms, and ripe olives
over both halves of bread. Cover with shredded
cheese. Place on cookie sheet and bake for 20
minutes, or until cheese is melted and bubbly. Slice
to serve.

Cheese Straws

350 degrees F.
About 4 dozen

    ¾ cup flour
    1¼ teaspoons baking powder
    ¼ teaspoon salt
    Dash of cayenne pepper
    ¼ cup (½ stick) cold butter or margarine
    ½ to ¾ cup shredded sharp cheese
    2 eggs
    2 teaspoons water
    Paprika, if desired

Sift together the flour, baking powder, salt, and
cayenne pepper. On medium speed of electric mixer,
cream the butter or margarine. Reduce speed to low
and blend in the cheese, then the dry ingredients.
Add eggs and water. Dough should be about the consistency of pie dough. Gather it together into a
smooth ball, wrap in plastic film (or wax paper), and
chill. Roll dough about ¼ inch thick and cut into
strips 4 inches long and about 1 inch wide. Sprinkle
with paprika, if desired, and bake on an ungreased
baking sheet for 10 to 15 minutes, or until lightly
brown.

Note: Sharp cheese is more costly than either mild
or medium cheese. These less expensive cheeses may
be used, if desired, and the flavor can be picked up
with a little dry mustard, cayenne pepper, and salt. In
the above recipe, about ¼ teaspoon dry mustard
would be a good beginning. Add more or less the
second time around, as desired.

Variation: Use 1 cup biscuit mix; add to it the
shredded cheese, cayenne pepper, eggs, water, and
paprika.

Graham Crackers

375 degrees F.

    ½ cup evaporated milk or ¼ cup nonfat dry
        milk powder plus ½ cup water
    2 tablespoons lemon juice or vinegar
    1 cup brown sugar
    ½ cup honey
    1 cup vegetable oil
    2 teaspoons vanilla
    2 eggs, beaten lightly
    1 teaspoon salt
    1 teaspoon baking soda
    6 cups whole wheat flour (about)

Mix together milk and lemon juice or vinegar; let stand. Beat well in a large bowl the brown sugar, honey, oil, vanilla, and eggs. Sift or stir salt and soda into part of flour. Add sifted flour mixture and milk mixture to bowl and mix well. Add additional flour as needed to make a stiff dough.

Divide dough in 4 equal parts and place each on a greased and floured cookie sheet. Roll each to about ⅛-inch thickness. Prick every 1 or 2 inches with fork tines. Bake 15 minutes, or until light brown. Cut in squares immediately.

Honey or Maple Butter

About 2 cups

    ½ cup butter
    ¼ teaspoon vanilla
    1 egg yolk
    ¾ cup honey or ½ cup maple or maple-blended syrup

Whip butter until fluffy. Add vanilla and egg yolk. Add honey gradually while whipping. Store in refrigerator.

Note: When making maple butter, omit the vanilla.

Pies, Cakes, and Cookies

General Directions for Making Pastry

Make a marvelous pie, and you are practically assured of being considered a marvelous cook. Good pie and good bread are the usual trademarks of a good cook. With both pies and bread you can do very well by bringing the products home from the store already prepared and ready for you to add your special touches. You will find recipes to help you do just that throughout this book, but in this section are "do-it-from-scratch" tips for your own elegant, flaky pie crust.

The recipe for good pie crust isn't as important as the technique. Some people make melt-in-the-mouth pastry using a basic pastry recipe; you'll find it here. Or try one of the several variations that women use to assure them of "the best."

Handling the crust and getting it rolled out are troublesome to many of us. Having the right equipment helps solve this problem. A pastry canvas and a stockinette rolling pin cover make the job much easier and are not expensive.

Hydrogenated shortening, such as Crisco, is an ideal fat for pies, though some cooks still swear by lard or a combination of fats. If you feel adventuresome, experiment; or try a variation that claims to make never-fail pastry.

You can crumble very cold fat into the dry ingredients using a mixer at low speed. Just don't overdo it. You're after a crumbled mixture, not a creamed one. We use a mixer to make up quantity recipes. Also, most of the food processors give special directions for making pastry.

For a 2-crust pie: Roll pastry very thin (less than ⅛ inch). Roll from the center toward the edge to keep it round and evenly thin, decreasing pressure toward edges. A bottom crust should be about 2 inches greater in circumference than the pie pan (11 inches for a 9-inch pan). Then ease the pastry into the pan so that it fits well into the curve of the pan. (An air space along this curve will cause your shell to shrink and to flatten out.) Trim off excess with knife.

Moisten with water the top edge of the pastry along the rim of the pan. Fill the shell. Roll out the top crust, again very thin, and slightly larger than pan size. Cut slits near the center of the top crust or make any decorative cut design desired. Fold the pastry in half or drape carefully over your rolling pin, and center the crust over the filling. Press the top crust to the bottom crust firmly on the rim of the pan. Trim the top crust with scissors so that it overhangs about ½ inch. Then fold overhanging top crust under bottom crust, press together well, and flute the edge in any desired pattern. Open slits in the top crust so steam can escape during baking.

Bake at 425 degrees F. for 40 to 60 minutes, depending on the filling, or until thick bubbles appear through the slits and a fork carefully inserted proves the fruit to be tender. Hard fruits such as apples are better if cooked slightly to soften before they go into the pie.

For a pie shell: Proceed the same as for a two-crust pie, allowing the bottom crust to overhang about an inch. Fold the edge under to the rim and flute so it stands above the rim. Prick the crust all over with a fork. If all the air under the crust has been removed and the dough has been eased and pricked well, your crust won't shrink as it bakes. Bake in a hot oven, 425 degrees F., for 12 to 15 minutes, or until lightly browned. If you have trouble with shrinkage, place a square of waxed paper over the unbaked shell and fill with dry rice or beans. Bake for about 10 minutes; then remove shell from oven and carefully remove the paper and its contents. Return shell to oven. It should be set by then and will continue baking without shrinking. (Keep rice or beans to use the next time.) Remove pie crust from oven and fill according to directions in your single-crust pie recipe.

For tart shells: Follow the same as for pie shell, except cut the pastry to fit the pan being used, allowing a slight overhang to compensate for shrinkage. Sometimes it is easier to fit pastry snugly on the back of a tart pan, especially the fluted kind, and bake upside down with pans set on a baking sheet.

Southern Pecan Pie (p. 107)

Basic Pastry

9-inch pie pan
1 double-crust pie or 2 pie shells

    2¼ cups flour (not sifted, but spooned into
       measuring cup)
    1 teaspoon salt
    ¾ cup shortening
    ⅓ cup cold water (about)

Combine flour and salt. Cut in about half the shortening with pastry blender (if fat is very cold, this can be done with mixer, but do it carefully in order to keep the mixture like coarse meal). Add remaining shortening in several pieces and cut until mixture is the size of large peas.

Sprinkle with water, a small amount at a time, mixing lightly with a fork until particles are moistened and cling together when pastry is pressed gently into a ball. Amount of water needed will vary slightly. Too much water results in a hard, "papery" crust. Cover dough with a damp cloth and let stand a few minutes. Handle, roll, and bake according to general directions, above.

Never-Fail Pie Crust

2 double-crust pies or 5 8-inch pie shells

    4 cups flour (not sifted, but spooned into measuring
       cup)
    1 tablespoon sugar
    2 teaspoons salt
    1¾ cups solid vegetable shortening
    1 tablespoon vinegar
    1 egg
    ½ cup water

Mix flour, sugar, and salt. Add shortening, and mix with fork or pastry cutter until ingredients are crumbly. (Electric mixer may be used; see general directions.)

Beat together vinegar, egg, and water. Combine with flour and fat mixture, stirring with fork to moisten ingredients. Shape with hands into 5 flat, round patties ready for rolling. Wrap each patty in foil or plastic wrap and store in freezer until ready to use. When ready to roll pie crust, remove pastry from freezer and thaw in refrigerator. Handle, roll, and bake according to general directions for pastry, above.

Basic Crumb Crust

9-inch or 8-inch pie pan
375 degrees F.

    1¼ cups graham cracker crumbs
    2 tablespoons sugar
    ⅓ cup butter or margarine, softened

Combine crumbs and sugar. Add softened butter, and mix well. Press firmly into bottom and up the sides of pie pan, using the back of a spoon or bottom of a smooth measuring cup. Chill 1 hour before using. For a firmer crust, bake 5 to 8 minutes before chilling.

For an 8-inch pie: Use 1 cup crumbs, 2 tablespoons sugar, and ¼ cup softened butter.

For Gingersnap Crust: Use recipe for 9-inch pie, increasing sugar to 3 tablespoons and reducing butter to ¼ cup. For an 8-inch Gingersnap Crust, use 1 cup crumbs, 2½ tablespoons sugar, and 3 tablespoons softened butter.

For Vanilla or Chocolate Wafer Crust: Use recipe for 9-inch pie, reducing sugar to 1 tablespoon and butter to ¼ cup. For an 8-inch wafer crust, use 1 cup crumbs, 1 tablespoon sugar, and 3 tablespoons softened butter.

Basic Cream Pie Filling

Filling for 1 9-inch pie

    ⅔ cup sugar
    ⅓ cup flour
    ½ teaspoon salt
    2 cups milk
    2 eggs, slightly beaten
    2 tablespoons butter or margarine
    1 teaspoon vanilla
    1 9-inch baked pie shell
    1 cup whipping cream

Mix sugar, flour, and salt in 2-quart saucepan. Add milk gradually, stirring to blend thoroughly. Bring to a full boil over medium heat, stirring constantly. Reduce heat to low; cover pan and let stand 5 minutes. Add some of the hot mixture to eggs, gradually, then add to cooked filling. Bring again to a boil, stirring constantly, and cook 1 minute longer. Remove from heat, and stir in butter and vanilla. Cool about 5 minutes, then pour into cooled pie shell. Just before serving, top with sweetened whipped cream.

Chocolate Cream Pie

Make Basic Cream Pie Filling, adding ½ to ⅔ cup chocolate chips with butter and vanilla; stir until chips are melted. Chill.

Black and White Pie

Make Basic Cream Pie Filling. Pour half the vanilla filling into the shell. Add ¼ to ⅓ cup chocolate chips to remaining filling, and stir until chips are melted. Pour on top of vanilla filling. Chill.

Banana Cream Pie

Make Basic Cream Pie Filling. Before pouring filling into pie shell, slice 2 bananas into shell. Top filling with whipped cream.

Coconut Cream Pie

Make Basic Cream Pie Filling, adding ½ cup flaked coconut, toasted or not, to filling before pouring it into shell.

Afton's Fresh Peach Pie

9-inch pie pan

    1 baked pie shell
    3 large peaches
    2 soft peaches
    1 cup sugar
    2 tablespoons cornstarch
    ½ cup water
    1 teaspoon almond extract
    2 tablespoons butter

Slice the three large peaches into baked pie shell. If the peaches are very juicy, lightly brush the pie shell with soft butter before adding peaches. In a small saucepan, mash the soft peaches; add sugar, cornstarch, and water. Cook over medium heat to boiling point, stirring constantly. Boil 1 minute, or until thick and clear. Remove from heat and add almond extract and butter. Pour over peaches in pie shell and chill for several hours until set. Serve with whipped cream, if desired.

Southern Pecan Pie

9-inch pie pan
350 degrees F.

    1 9-inch unbaked pie shell
    1 cup pecans
    4 eggs, slightly beaten
    ¼ cup melted butter (no substitute)
    ¾ cup light corn syrup (dark may be used)
    ⅞ cup granulated sugar or 1 cup brown sugar
    1 teaspoon vanilla

Spread pecans over the bottom of the unbaked pie crust. Beat eggs slightly. Add melted butter, corn syrup, and sugar; blend well. Stir in vanilla. Pour egg mixture over pecans in pie shell. Bake for 45 to 60 minutes until center of pie is set. Cool before serving. Serve garnished with slightly sweetened whipped cream.

Apple Pie

9-inch pie pan
425 degrees F.

    4 to 5 cups tart apples, peeled, cored, and sliced
    ¼ to ½ cup water
    ¾ to 1 cup sugar
    1 to 2 tablespoons flour
    ½ to 1 teaspoon cinnamon
    ⅛ teaspoon salt
    1 tablespoon lemon juice
    2 tablespoons butter or margarine
    Pastry for 2-crust 9-inch pie

Steam or simmer apples gently in water until they wilt and begin to become transparent. (This is a partial cooking only, so that apples will cook thoroughly in the pie.)

Combine the sugar, flour, cinnamon, and salt. Mix well. Spread half over the pastry-lined pie pan. Lift apples from cooking liquid into crust. Add ¼ cup of the cooling liquid. Sprinkle with remaining sugar mixture, then with lemon juice; dot with butter. Roll, fit, and seal top crust. Brush with milk and sprinkle with sugar, if desired. Bake on lower shelf of oven for 30 to 40 minutes, or until nicely browned.

Note: Apple pie is only as good as the apples it is made with. Tart, juicy apples are desirable, and some judgment is necessary as to amounts of sugar and thickening when sweeter, less juicy apples are used.

Quick Cookie Apple Pie

9-inch pie pan
350 degrees F.

    6 tart, juicy apples, peeled, cored, and sliced
    Sugar
    Nutmeg
    Butter
    ½ cup butter or margarine
    ½ cup brown sugar
    1 cup flour

Layer apples in buttered pie pan. Sprinkle with sugar and nutmeg; dot with butter. Repeat layers. Cream ½ cup butter with brown sugar until well blended and fluffy. Add flour; mix well. Take a small amount of the mixture in your hands and lightly pat into a thin circle, about 3 inches in diameter. Lay on top of apples. Repeat making circles, and lay them on apples with edges overlapping. Cover top of pie this way. Bake 35 to 60 minutes, or until apples are soft and cookies on top are crisp and lightly brown. Pie is best served warm. If made ahead, reheat. Pie freezes well.

Maple-Apple Flan

9-inch pie or flan pan
425 degrees F.

    Pastry for 1 9-inch pie
    4 tart apples
    1 cup maple or maple-blended syrup
    ⅛ teaspoon salt
    2 tablespoons raisins
    1 tablespoon butter or margarine

Roll pastry 1 inch larger than pan. Line pan with pastry. Fold overhang and crimp along edge of pan.
Peel, core and quarter apples; cut into thick wedges. Heat syrup and salt to the boiling point. Add half the apple slices, and simmer until apples are slightly glazed, 5 to 7 minutes. Repeat with remaining apples. Remove apples from syrup; arrange in rows on pastry so that slices overlap slightly. Sprinkle on raisins. Let butter melt in syrup, then pour over apples. Bake 25 to 30 minutes, or until pastry is cooked and apples are slightly browned.

Rhubarb Surprise Pie

9-inch pie pan
350 degrees F.

    1 cup flour
    1 teaspoon baking powder
    ½ teaspoon salt
    3 tablespoons butter or margarine
    1 egg, beaten
    2 tablespoons milk
    3 cups diced raw rhubarb
    1 package (3 ounces) strawberry-flavor gelatin
    ½ cup flour
    1 cup sugar
    ½ teaspoon cinnamon
    ¼ cup butter or margarine, melted

Sift together 1 cup flour, baking powder, and salt. Cut in butter. Add egg and milk; mix. Press into a greased pie pan. Arrange rhubarb in pie shell. Sprinkle with gelatin. Combine remaining ingredients; sprinkle on top of pie. Bake 50 minutes or until rhubarb is tender.

Butterscotch Pie

9-inch pie pan

    ¾ cup sugar
    2 tablespoons cornstarch
    3 tablespoons flour
    2 cups milk
    3 tablespoons butter or margarine
    ¾ cup brown sugar
    2 egg yolks
    ½ teaspoon vanilla
    ¼ teaspoon salt
    1 9-inch baked pie shell

In a saucepan, combine sugar, cornstarch, flour, and milk. Cook, stirring, until thick and smooth. Set aside.
In a small frying pan, cook butter and brown sugar until bubbly and caramelized, taking care not to burn. Pour into sugar-milk mixture and stir well. Beat egg yolks and add a small amount of hot mixture; return mixture to pan. Cook until mixture holds boil 1 minute and is thick and smooth. Add vanilla and salt and pour into pie shell. Cool well before cutting (3 to 4 hours).
Variation: Add toasted pecans or walnuts.

Lemon Meringue Pie

The secret of successful lemon pie is to be sure the filling is thick enough and the raw starch taste cooked out *before* you add the egg yolk or lemon juice. Overcooking the egg yolk will cause lumpy filling, and the lemon juice will break down the starch, resulting in a thin, syrupy filling.

9-inch pie pan

1½ cups sugar
5 tablespoons cornstarch
Pinch of salt
1½ cups boiling water
3 egg yolks, slightly beaten
6 tablespoons lemon juice
Grated rind from one lemon
1 tablespoon butter or margarine
1 9-inch baked pie shell, cooled
3 egg whites
¼ teaspoon cream of tartar
6 tablespoons sugar

Blend sugar, cornstarch, and salt in 2-quart saucepan. Add boiling water; stir and cook on medium-high heat until mixture boils and is thick. Put lid on pan; turn heat to very low and let mixture cook 10 minutes, stirring once.

Stir about ½ cup of the hot mixture into the egg yolks, then return mixture to pan and continue cooking for a minute or two, stirring constantly. Remove from heat, and stir in lemon juice, rind, and butter, and stir until butter is melted. Pour into pie shell.

Make meringue: Beat 3 egg whites with cream of tartar until foamy and about double in volume (use small bowl of electric mixer). Add sugar gradually, about 1 tablespoon at a time, beating all the while with mixer set at highest speed until sugar completely dissolves and meringue stands in firm peaks. Spread meringue on pie filling, being sure to seal it to the shell. Swirl meringue into a pretty design with peaks and valleys.

Return to oven and bake either at 375 degrees F. for 15 to 20 minutes or at 425 degrees F. for 3 to 5 minutes. Let peaks of meringue brown to a delicate golden color. Remove pie from oven and cool on a rack for at least 4 hours before serving. (*Note:* We prefer the lower-temperature, longer-time method; there is less chance of soft, uncooked egg white, although greater shrinkage usually results with this method.)

Fresh Lime Meringue Pie

Make as for Lemon Meringue Pie, substituting lime juice for lemon juice and using 1 teaspoon fresh grated lime peel. Add two drops of green food coloring if deeper color is desired.

Lemon Meringue Party Pie

9-inch pie pan

1 9-inch baked pie shell, cooled
1 package (3 ounces) lemon pudding and pie filling (the kind you have to cook)
¾ cup sugar
½ cup cold water
3 egg yolks, slightly beaten
2 cups water
1 tablespoon butter
Grated rind from 1 lemon
2 tablespoons lemon juice
3 egg whites
¼ teaspoon cream of tartar
6 tablespoons sugar

Prepare pie shell. Mix contents of pudding and pie filling package with sugar. Add ½ cup water and blend well. Add egg yolks, then 2 cups water. Cook and stir over medium high heat until mixture comes to a *full* boil (bubbles break across the entire surface). Remove from heat; add butter, lemon rind, and juice. Stir until well blended. Pour into pie shell.

Make and bake meringue as for Lemon Meringue Pie (above).

Note: If you have trouble making Lemon Meringue Pie from scratch, this recipe is practically fool-proof and will stand with the best.

Lemon Chess Pie

9-inch pie pan
400 degrees F., then 325 degrees F.

2 tablespoons butter or margarine
2 cups sugar
1 tablespoon flour
1 tablespoon cornmeal
3 eggs
¼ cup milk
1 tablespoon grated lemon peel
4 tablespoons lemon juice
1 unbaked pie shell

Melt butter; add sugar, flour, and cornmeal, and blend well. Beat eggs until well blended; add milk, lemon peel, and lemon juice. Pour into sugar mixture and mix well. Pour into pie shell, and bake at 400 degrees F. for 10 minutes. Reduce heat and bake at 325 degrees F. for 30 to 45 minutes, or until pie is set in center.

Basic Fresh Fruit Pie

9-inch pie pan
425 degrees F.

    1 quart fresh fruit (see below)
    1 to 3 tablespoons lemon juice
    ¾ to 1 cup sugar, depending on tartness of fruit
    2 to 3 tablespoons Minute Tapioca
    1 to 2 tablespoons butter
    Pastry for 2-crust 9-inch pie

Prepare fruit. Add lemon juice, the larger quantity for fruits that are more bland. Combine sugar and tapioca, the larger quantity depending on juiciness and tartness of fruit. Add sugar-tapioca mixture and lemon juice to fruit in large bowl; mix gently. Immediately fill unbaked pie shell, letting fruit hump a little in center. Dot with butter. Place top crust over filling, sealing edges well. Bake 40 to 60 minutes or until done. See general directions for pastry.

Fruits to Use

    Apricots, washed, pitted, sliced and seasoned, if
      desired
    Peaches, skinned, pitted, and sliced
    Tart plums, washed, pitted, and sliced
    Pears, skinned, cored, and sliced
    Rhubarb, washed, trimmed, and cut in about ½-inch
      pieces or chopped
    Cherries, washed, stoned (tart pie cherries are best)
    Berries (raspberries, boysenberries, blueberries,
      sliced strawberries, gooseberries, etc.), washed

Note: About ¼ teaspoon salt and ½ teaspoon each cinnamon and nutmeg are especially good with apricots; you may also wish to use with peaches and pears. A dash of ground cloves is nice with plums. For fresh apple pie, see recipe below.

Chocolate Mint Ice Cream Pie

9-inch pie pan
8 to 10 servings

    2 squares (2 ounces) baking chocolate
    2 tablespoons butter or margarine
    ½ cup sugar
    1 tablespoon cornstarch
    Dash of salt
    1 cup milk
    ½ teaspoon vanilla
    3 pints peppermint stick ice cream
    1 baked pie shell
    Chopped nuts, optional

Melt chocolate and butter in small saucepan over low heat. Stir so that chocolate won't burn. Mix sugar and cornstarch well; stir into chocolate with salt and milk. Cook over medium heat, stirring constantly, until thickened; cook an additional 2 minutes. Add vanilla. Remove from heat and cool.

Pour ½ cup of chocolate mixture into pie shell, coating sides and bottom. Freeze. Scoop 1½ pints ice cream into shell (don't smooth the ice cream; leave it piled in scoops, although you will have to cover bottom of shell well and press scooped ice cream down to get it all in). Drizzle ½ cup of the remaining chocolate syrup over ice cream. Freeze. Scoop remaining 1½ pints ice cream into shell; pour remaining sauce over top. Freeze. Sprinkle chopped nuts over top of pie, if desired.

Fresh Fruit Tart

10-inch pie pan
8 servings

    2 tablespoons butter or margarine
    2 cups miniature marshmallows (or 20 regular
      marshmallows)
    2½ cups toasted rice cereal (Rice Krispies)
    1 package (3½ ounces) vanilla instant pudding mix
    1¼ cups milk
    1 cup whipping cream
    1 teaspoon almond extract
    1½ pounds sweet cherries

In 2-quart saucepan over low heat, melt butter or margarine. Add marshmallows; heat until marshmallows are melted, stirring frequently. Remove from heat; stir in cereal until well mixed. With buttered hands, pat mixture into greased 10-inch tart pan or 9-inch pie pan.

In a large bowl with mixer at high speed, beat

pudding mix and milk, cream, and almond extract for 5 minutes or until stiff peaks form. Spoon mixture into cereal crust. Refrigerate.

Remove pits from washed cherries. Gently press cherries into cream filling.

Note: Sliced strawberries or peaches, raspberries, or other fresh fruit may be used. Sweeten, if desired.

Puff Pie Shell

9-inch pie pan
425 degrees F.

    ¼ cup butter
    ½ cup boiling water
    ½ cup flour
    2 eggs

Combine butter and boiling water in saucepan. Bring to a boil. Reduce heat and add flour all at once, stirring rapidly. Cook and stir until mixture pulls away from sides of pan in smooth, compact mass, about 2 minutes. Remove from heat. Add eggs, one at a time, beating thoroughly after each. Then beat steadily until mixture is satiny and breaks off when spoon is raised.

Spread most of dough evenly over bottom and sides of pie pan and drop remaining dough by spoonfuls around rim. Bake 35 minutes. Remove from oven, and prick bottom and sides with a fork. Bake another 5 minutes, or until dry and crisp. Cool before filling.

Glazed Cream Puff Pie

1 9-inch pie

    1 package (3¾ ounces) vanilla pudding and pie
      filling (not instant)
    2 cups milk
    1 baked Puff Pie Shell, cooled
    1 package (3 ounces) raspberry-flavor gelatin
    1 cup boiling water
    8 to 12 ice cubes
    1 banana
    Sweetened whipped cream

Combine pie filling mix and milk in saucepan. Cook and stir over medium heat until mixture comes to a full boil. Cool about 5 minutes, stirring once or twice. Pour into Puff Pie Shell. Chill.

Dissolve gelatin completely in boiling water. Add

ice cubes and stir constantly for 2 to 3 minutes, or until gelatin starts to thicken. Remove unmelted ice.

Slice banana over pie filling. Cover with gelatin. Chill until set, about 30 minutes. Garnish with sweetened whipped cream.

Fruit in Easy Puff Shell

Deep 9- or 10-inch pie pan or iron frying pan
450 degrees F.

    2 tablespoons butter or margarine
    2 or 3 eggs
    ½ cup milk
    ½ cup flour
    ¼ teaspoon salt
    Fresh fruit
    Sugar
    Whipped cream

Melt butter in pie pan; remove from heat and tilt pan to coat surface. Set aside. Beat eggs; add milk, flour, and salt. Beat until smooth. Pour melted butter from pan into mixture and blend. Pour mixture into buttered pan. Bake on lower rack 20 minutes or until golden color on tips of puffs; reduce heat to 325 degrees F. (if center is too puffed, prick with a fork). Bake 10 to 15 minutes longer.

Serve warm, filled with fresh fruit, sugar, and whipped cream. Raspberries, strawberries, or sliced peaches (drizzled with lemon juice) make a beautiful dessert, Sunday night snack, or special breakfast.

Meringue Shells

375 degrees F.
6 to 8 shells or 9- to 10-inch pie pan

    4 egg whites
    ¼ teaspoon salt
    ¼ teaspoon cream of tartar
    1 cup sugar
    ½ teaspoon vanilla

In small bowl of electric mixer beat egg whites at highest speed until foamy. Add salt and cream of tartar, then sugar gradually, beating continuously until thick and glossy, 8 to 10 minutes in all.

Line cookie sheet with brown paper or foil. For individual shells, divide meringue mixture evenly into piles, set well apart. With the back of a spoon, form a shell from each pile of meringue, smoothing the center and piling up the sides. For a large pie, shape all meringue into one shell or pile into buttered pie pan. Place in preheated oven. Immediately turn off heat. Leave shells in oven overnight, or until they completely dry out (3 hours or more). Remove shells from oven and lift them carefully from the paper. Cool. Fill as desired with fresh fruit, ice cream, French Chocolate Creme, etc.

Note: Meringues may also be baked in an oven set at 275 degrees F. for one hour, or until completely dry. If served immediately, shells are crisp. They become soft when filled and refrigerated.

French Chocolate Creme

    1 package (12 ounces) chocolate chips
    ¼ cup water
    ½ teaspoon rum extract (optional) or vanilla
    1 cup whipping cream, whipped

Melt chocolate chips over hot water, or in a heavy pan on low heat, stirring often. Add water and the extract; beat until smooth. Cool slightly. Fold the whipped cream into the chocolate mixture. Pour into cooled meringue shells. Chill.

Meringue Cookies

Make meringue as for shells. Add 1¼ cups coarsely chopped nuts and 1 cup chocolate chips. Drop by teaspoonfuls on greased cookie sheet and bake until set, about 10 minutes.

Lemon Angel Pie

    4 egg yolks
    ¼ to ½ cup sugar
    ¼ cup lemon juice
    2 teaspoons lemon rind
    ¼ cup water
    1½ cups whipping cream
    2 tablespoons powdered sugar
    ¼ teaspoon lemon extract
    Meringue Shells (above)

Beat egg yolks until thick over very low heat or in double boiler. Beat in sugar, lemon juice, lemon rind, and water. Stir until mixture thickens, then cool.

Whip cream. Add powdered sugar and lemon extract. Put half of whipped cream in meringue shells, then all of filling, then rest of whipped cream.

Note: Make this pie the day before you need it. It will keep in good condition for 2 to 3 days.

Berry Angel Pie

Instead of lemon filling in Lemon Angel Pie (above), spread a layer of halved strawberries or whole raspberries over the first layer of cream. Sprinkle lightly with sugar and cover with second layer of cream.

Baklava

9×13×2-inch baking pan
350 degrees F.

    1 pound butter (no substitutes)
    1 pound ground walnuts
    1 pound ground almonds
    1 tablespoon cinnamon
    ½ teaspoon ground cloves
    1 package (16 ounces) filo pastry sheets

Melt butter in small saucepan. Cool. Pour off clear butter oil for use on filo. Discard milk solids.

Mix walnuts and almonds together. Mix cinnamon and cloves together.

Prepare filo according to package directions. Line baking pan with filo and brush with butter oil. It is important that the filo be completely covered with butter to prevent its drying out.

Sprinkle filo with nut mixture, then with spice mixture. Repeat, alternating layers of filo, nuts, and spices, using two sheets of filo per layer and brushing each layer of filo thoroughly with butter. Top with 3 to 5 sheets of filo. Cut into squares or diamonds with a very sharp knife. Bake for 1 hour. Prepare Syrup (below) and cool. Pour half of the cool syrup over hot baklava. Cool for 1 hour and cover with remaining syrup.

Syrup

    6 cups sugar
    3 cups water
    1 slice fresh lemon
    1 stick cinnamon

Combine ingredients and boil together until sugar is dissolved. Cool.

Applesauce Cake

9×13×2-inch cake pan
350 degrees F.

½ cup (1 stick) margarine
1 cup sugar
1½ cups thick applesauce
1 egg
1 teaspoon vanilla
2 cups flour
1 teaspoon soda
1 teaspoon cinnamon
⅓ teaspoon allspice
¼ teaspoon salt
2 tablespoons cocoa
1 cup raisins
¾ cup chopped nuts

Combine margarine, sugar, applesauce, egg, and vanilla and beat until creamy. Sift flour, soda, cinnamon, allspice, salt, and cocoa, and add to creamed mixture. Fold in raisins and nuts. Pour into greased pan and bake about 45 minutes, or until cake tests done.

Frost with your favorite butter cream or cream cheese frosting (see Index).

Cherry Nut Cake

10-inch tube pan or 2 8×4×3-inch loaf pans
325 degrees F.

1 cup (½ pound) butter
1½ cups sugar
6 eggs
4 cups flour
1 teaspoon baking powder
2 teaspoons nutmeg
½ teaspoon salt
¼ cup maraschino cherry juice
5 cups maraschino cherries, well drained
4 cups coarsely chopped pecans

Cream butter and sugar until fluffy. Add eggs, one at a time, beating well after each. Sift 2 cups flour, baking powder, nutmeg, and salt together and add to creamed mixture, beating until smooth. Stir in cherry juice. Combine cherries and nuts and toss with the remaining 2 cups of flour. Stir into batter.

Bake in well-greased and floured tube pan or in two loaf pans for 1 hour, or until cake tests done. Remove from pan and cool for 1 hour. Wrap tightly and allow to "ripen" for a few days to develop flavor and texture.

Pineapple Carrot Cake

9×13×2-inch baking pan
350 degrees F.
18 to 24 servings

2 cups flour
2 teaspoons baking soda
2 teaspoons cinnamon
½ teaspoon salt
3 eggs
¾ cup salad oil
¾ cup buttermilk
2 cups sugar
2 teaspoons vanilla
1 can (8 ounces) crushed pineapple, drained
2 cups shredded carrots
1 cup flaked coconut
1 cup chopped nuts

Sift flour, soda, cinnamon, and salt together and set aside. In a large bowl, beat eggs; add oil, buttermilk, sugar, and vanilla; mix well. Add dry ingredients and mix well. Add pineapple, carrots, coconut, and nuts; mix well.

Pour into generously greased baking pan; bake for 1 hour, or until toothpick comes out clean when cake is tested. Prepare Glaze (below).

Glaze

1 cup sugar
½ teaspoon baking soda
½ cup buttermilk
¼ pound butter or margarine
1 tablespoon corn syrup
1 teaspoon vanilla

Combine all ingredients and boil for 1 minute. Remove cake from oven and, while hot, pour glaze over cake. Cool completely. Frost with Orange Cream Cheese Frosting (below).

Orange Cream Cheese Frosting

¼ pound butter or margarine
1 package (8 ounces) cream cheese
1 teaspoon vanilla
2 cups powdered sugar
1 teaspoon orange juice
1 teaspoon orange peel

Combine butter and cream cheese. Add vanilla, powdered sugar, orange juice, and orange peel, and beat until thick and smooth.

Picnic Cake

9×13×2-inch baking pan
350 degrees F.
18 to 24 servings

    1 cup cut-up dates
    1½ cups boiling water
    1 teaspoon soda
    1 cup sugar
    ¾ cup shortening
    2 eggs, beaten
    1 teaspoon vanilla
    1¾ cups flour
    1 teaspoon cinnamon
    ½ teaspoon salt
    ½ cup brown sugar
    ½ cup chopped nuts
    1 package (6 ounces) chocolate chips

Combine dates, boiling water, and soda, and set aside to cool. Combine sugar and shortening and blend well; add eggs and vanilla. Combine flour, cinnamon, and salt, and add to sugar mixture. Mix well, then pour into well-greased pan. Combine brown sugar, nuts, and chocolate chips, and sprinkle over top of cake. Bake for 30 to 40 minutes, or until cake tests done.

Pioneer Cake

2 9×3×4½-inch bread pans or 1 tube pan
375 degrees F.
2 loaves

    1 package dry yeast
    2 tablespoons warm water
    1⅓ cups milk, warm
    ⅔ cup sugar
    ⅓ cup butter or margarine, melted
    1 egg
    ½ cup raisins
    ½ teaspoon salt
    ¼ teaspoon cardamom, nutmeg, or mace
    3 to 4 cups flour
    ¼ cup whipping cream or 2 tablespoons butter,
       melted
    2 to 3 tablespoons sugar

Sprinkle yeast on warm water in a pre-warmed large bowl. Let stand several minutes. Add warm milk, ⅔ cup sugar, ⅓ cup butter, egg, raisins, salt, spices, and flour; adjust amount of flour to make a thick batter but not a dough. Cover and let rise until doubled in bulk. Stir down gently; place in greased bread pans. Gently brush tops with whip-ping cream or melted butter. Sprinkle sugar on top. Let rise in pans until doubled. Bake 40 minutes. Turn out on cake rack to cool.

Variation: Omit raisins and cardamom. Add ½ cup chopped walnuts or pecans, ⅛ teaspoon nutmeg, and the grated rind from ½ lemon.

Carrot Cake

10-inch Bundt pan, or 9×13×2-inch baking pan
400 degrees F.
20 servings

    3 cups finely shredded carrots
    1 cup nuts, chopped
    1¾ cups sugar
    1 cup salad oil
    4 eggs
    2 cups flour
    1 teaspoon salt
    2 teaspoons soda
    2 teaspoons cinnamon

Prepare carrots and nuts. Mix sugar, oil, and eggs in large bowl of electric mixer. Sift dry ingredients and beat with egg mixture. Add carrots and nuts. Blend gently. Pour batter into well-greased pan (greased and floured, if a Bundt pan is used). Bake until cake tests done (50 to 60 minutes for 10-inch Bundt pan).

Cream Cheese Frosting

    ½ package (4 ounces) cream cheese
    3 tablespoons butter or margarine
    1 cup powdered sugar
    ½ teaspoon vanilla
    ½ cup nuts, chopped

Blend cream cheese and butter until smooth. Beat in remaining ingredients.

Chocolate Rocky Road Cake

8×8×2-inch baking pan
350 degrees F.
9 servings

> ¼ cup butter or margarine
> ¼ cup salad oil
> 1 square baking chocolate
> ½ cup water
> 1 cup flour
> 1 cup minus 2 tablespoons sugar*
> ½ teaspoon salt
> 1 egg, beaten
> ¼ cup buttermilk blended with ½ teaspoon soda
> ¾ teaspoon vanilla

In a small saucepan over low heat, combine butter, oil, and chocolate. Stir until solids are melted. Add water, and stir until smooth and thick. Remove from heat and cool for 10 minutes. Sift flour, sugar, and salt together into a large mixing bowl. Add chocolate mixture. Add egg and beat until smooth; stir in buttermilk-soda mixture and vanilla.

Pour batter into well-greased baking pan and bake 30 to 35 minutes, or until cake tests done. Remove from oven and cool in pan set on a cake rack. Frost with Rocky Road Frosting (below).

For altitudes to 3500 feet, use 1 cup sugar. For altitudes over 5000 feet, see index for Altitude Adjustments.

Rocky Road Frosting

> 1 square baking chocolate
> ¼ cup butter or margarine
> 3 tablespoons buttermilk
> ½ teaspoon vanilla
> 1¾ cups (about) powdered sugar
> ⅓ cup miniature marshmallows or snipped large marshmallows
> ¼ cup nuts, coarsely chopped

Melt chocolate and butter over low heat, stirring frequently. Add buttermilk and vanilla. Pour mixture over powdered sugar in mixing bowl. Beat until smooth and of good spreading consistency (a little thin before marshmallows and nuts are added). Stir in marshmallows and nuts. Spread frosting on cake quickly, making peaks and valleys as you go. Try not to go over what you have already swirled, or you lose the gloss.

Note: Cocoa (not a mix) may be used in place of chocolate. Use 2 tablespoons in the cake, sifted with the dry ingredients, and 2 tablespoons in the frosting, mixed with the powdered sugar.

Fruit Cocktail Pudding Cake

8×8-inch baking pan
350 degrees F.
12 servings

> 1½ cups flour
> 1 cup sugar
> ¾ teaspoon salt
> 1 teaspoon baking soda
> 1 teaspoon vanilla
> 1 teaspoon almond extract (optional)
> 1 egg, slightly beaten
> 1 can (16 ounces) fruit cocktail, undrained
> ⅓ cup brown sugar
> ⅓ cup chopped nuts
> Whipped cream, ice cream, or a pudding sauce

Sift flour, sugar, salt, and baking soda together. Combine vanilla, almond extract, egg, and fruit cocktail. Add to flour mixture and blend well. Pour into greased pan. Sprinkle top of batter with brown sugar, then with nuts. Bake about 40 minutes, or until well browned and set. Serve warm with whipped cream, ice cream, or pudding sauce, if desired.

Hummingbird Cake

10-inch tube cake pan or Bundt pan
350 degrees F.
18 to 24 servings

> 3 cups flour
> 2 cups sugar
> 1 teaspoon baking soda
> 1 teaspoon cinnamon
> 1 teaspoon salt
> 1½ cups salad oil
> 1½ teaspoons vanilla
> 3 eggs, slightly beaten
> 1 can (8 ounces) crushed pineapple, undrained
> 2 cups diced bananas (about 3 bananas)
> 1 cup chopped nuts

Combine flour, sugar, baking soda, cinnamon, and salt in a large mixing bowl. Add oil, vanilla, eggs, undrained pineapple, bananas, and nuts, and stir well. Batter will be thick. Pour into well-greased and floured tube pan and bake for 1 hour and 10 minutes, or until cake tests done and is browned. Cool completely in pan. This cake is very moist and will store well if kept in a cool place.

Black Forest Cake

2 9-inch round cake pans
375 degrees F.
12 servings

    1 chocolate-flavored cake mix (2-layer size)
    3 cups whipped topping
    1 can (21 ounces) cherry pie filling

Make chocolate cake according to package directions, adjusting for altitude, if necessary. Bake and cool on rack. Slice each layer horizontally through center to make 4 thin layers. Spread about ½ cup whipped topping over bottom layer; top with small amount of pie filling. Place on next layer and repeat topping and filling. Finish last layer with whipped topping piled up around edge and with filling deeper in center. Chill.

Poppy Seed Cake

Bundt pan
350 degrees F.

    1 package lemon cake mix (extra moist), 2-layer size
    1 package (3¾ ounces) lemon instant pudding
    4 eggs
    ½ cup salad oil
    2 to 4 tablespoons poppy seeds
    1½ cups water

Combine all ingredients, making high altitude adjustments as package directs, if necessary. Beat according to package directions. Pour into well-greased and floured Bundt pan. Bake about 50 minutes, or until cake tests done. Remove from oven and let stand 10 to 15 minutes; then turn out of pan onto wire rack to cool completely. Sprinkle with powdered sugar.

Variation of Poppy Seed Cake

    1 package yellow cake mix (2-layer size)
    1 package (3¾ ounces) French vanilla
      instant pudding
    4 eggs
    ½ cup salad oil, or use melted margarine
    2 to 4 tablespoons poppy seeds
    ½ cup water
    1 cup sour cream
    ½ teaspoon rum extract
    Powdered sugar (optional)

Mix and bake as above. When cake is cool, dust lightly with powdered sugar, if desired.

Old-Time Poundcake

10-inch tube or Bundt pan
350 degrees F.

    1 cup butter
    2 cups sugar
    4 eggs
    1 teaspoon vanilla
    ½ teaspoon lemon extract or 1 teaspoon grated
      lemon peel
    3 cups flour
    ½ teaspoon baking soda
    ½ teaspoon baking powder
    ½ teaspoon salt
    1 cup buttermilk

Cream butter and sugar until fluffy. Add eggs, one at a time, beating at least 1 minute after each. Beat 3 more minutes. Blend in vanilla and lemon juice. Combine flour, baking soda, baking powder, and salt. Add dry ingredients alternately with buttermilk, beginning and ending with dry ingredients, beating 1 minute after each addition.

Pour into a well-greased and floured 10-inch tube pan or Bundt pan. If a slightly crisp crust is desired, use butter to grease the pan. Bake at for 1 hour and 10 minutes, or until cake tests done. Cool in pan for 10 minutes, and remove from pan to cool thoroughly before cutting.

Fruit Shortcake

Mary Ann pan or 9-inch cake pan
375 degrees F.
6 to 8 servings

    1 egg, lightly beaten
    ⅔ cup milk
    1½ cups biscuit mix
    ¼ cup sugar
    2 tablespoons butter or margarine, melted
    Fruit filling
    Whipped cream

Combine egg and milk. Add biscuit mix, sugar, and butter, and stir to blend well. Should be a soft, sticky dough. Add a little more milk, if needed. Pour into a well-greased fluted Mary Ann or flan pan, or into a 9-inch cake pan, and bake about 25 minutes or until lightly browned. Slice the 9-inch layer horizontally. Fill with fresh fruit, strawberries, raspberries, or sliced peaches, or use 1 can of pie filling. Top with whipped cream.

Shortcake is always best when baked at the last

Strawberry Cake (p. 118), Black Forest Cake (p. 116),
Poppy Seed Cake (p. 116)

minute, then filled and served while it is still warm.

Individual Shortcakes: Reduce milk slightly so that you can knead the dough lightly on a floured board. Roll or pat to about ½ inch thickness and cut with a 2-inch cookie cutter. Bake 10 to 15 minutes, or until lightly browned. Slice horizontally, adding crushed fruit and whipped cream between and on top.

Spanish Cake

8×8×2-inch cake pan
350 degrees F.

    1 cup sugar
    ½ cup (¼ pound) butter or margarine
    2 egg yolks
    1 cup flour
    1 teaspoon baking powder
    1 tablespoon cinnamon
    ½ cup milk
    2 egg whites, stiffly beaten

Cream sugar and butter. Add egg yolks and beat well. Sift flour, baking powder, and cinnamon together. Add alternately with milk. Fold in egg whites. Bake in greased pan for about 30 minutes, or until cake tests done. Remove from oven and spread on Broiled Topping (below) immediately. Put under broiler until bubbly (watch carefully—this takes only a minute or two!).

Broiled Topping

    ⅔ cup brown sugar
    3 tablespoons soft butter or margarine
    ⅛ teaspoon cream of tartar
    ½ teaspoon vanilla
    3 tablespoons cream (about)

Combine brown sugar, butter, cream of tartar, and vanilla. Add cream to make spreading consistency.

Strawberry Cake

2 9-inch round cake pans
375 degrees F.

    1 package white cake mix, with high-altitude
        addition of flour (2 to 3 tablespoons)
    ½ of a 3-ounce box strawberry-flavor gelatin (stir
        contents before measuring)
    3 eggs
    ½ cup water

    ⅓ cup salad oil
    ½ of 10-ounce package frozen strawberries or
    ½ cup crushed fresh strawberries

Combine all ingredients and beat for two minutes. Bake in two 9-inch round cake pans, which have been well greased and floured, for 30 minutes, or until cake tests done. Cool in pans for 5 minutes, and remove to cake racks to cool completely. Frost with Strawberry Frosting (below).

Strawberry Frosting

    4 cups powdered sugar
    ¼ cup (½ stick) butter or margarine, softened
    ½ of a 10-ounce package frozen strawberries,
        thawed

Combine all ingredients and beat until smooth. If not of proper consistency, add a few drops of milk or water.

Brown Sugar Pecan Peach Shortcake

8-inch round cake pan
375 degrees F.

    1½ cups flour
    1 tablespoon baking powder
    ½ teaspoon salt
    ¼ teaspoon baking soda
    ½ cup firmly packed brown sugar
    ½ cup (¼ pound) margarine or butter
    ½ cup coarsely chopped pecans
    1 egg
    ¾ cup milk
    6 to 8 peaches, sliced
    1 cup cream, whipped

Combine flour, baking powder, salt, and baking soda in mixing bowl. Cut in brown sugar and margarine until mixture looks like meal. Stir in pecans. Combine egg and milk, and stir into flour mixture just until blended. Pat into cake pan.

Bake 20 to 25 minutes, or until pick inserted in center comes out clean. Cool on rack. To serve, cut in wedges and top with sliced peaches and whipped cream.

Carob Cake

9×13×2-inch baking pan
400 degrees F.

    2 cups flour
    2 cups sugar
    ½ pound butter or margarine
    ¼ cup carob powder
    1 cup water
    2 eggs
    1 teaspoon vanilla
    1 teaspoon baking soda
    1 teaspoon cinnamon
    ½ cup buttermilk

Combine flour and sugar and mix well. Combine butter, carob powder, and water, and bring to a boil. Pour over flour-sugar mixture and beat until smooth. Add eggs, vanilla, soda, cinnamon, and milk; beat until smooth. Pour into well-greased baking pan, and bake for 20 to 25 minutes. Five minutes before cake is done, make frosting (below) and pour over cake as soon as it is removed from the oven.

Carob Frosting

    ¼ pound butter or margarine
    ¼ cup carob powder
    ⅓ cup milk
    1 teaspoon vanilla
    4 cups powdered sugar
    1 cup nuts, coarsely chopped

Combine butter, carob powder, and milk in saucepan and bring to a boil. Add vanilla and powdered sugar, and beat with electric mixer or by hand until smooth. Stir in nuts. Spread over hot cake. This cake always seems to be more moist and to have a better flavor the day after it is baked.

Note: This is a delicious cake to satisfy that chocolate craving for those who cannot eat chocolate. Carob powder may be purchased in many supermarkets and in health food stores.

"Any Old Fruit" Loaves

8½×4½-inch or 9×5-inch loaf pans
350 degrees F.
2 to 3 loaves

    1 quart home-canned fruit, undrained
    2 cups sugar
    1 cup oil
    4 cups flour
    4 teaspoons soda
    4 teaspoons cinnamon
    2 teaspoons nutmeg
    ¾ teaspoon cloves
    1 cup nuts, chopped (optional)
    1 cup raisins (optional)

Use old canned fruit (discolored but not spoiled). Purée it in a blender or food mill. Measure 4 cups. Mix together sugar and oil. Sift together dry ingredients. Add to sugar-oil mixture alternately with puréed fruit. Add nuts and raisins. Mix well. Pour into loaf pans that have been greased and floured. Bake about 1 hour, or until cake tests done. Let cool in pans 10 minutes. Turn out on cooling rack.

To use same recipe for cake, bake in a 9×13×2-inch pan about 45 minutes. Frost, when cool, with Cream Cheese Frosting (check Index for page).

Raisin Cupcakes

12-cup muffin pan
375 degrees F.

    1 cup raisins
    1 cup water
    ¼ cup butter or margarine
    ¾ cup sugar
    1 egg, beaten
    1½ cups flour
    1 teaspoon baking powder
    1 teaspoon baking soda
    1 teaspoon nutmeg
    1 teaspoon cinnamon
    ½ teaspoon salt
    ½ cup raisin water

Simmer raisins in water 5 minutes. Cool. Cream butter and sugar well; add egg, and beat until fluffy.

Sift dry ingredients together, then add to creamed mixture alternately with raisins and the raisin water. Beat well after each addition.

Divide batter into 12 muffin cups, either well greased or lined with fluted paper cups. (We prefer the fluted paper.) Bake for 20 to 25 minutes, or until cakes test done.

Cranberry Cream Roll

15½ × 10½ × 1-inch jelly roll pan
400 degrees F.
8 servings

Sponge Cake

    4 large eggs
    ¾ teaspoon baking powder
    ¼ teaspoon salt
    ¾ cup sugar
    1 teaspoon vanilla
    ¾ cup flour
    1 cup finely chopped nuts (optional)

Line pan with wax paper, then grease paper lightly. Beat eggs, baking powder, and salt with electric mixer at high speed, adding sugar gradually. Continue beating until thick and lemon-colored. Fold in vanilla and flour.

Pour into pan. Sprinkle nuts over top. Bake for 13 minutes, or until cake tests done (don't overbake). Loosen edges and immediately turn upside down on a towel sprinkled with powdered sugar. Carefully peel off wax paper. Roll jelly roll fashion, starting at narrow end. Cool on rack. Unroll. Spread with Cream Cheese Filling, then spread with Cranberry Filling. Reroll. Chill for several hours. (Freeze, if desired.) Garnish with whipped cream, if desired.

Cream Cheese Filling

    ¼ cup butter or margarine
    1 package (8 ounces) cream cheese
    ⅔ cup sifted powdered sugar
    ½ teaspoon vanilla

Cream butter and cream cheese until fluffy; beat in powdered sugar and vanilla. Spread on cake roll (above).

Cranberry Filling

    ⅔ cup water
    ½ cup sugar
    2 cups fresh cranberries
    1 tablespoon plus 1 teaspoon cornstarch
    1 tablespoon water
    ½ cup heavy cream, whipped (optional)

Combine water and sugar; bring to boil. Add cranberries, and cook just until skins pop. Drain off juice thoroughly into another saucepan. Combine cornstarch and 1 tablespoon water; stir into juice. Cook over medium heat, stirring, until thickened and clear. Stir carefully into cranberries to keep berries whole.

Easy Chocolate Log

15 × 10 × 1-inch jelly roll pan
375 degrees F.

    ¼ cup butter or margarine
    1 cup chopped nuts
    1⅓ cups flaked coconut
    1 can (14 ounces) sweetened condensed milk
    3 eggs
    1 cup sugar
    ¾ cup flour
    ⅓ cup cocoa
    ¼ teaspoon salt
    ¼ teaspoon baking soda
    1 teaspoon vanilla
    ⅓ cup powdered sugar

Line jelly roll pan with aluminum foil. In the pan, melt the butter and add, in layers, the chopped nuts, coconut, and sweetened condensed milk.

In a mixing bowl, beat the eggs and gradually add sugar. Beat two minutes. Combine flour, cocoa, salt, and soda, and add to the egg mixture. Stir in vanilla, and pour cake mixture evenly over the mixture in the pan.

Bake 15 to 20 minutes. Remove from oven, and sprinkle surface of cake with powdered sugar. Cover with a towel; place cookie sheet over towel and invert. Remove pan and foil. Starting with the end, roll up as for a jelly roll, being careful not to roll towel with cake. Leave wrapped in towel until completely cool. Slice in ½-inch slices to serve.

Grandma Grover's Cake Doughnuts

375 degrees F.
2 to 2½ dozen

    4 cups flour
    1 cup sugar
    3 teaspoons baking powder
    1½ teaspoons nutmeg
    1 teaspoon salt
    2 eggs, well beaten
    1 cup milk (about)

¼ cup heavy cream
Oil for frying

Mix flour, sugar, baking powder, nutmeg, and salt in large mixing bowl. Combine eggs, milk, and cream; add to flour mixture, mixing just enough to form a soft dough. Turn out on lightly floured board and knead gently 15 to 20 turns, or just until dough can be handled easily. (If dough is too soft to knead, cover and chill for 30 minutes.)

Roll out ⅜ inch thick and cut with floured 2¾-inch doughnut cutter. Fry in deep fat, or in at least 1 inch of hot fat, until golden brown, about 2 minutes on each side, turning only once. Drain on absorbent paper. If desired, doughnuts may be rolled in granulated or powdered sugar or a mixture of granulated sugar and cinnamon.

Cake Frostings

What's a cake without a frosting? Today you can have both cake and frosting quite easily from a package. Frosting cannisters require only a pull tab to deliver their creamy goodness all ready for spreading.

For those who prefer to make their own frosting, the following group of frostings, courtesy of General Foods Consumer Center, is representative of some old favorites. The directions provide a few tips for excellent results. For example, in the classic Seven-Minute Frosting (don't even try it unless you have an electric beater), you find the tip that is responsible for all those beautiful mountains of fluff the television commercials show. The trick is to remove the mixture from its cooking pan to a cool bowl for a final few minutes of beating to smooth and stabilize it. And creamy frostings contain an egg or just the egg white to make them smooth and so that the powdered sugar is not grainy.

Frosting recipes that go with special cakes are shown with the cake recipe.

Glossy Powdered Sugar Glaze

⅓ cup

1 tablespoon hot milk (about)
1 cup powdered sugar

Add milk gradually to powdered sugar in small bowl. Blend until mixture is thin enough to spread over cake.

Fluffy Butter Frosting

2¼ cups

6 tablespoons butter or margarine
¼ teaspoon salt
1 teaspoon vanilla
1 pound (about 4 cups) powdered sugar
2 egg whites, unbeaten
1 tablespoon milk (about)

Cream butter, salt, and vanilla together. Add sugar alternately with egg whites, beating well after each addition. Add milk, and beat until smooth and of spreading consistency. Makes enough to cover tops and sides of two 8- or 9-inch layers.

Fluffy Chocolate Butter Frosting

Use recipe for Fluffy Butter Frosting, adding 3 squares unsweetened chocolate, melted, to the sugar-egg white mixture. Beat well. Increase milk to 2 or 3 tablespoons; add to chocolate mixture, and beat until frosting is of spreading consistency. Makes 2½ cups, or enough to frost tops and sides of two 8- or 9-inch layers.

Butter Cream Frosting

2½ cups

½ cup (¼ pound) butter or margarine
⅛ teaspoon salt
1 pound (about 4 cups) powdered sugar
2 egg yolks, unbeaten, or use 1 whole egg*
1 teaspoon vanilla
2 tablespoons milk (about)

Cream butter until soft. Add salt and part of sugar gradually, blending after each addition. Then add egg yolks and vanilla; blend well. Add remaining sugar, alternately with milk, until of right consistency to spread, beating after each addition until smooth. Makes enough to frost tops and sides of three 8-inch or two 9-inch layers, two 9×9×2-inch square cakes, one 13×9×2-inch cake, or the tops of 3 dozen cupcakes.

*Or egg may be eliminated and milk increased slightly.

Lemon Butter Cream Frosting

Use recipe for Butter Cream Frosting, substituting 1 teaspoon grated lemon rind for the vanilla.

Orange Butter Cream Frosting

Use recipe for Butter Cream Frosting, substituting 1 teaspoon grated orange rind for the vanilla. If desired, orange juice may be used in place of the milk.

Chocolate Butter Cream Frosting

Use recipe for Butter Cream Frosting, increasing milk to about 4 tablespoons and adding 3 squares unsweetened chocolate, melted, after first addition of sugar. Makes 2¾ cups.

Easy Chocolate Frosting

2 cups

3 to 4 squares unsweetened chocolate
3 tablespoons butter or margarine
4 cups powdered sugar
⅛ teaspoon salt
7 tablespoons milk
1 teaspoon vanilla

Melt chocolate and butter over hot water. Combine sugar, salt, milk, and vanilla; blend. Add melted chocolate and butter and mix well. Let stand, stirring occasionally, until of right consistency to spread. If necessary, place bowl in pan of ice and water to hasten thickening. Makes enough to cover tops and sides of two 8- or 9-inch layers.

Chocolate Cream Cheese Frosting

2 cups

2 packages (4 ounces each) Baker's German's Sweet Chocolate
2 packages (3 ounces each) cream cheese
2 tablespoons light cream
2 cups powdered sugar
¼ teaspoon salt
1 teaspoon vanilla

Place chocolate in small bowl and set over hot water until melted. Cool slightly. Add cream cheese and cream; blend. Add sugar gradually, mixing well. Then add salt and vanilla.

Makes enough to spread on tops and sides of two 8- or 9-inch layers, or the tops of about 30 cupcakes.

Note: Divide all ingredients in half, except salt, to make about 1 cup frosting, or enough to cover top of 8- or 9-inch square cake. Make this frosting for Sunday-best cakes. It's expensive but worth every cent.

Quick Caramel Frosting

2 cups

⅔ cup butter or margarine
1 cup firmly packed brown sugar
⅓ cup evaporated milk (or fresh, whole milk)
3 cups powdered sugar (about)

Melt butter in saucepan. Add brown sugar; cook over low heat 2 minutes, stirring constantly. Add milk, and cook and stir until mixture comes to a boil. Remove from heat, and cool about 10 minutes. Gradually add powdered sugar until frosting is of right consistency to spread, beating well after each addition. Makes enough to cover tops and sides of two 8- or 9-inch layers, or top and sides of a 9×9×2-inch cake.

Fluffy Seven-Minute Frosting

5⅓ cups

2 egg whites, unbeaten
1½ cups sugar
Dash of salt
½ cup water
1 tablespoon light corn syrup
1¼ teaspoons vanilla

Combine egg whites, sugar, salt, water, and corn syrup in top of double boiler. Beat with electric beater about 1 minute to mix thoroughly. Then place over boiling water and beat constantly 7 minutes, or until frosting will stand in stiff peaks. (Stir frosting up from bottom of pan occasionally.)

Remove from boiling water. For a very smooth and satiny frosting, pour in large bowl for final beating. Add vanilla and beat 1 minute, or until thick enough to spread. Makes enough for tops and sides of two 8- or 9-inch layers, top and sides of a 13×9×2-inch cake, or 2 dozen cupcakes.

Note: Make this frosting only if you have an electric beater!

Sea Foam Frosting

Use brown sugar instead of white, ⅓ cup water, and 1 teaspoon vanilla. Otherwise, use ingredients and method as above. Makes 5¾ cups.

Sugarplum Frosting

Use recipe for Sea Foam Frosting. Just before spreading, fold in 1 cup cooked prunes, drained and cut in ½-inch pieces.

Praline Frosting

Prepare Sea Foam Frosting as directed. Just before spreading, fold in ¾ cup chopped pecans.

Fudge Sauce and Frosting

2½ to 3 cups

5 squares unsweetened baking chocolate
½ cup (¼ pound) butter or margarine
3 cups powdered sugar
1⅔ cups (13½-ounce can) evaporated milk
1¼ teaspoons vanilla

Melt chocolate and butter in saucepan. Remove from heat. Add powdered sugar alternately with milk, blending well after each addition. Bring to a boil over medium heat, stirring constantly. Then cook and stir about 5 minutes, or until mixture thickens and is creamy. Remove from heat; stir in vanilla.

To use as sauce: Spoon warm sauce over ice cream, cake, and other desserts, allowing 2 to 3 tablespoons per serving. Sauce may be prepared in advance; cover and store in refrigerator. Reheat over hot water, stirring frequently. It's marvelous for hot-fudge sundaes.

To make frosting: Cool 2 cups sauce thoroughly, to room temperature. Then add 2 cups powdered sugar, blending well. Makes enough to cover tops and sides of two 8- or 9-inch layers.

To make glaze: Cool 2 cups sauce to lukewarm. Then add 2 cups powdered sugar, blending well. Use on angel food or pound cake, eclairs, cream puffs, and other desserts.

Marilyn's Peanut Butter Fudge Frosting

2½ cups

½ cup brown sugar
2 tablespoons butter
¼ cup milk
3 tablespoons cocoa
1 teaspoon vanilla
⅔ cup chunky peanut butter
Powdered sugar

Combine brown sugar, butter, and milk, and bring to a full rolling boil. Add cocoa, vanilla, and peanut butter. Remove from heat, and add powdered sugar to spreading consistency.

Brownie Drops

350 degrees F.
About 36 cookies

2 packages (4 ounces each) Baker's German's Sweet Chocolate
1 tablespoon butter or margarine
2 eggs
¾ cup sugar
¼ cup flour
¼ teaspoon baking powder
¼ teaspoon cinnamon
⅛ teaspoon salt
½ teaspoon vanilla
¾ cup pecans, finely chopped

Melt chocolate and butter over low heat. Stir, then cool. Beat eggs until foamy; then add sugar, 2 tablespoons at a time, and beat until thickened (5 minutes on electric mixer). Blend in chocolate-butter mixture. Add flour, baking powder, cinnamon, and salt; blend. Stir in vanilla and nuts. Drop from teaspoon on greased cookie sheet. Bake until cookies feel set when very lightly touched, about 8 to 10 minutes.

Oatmeal Cookies

400 degrees F.
3½ dozen cookies about 2½ inches in diameter each

1 cup raisins
1 cup water
2 cups flour
½ teaspoon baking soda
½ teaspoon salt
½ teaspoon allspice
½ teaspoon cloves
½ teaspoon nutmeg
1 teaspoon cinnamon
1 cup sugar (white or brown)
1 cup fat (butter, margarine, or hydrogenated
  vegetable fat)
2 to 3 eggs
⅓ cup raisin liquid
2 cups quick-cooking oatmeal
½ cup dates, cut-up, or chocolate chips (optional)
1 cup chopped nuts (optional)

In a small saucepan with a tight lid, heat raisins and water to boiling. Remove from heat; cool. Measure ⅓ cup of raisin liquid and reserve; drain raisins.

Sift dry ingredients into large mixer bowl. Add fat. Beat on low speed until well blended. Add eggs and raisin liquid. Beat at medium speed 2 minutes or until light and smooth. Add oatmeal, raisins, dates, and nuts; mix well by hand.

Drop by heaping teaspoons two inches apart on greased cookie sheet. Bake 10 to 15 minutes, or until delicately brown. Cool on cake rack. For a soft cookie, store in an air-tight container.

Oatmeal Crisps

325 degrees F.
About 6 dozen

1 cup brown sugar
1 cup minus 2 tablespoons white sugar
1 cup (½ pound) butter or margarine
2 eggs, beaten
1½ cups flour
½ teaspoon salt
1¾ teaspoons baking soda
1 teaspoon vanilla
1 cup nuts, finely chopped
2 cups oatmeal

Cream sugars and butter. Add eggs. Sift flour, salt, and baking soda together and add to creamed mixture. Stir in vanilla, nuts, and oats. Drop from

teaspoon on greased cookie sheet. (These cookies spread, so allow room.) Bake 10 minutes or until light golden brown. Remove to cooling rack.

Krispie Oatmeal Cookies

375 degrees F.
About 8 dozen

1 cup sugar
1 cup brown sugar
1 cup (½ pound) margarine
1 cup oil
1 egg, slightly beaten
1 teaspoon vanilla
1 cup Rice Krispies
1 cup quick oatmeal
3½ cups flour
¾ teaspoon salt
1 teaspoon soda
1 teaspoon cream of tartar
1 cup coconut

Blend sugars well; cream with margarine, then add oil. Blend in egg, vanilla, Rice Krispies, and oatmeal. Sift flour, salt, soda, and cream of tartar together and add to sugar mixture. Mix well. Add coconut. Drop from teaspoon on ungreased cookie sheet. Bake about 12 minutes, or to desired brownness. Remove to cooling rack.

Chewy Oatmeal Cookies

350 degrees F.
4 to 5 dozen

½ to 1 cup water
½ to 1 cup raisins*
1 cup flour
½ teaspoon baking soda
1 teaspoon salt
¾ cup shortening
½ cup sugar
1 cup brown sugar
1 egg, beaten
1 teaspoon vanilla
3 cups quick-cooking oats, uncooked
½ to 1 cup nuts (optional)

In a small saucepan, boil raisins and water together, covered, 2 minutes. Remove from heat and cool.

Sift flour, soda, and salt together. Reserve.

Cream shortening and sugars thoroughly. Add egg and vanilla; combine well. Mix in ¼ cup of the raisin water, oats, and flour mixture. Add well-drained raisins and nuts. Drop by teaspoonfuls onto greased cookie sheets. Bake 12 to 15 minutes, or until lightly browned and set. Don't overbake, and you have a moist, chewy cookie.

Replace raisins with chocolate chips and substitute ¼ cup water. Or replace raisins with flaked coconut, cut; substitute ¼ cup water.

Soft Ginger Cookies

375 degrees F.
3 dozen cookies

   ¾ cup shortening
   1 cup sugar
   1 egg, beaten slightly
   4 teaspoons molasses
   2 cups flour
   2 teaspoons baking soda
   ½ teaspoon salt
   ½ teaspoon ginger
   1 teaspoon cinnamon

Cream shortening and sugar. Add egg and molasses and mix well. Combine dry ingredients and add, blending well. Drop from teaspoon on greased cookie sheet; bake 6 to 9 minutes. Cookies should be soft, so avoid over-cooking them and allowing them to dry out.

Breakfast Cookies

400 degrees F.
4 dozen

   1¼ cup brown sugar
   ½ cup (¼ pound) margarine
   2 eggs, beaten
   3 cups flour
   2 teaspoons baking powder
   ⅛ teaspoon soda
   ½ cup non-fat dry milk
   6 tablespoons molasses
   2 cups quick rolled oats
   1 cup raisins or dates or dried apricots
   1 cup nuts, chopped

Cream sugar and margarine; add eggs. Combine dry ingredients and add to sugar mixture alternately with molasses. Stir in oats, dried fruit, and nuts. Dough will be very stiff. Drop from teaspoon on lightly greased cookie sheet. Bake 10 to 12 minutes, or until lightly browned.

Note: These cookies are full of nutritious goodies that make them an adequate breakfast with a glass of milk.

Jam Cookies

350 degrees F.
About 2 dozen cookies

   ½ cup shortening
   1 cup thick jam
   ¼ cup sugar (optional)
   1 egg, beaten
   2 cups flour
   1 teaspoon baking soda
   1 teaspoon salt
   1 teaspoon vanilla*
   ½ cup nuts, chopped
   ¾ cup chocolate chips (optional)

Cream shortening. Add jam and sugar, then egg. Sift together flour, soda, and salt. Add to creamed mixture. Mix well. Add vanilla, nuts, and chocolate chips. Drop from teaspoon on greased cookie sheet. Bake 10 to 15 minutes, or until done. This is a moist cookie and will keep well. It is a good way to use up old jam that may have discolored.

Some jams may be very mild in flavor. About ¼ teaspoon allspice, cinnamon, or cloves (or combination) will pick up the flavor of dark fruits, such as plums. Grated rind of a lemon or orange (about ½ teaspoon) will help peach, apricot, or pear jam.

Joan's Lemonade Cookies

Cookie sheet
375 degrees F.
4 dozen cookies

   1 cup butter
   1 cup sugar
   2 eggs, beaten
   3 cups flour
   ½ teaspoon salt
   1 teaspoon baking soda
   1 can (6 ounces) frozen lemonade concentrate, thawed
   ½ teaspoon grated lemon rind (optional)

Cream butter and sugar; beat in eggs. Mix flour, salt, and soda, then add alternately with ½ cup concentrate. Add grated rind. Drop from teaspoon 2 inches apart on ungreased cookie sheet. Bake 8 to 10 minutes, or until lightly browned around edges. Brush hot cookies lightly with remaining concentrate, then sprinkle with sugar.

Easy Raisin-filled Cookies

350 degrees F.
About 3 dozen cookies

>   2 cups shortening (use half butter or margarine,
>   if desired)
>   1 cup sugar
>   1 cup brown sugar
>   2 eggs, slightly beaten
>   2 teaspoons vanilla
>   6 cups flour
>   1 teaspoon salt
>   1 teaspoon baking soda
>   6 tablespoons milk

Cream shortening and sugars; add eggs and vanilla and blend well. Sift dry ingredients and add alternately with milk. Shape into rolls 2½ to 3 inches in diameter for large cookies. Wrap in foil or waxed paper; put in freezer. When firm, slice ⅛- to ¼-inch thick. Place half of slices on cookie sheets. Spoon about 1 teaspoon of raisin filling (or firm jam) on each slice, then cover with a second slice. Bake 12 to 17 minutes, or until cookies are lightly browned and do not collapse when touched with finger. Store tightly covered if a soft cookie is desired.

Raisin Filling

>   2 cups raisins, ground
>   1 cup water
>   ½ to ¾ cup sugar
>   1 tablespoon flour
>   1 teaspoon vanilla
>   1 cup nuts, chopped

Combine all ingredients, and simmer until blended and thickened. Cool.

Jumbo Raisin Cookies

375 degrees F.
About 4 dozen

>   2 cups raisins
>   1 cup water
>   3¾ cups flour (white or part whole wheat)
>   1 teaspoon baking powder
>   1 teaspoon baking soda
>   1 teaspoon salt
>   ½ teaspoon cinnamon
>   ½ teaspoon nutmeg
>   1 cup shortening or margarine
>   1¾ cups sugar
>   2 eggs, slightly beaten
>   1 teaspoon vanilla
>   ½ cup nuts, chopped

Bring raisins and water to a boil in a small saucepan with a tight lid. Simmer 2 to 3 minutes. Cool. Sift together flour, baking powder, soda, salt, cinnamon, and nutmeg. Cream shortening and sugar until light and fluffy. Add eggs and vanilla, and mix well. Stir in raisins and any remaining water. Gradually add the flour mixture, blending thoroughly after each addition. Stir in nuts. Drop from tablespoon 1 inch apart on greased cookie sheet. Bake 12 to 15 minutes, or until lightly browned.

Jumbo Oatmeal Raisin Cookies: Make as above, except use 2 cups flour and 2½ cups oatmeal.

Noels

400 degrees F.
3 dozen cookies

>   ⅓ cup butter or margarine
>   1 teaspoon vanilla
>   ¾ cup brown sugar
>   1 egg, beaten
>   1½ cups flour
>   ½ teaspoon salt
>   ¼ teaspoon baking powder
>   ½ teaspoon baking soda
>   ½ cup sour cream
>   36 pitted dates
>   36 pecan or walnut halves
>   Frosting

Cream butter, vanilla, and brown sugar. Add egg, and beat well. Sift dry ingredients, and add alternately with sour cream.

Stuff each date with a nut half. Drop stuffed dates into dough and roll with a fork until completely coated with dough. Drop from teaspoon on well-greased cookie sheet. Bake for about 10 minutes, or until lightly browned. Cool, and spread with Noel Frosting (below).

Variation: Chop dates and nuts, and fold into dough. Drop from teaspoon on cookie sheet and bake.

Noel Frosting

>   2 tablespoons butter or margarine, melted and
>   browned slightly
>   1 cup powdered sugar (about)
>   1 teaspoon vanilla
>   1 teaspoon cream or milk

Combine all ingredients and blend until smooth. Glaze cookies.

Snowballs

400 degrees F.
3 dozen cookies

    1 cup (½ pound) butter or margarine
    ½ cup powdered sugar
    1 teaspoon vanilla
    2¼ cups flour
    ¼ teaspoon salt
    ¾ cup finely chopped nuts
    Powdered sugar

Cream butter, sugar, and vanilla well. Stir flour and salt together and blend in. Mix in nuts. Chill dough. Roll dough into small balls using about 1 teaspoon of dough for each cookie, and place on ungreased cookie sheet. Bake for 10 to 12 minutes, or until set but not brown. While warm, roll in powdered sugar. Cool. Roll in powdered sugar again.

Chocolate Snowballs: Add ½ cup chocolate chips to dough.

Christmas Kisses

350 degrees F.
3 dozen cookies

    ½ cup (¼ pound) butter or margarine
    ⅓ cup peanut butter
    ½ cup sugar
    ½ cup brown sugar, packed
    1 egg
    1 teaspoon vanilla
    1¾ cups flour
    1 teaspoon baking soda
    ½ teaspoon salt
    36 chocolate candy kisses

Cream butter and peanut butter. Add sugars and cream together. Beat in egg and vanilla. Combine flour, baking soda, and salt; mix well with sugar mixture.

Shape into 1-inch balls; roll in granulated sugar. Bake on ungreased cookie sheet 8 minutes. Remove from oven and top each cookie with a chocolate kiss, pressing down into cookie. Return to oven and bake 3 to 6 minutes longer, or until kiss is melted slightly.

Linzer Cookies

375 degrees F.

    ½ cup butter or margarine
    ¼ cup sugar
    1 egg
    1 teaspoon vanilla
    ¼ teaspoon almond extract
    ½ teaspoon salt
    1¼ cups sifted cake flour
    ¾ cup fine dry bread crumbs
    1 cup very finely ground blanched almonds*
    Powdered sugar
    ¾ cup red raspberry jam

Cream butter until softened. Gradually add sugar, creaming together until light and fluffy. Add egg and beat well. Stir in flavorings and salt. Add flour, bread crumbs, and almonds; stir until well blended.

Roll out half of the dough at a time on a board that has been lightly dusted with flour and then sprinkled with granulated sugar (dough should be about the thickness of pie crust, less than ⅛ inch). Cut into round cookies, using a 3½-inch scalloped cutter. Cut a hole in the centers of half the cookies, using a plain 1½-inch round cutter.

Place cookies on a lightly greased cookie sheet. Bake about 7 minutes. Remove from sheet and cool on racks. Sift powdered sugar over cookies with a hole in the center. Spread about 1 tablespoon jam over the bottom of the whole cookies. Center sugar-sprinkled cookies over jam cookies; press together. Makes 1 dozen cookies.

Sift ground almonds to remove any large pieces.

Surprise Balls

15 servings

    1 pint frozen whipped topping, or ½ pint whipping
      cream, whipped
    1 package (10½ ounces) miniature marshmallows
    ½ cup crushed peppermint stick candy
    ½ cup chopped nuts
    1 cup crushed chocolate cookie crumbs, or 1 cup
      vanilla wafer crumbs, or 1 cup finely chopped nuts

Mix whipped topping or whipped cream, marshmallows, crushed candy, and nuts; cover and refrigerate overnight. The next day, make golf-ball-size portions out of the chilled mixture. Roll each ball in cookie crumbs or nuts. Freeze until firm.

Note: The balls can be eaten without freezing if they are kept refrigerated.

Pecan Pie Cookies

375 degrees F.
4 dozen cookies

    1 cup (½ pound) butter or margarine
    ½ cup sugar
    ½ cup light corn syrup
    2 eggs, separated
    2½ cups flour
    Pecan Filling (below)

Cream butter and sugar together. Add corn syrup and egg yolks; beat until thoroughly blended. Stir in flour gradually. Chill dough for several hours.

Beat egg whites slightly. Using 1 tablespoon of dough for each cookie, roll into balls. Brush lightly with egg white. Place two inches apart on greased cookie sheet. Bake five minutes. Remove from oven.

Place a ball of Pecan Filling (below) made from ½ teaspoon of filling into the center of each cookie, pressing about halfway down into the cookie. Do not press completely through cookie. Return cookies to oven and bake 5 minutes longer, or until lightly browned. Cool on rack. Cookies will store for weeks if kept in a tightly closed container.

Pecan Filling

    ½ cup powdered sugar
    ¼ cup butter
    3 tablespoons corn syrup
    ½ cup finely chopped pecans

Combine sugar, butter, and corn syrup in a small saucepan; stir to blend. Cook over medium heat, stirring occasionally, until mixture reaches a full boil. Remove from heat, and stir in pecans. Chill. Using ½ teaspoon of mixture, roll into small balls and press into each cookie to form filling.

Apricot Bars

9×9×2-inch pan
350 degrees F.
About 32 1×2-inch strips

    ⅔ cup dried apricots
    ½ cup (1 stick) butter or margarine
    ¼ cup sugar
    1 cup flour
    ⅓ cup flour
    ½ teaspoon baking powder
    ¼ teaspoon salt

    1 cup brown sugar
    2 eggs, well beaten
    ½ teaspoon vanilla
    ½ cup chopped nuts
    Powdered sugar

Rinse apricots; cover with water, and boil 10 minutes. Drain, cool, and chop.

Mix butter, sugar, and 1 cup flour until crumbly. Pack into ungreased pan. Bake about 25 minutes, or until lightly browned.

Sift together ⅓ cup flour, baking powder, and salt. Gradually beat brown sugar into eggs. Add flour mixture, mix well. Mix in vanilla, nuts, and apricots. Spread over baked layer. Bake 30 minutes, or until done. Cool in pan, then cut into bars and dust with powdered sugar.

Lemon-Prune Bars

9×9×2-inch pan
350 degrees F.
9 to 16 bars, 3×3 or 4×4 inches

    1 cup brown sugar
    2 tablespoons butter or margarine
    3 eggs, well beaten
    1 cup flour
    ½ teaspoon baking powder
    ½ teaspoon baking soda
    ½ teaspoon salt
    ½ teaspoon nutmeg
    ¾ teaspoon cinnamon
    ¼ teaspoon cloves
    ¾ teaspoon vanilla
    ½ teaspoon grated lemon rind
    1 cup walnuts, chopped
    1½ cups chopped pitted prunes
    Lemon Frosting (below)

Add sugar and butter to eggs; beat well. Sift dry ingredients together, then add to sugar mixture. Stir in remaining ingredients, except frosting.

Spread into well-greased pan and bake 20 to 25 minutes, or until it tests done. Cool to lukewarm in pan. Spread with Lemon Frosting. Cut into bars.

Lemon Frosting

    3 cups powdered sugar
    3 tablespoons butter or margarine, melted
    3 tablespoons lemon juice (more, if desired)

Blend all ingredients until smooth.

Apricot Cookie Rolls

350 degrees F.
4 dozen cookies

½ cup flaked coconut
½ cup apricot preserves
¼ cup chopped nuts
1 cup butter or margarine
1 cup sour cream
½ teaspoon salt
2 cups flour

Combine coconut, preserves, and nuts. Chill.

Cream butter, sour cream, and salt; gradually stir in flour. Divide dough into fourths; chill thoroughly.

When ready to assemble cookies, roll one portion of dough at a time to ⅛-inch thickness. Cut into 2½-inch squares; spread each with ½ teaspoon of the coconut-apricot mixture. Starting with one corner, roll cookie to opposite corner. Moisten corner and seal. Bake on ungreased cookie sheets 16 to 18 minutes, or until lightly browned. Cool. Dust with powdered sugar.

Lemon Sponge Squares

9×9×2-inch pan
350 degrees F.
16 2-inch squares

1 cup flour
¼ cup sugar
½ cup butter or margarine
2 eggs
1 cup sugar
Grated rind from one lemon
¼ cup lemon juice
2 tablespoons flour
½ teaspoon baking powder
Powdered sugar

Blend 1 cup flour, ¼ cup sugar, and butter well. Press firmly into square pan and bake until lightly browned (15 to 20 minutes).

Beat together eggs, 1 cup sugar, rind, and lemon juice. Mix 2 tablespoons flour and baking powder; add to egg mixture. Pour over the baked crust; bake another 20 minutes, or until lightly browned and top seems set when touched with finger. Sprinkle a light dusting of powdered sugar on top. Cool, then cut into squares.

Brownies

350 degrees F.

	9 × 9 × 2-inch pan 20 brownies	9 × 13 × 2-inch pan or 10 × 15 × 1-inch pan 40 brownies
Unsweetened chocolate*	2 squares	4 squares
Butter or margarine	⅓ cup	⅔ cup
Flour	⅔ cup	1⅓ cup
Baking powder	½ teaspoon	1 teaspoon
Salt	¼ teaspoon	½ teaspoon
Eggs	2	4
Sugar	1 cup	2 cups
Vanilla	1 teaspoon	2 teaspoons
Nuts, chopped	½ cup	1 cup

Melt chocolate and butter over low heat. Mix flour with baking powder and salt. Beat eggs well; gradually beat in sugar. Blend in melted chocolate and vanilla. Mix in flour mixture. Add nuts. Spread in greased pan. Bake 25 minutes. Cool.

*Variation for cocoa: For each square of chocolate, substitute 3 tablespoons cocoa and 1 tablespoon butter. Add butter with other butter, and add cocoa with dry ingredients.

Glazed Cinnamon Bars

15×10×1-inch jelly roll pan
350 degrees F.
4 dozen bars

1 cup (½ pound) butter or margarine
1 cup brown sugar, firmly packed
1 egg, separated
1¾ cups flour
¼ teaspoon salt
3 teaspoons cinnamon
½ cup powdered sugar
1 cup chopped nuts

Combine butter, brown sugar, and egg yolk. Beat until creamy. Stir in flour, salt, and cinnamon. Mix well. Spread dough into lightly greased jelly roll pan. Beat egg white until foamy. Stir in powdered sugar. Spread egg-sugar mixture over batter. Sprinkle with chopped nuts. Bake 30 to 35 minutes. While hot, cut into bars. Remove from pan and cool on rack.

Coconut-Pecan Bars

350 degrees F.

	9 × 9 × 2-inch pan 32 1 × 2-inch bars	9 × 13 × 2-inch pan 48 1 × 2-inch bars
Flour	1 cup	1½ cups
Sugar	2 tablespoons	3 tablespoons
Salt	⅛ teaspoon	⅛ teaspoon
Butter or margarine	⅓ cup	½ cup
Eggs, slightly beaten	2	3
Brown sugar, firmly packed	1 cup	1½ cups
Pecans, chopped	½ cup	¾ cup
Angel Flake Coconut, cut fine	½ cup	¾ cup
Vanilla	½ teaspoon	¾ teaspoon

Sift flour, sugar, and salt into a bowl. Cut in butter as you would for pie crust, until the mixture resembles coarse meal. Press it firmly into the baking pan. Bake about 15 minutes, or until pastry is very faintly brown. In the meantime, combine eggs, brown sugar, nuts, coconut, and vanilla. Pour over partially baked pastry. Return to oven and bake about 30 minutes, or until topping is firm. Cool 15 minutes. Spread on Lemon Glaze, then cut into bars. Cool.

Lemon Glaze

For smaller pan, use 1 cup powdered sugar, ½ tablespoon lemon juice, and grated rind from ½ lemon. For larger pan, use 1½ cups powdered sugar, 1 tablespoon (about) lemon juice, and grated rind from one lemon. Blend powdered sugar, lemon juice, and rind. Add a drop or two of water, if necessary, so that glaze spreads easily.

Waffle-Iron Oatmeal Cookies

Waffle iron
30 to 40 cookies

⅔ cup butter or margarine
¾ cup sugar
2 eggs, beaten
2 cups quick oats
1¾ cups whole wheat flour
1 cup white flour
1 teaspoon salt
2 teaspoons cinnamon
1 teaspoon ginger
2 teaspoons baking powder
½ teaspoon baking soda
1 cup sour milk (add 1 tablespoon lemon juice or vinegar to milk) or buttermilk
1 cup raisins, plumped

Cream butter and sugar. Add eggs and mix well. Combine oats, flours, salt, cinnamon, ginger, baking powder, and baking soda, and add alternately with the sour milk. Stir in raisins. Heat waffle iron to medium heat. Drop a tablespoonful of dough on each section of the waffle iron, and bake 3 to 5 minutes. Serve warm.

Note: Waffle-iron cookies are easy and fun for children to bake.

Waffle-Iron Brownies

Waffle iron
24 servings

½ cup (¼ pound) butter or margarine
1 cup sugar
2 squares chocolate, melted
2 eggs, beaten
1 teaspoon vanilla
½ teaspoon almond extract
1 cup flour
½ teaspoon salt

Cream butter and sugar together. Add melted chocolate, beaten eggs, and vanilla and almond extracts. Combine flour and salt and add to the first mixture. Heat waffle iron to a low setting, as chocolate scorches easily. When iron is ready, drop a tablespoonful of dough on each section of waffle iron. Bake about 3 minutes.

Puddings and Desserts

Old-Fashioned Rice Pudding

1- or 1½-quart casserole
325 degrees F.
8 servings

3½ cups milk, scalded
¼ cup uncooked long-grain rice*
⅓ cup sugar
½ teaspoon salt
¼ teaspoon nutmeg
½ teaspoon vanilla
½ cup raisins (optional)

Combine all ingredients except vanilla and raisins. Bake 1½ hours (stir each ½ hour). Stir in vanilla and raisins and let cook another half hour, or until rice is tender. Don't stir again.

Converted rice may be used, but not rice that is broken and split.

Bread Pudding

2-quart casserole
350 degrees F.
6 servings

½ cup sugar
½ teaspoon cinnamon
¼ teaspoon salt
2 eggs
1 quart milk
1 teaspoon vanilla
8 slices bread, cut in cubes
½ cup raisins
2 tablespoons butter, melted

Mix sugar, cinnamon, and salt in a large bowl. Beat in eggs and slowly stir in milk and vanilla. Stir in bread cubes, raisins, and butter. Pour into baking pan.

Bake about 40 minutes or until knife inserted near center comes out clean. Don't overbake, or pudding will be watery.

Old-Time Christmas Pudding

About 6 servings

½ cup butter or finely ground suet
1 cup sugar
1 egg, beaten
2 cups raisins
½ cup flour
1 cup grated raw carrots
½ cup grated raw potato
½ cup grated raw apple
1 teaspoon baking soda
1 teaspoon cinnamon
1 teaspoon nutmeg
½ teaspoon salt
1 cup flour

Cream butter and sugar together. Add egg and mix well. Combine raisins and ½ cup flour, and stir into creamed mixture. Stir in carrots, potatoes, and apple. Combine soda, cinnamon, nutmeg, salt, and 1 cup flour. Stir into first combination and mix well. Steam for 2½ hours. See Steamed Chocolate Pudding for steaming directions.

Pearl's Lemon Pudding

9×13×2-inch baking pan
375 degrees F.

⅔ cup flour
2 cups sugar
4 eggs, separated
3 tablespoons butter, melted and cooled
Juice of 2 lemons (about ⅓ cup)
Grated rind of two lemons (about 2 teaspoons)
2 cups milk

Mix flour and sugar in large bowl. In a small bowl beat egg yolks. Add cooled melted butter and lemon juice and rind. Stir in milk. Add liquids to flour and sugar mixture. Beat egg whites until stiff and fold in. Pour into ungreased baking pan and bake 35 to 40 minutes or until set. Serve warm, with cream or whipped cream, if desired.

Steamed Chocolate Pudding

2-quart pudding mold, or 2 1-quart molds
12 servings

    3 squares unsweetened chocolate
    2 cups flour
    2 teaspoons baking powder
    ½ teaspoon baking soda
    ¼ teaspoon salt
    ⅓ cup butter or other shortening
    1 cup sugar
    1 egg, slightly beaten
    1 cup milk
    1 teaspoon vanilla
    Whipped cream, or any desired sauce

Melt chocolate over low heat. Sift flour with baking powder, soda, and salt. Cream butter. Gradually add sugar; cream together thoroughly. Add egg and melted chocolate, beating until smooth. Add flour mixture alternately with milk, beating well after each addition. Blend in vanilla. Steam 1¾ to 2 hours, or until cake tester inserted into center comes out clean. Let pudding stand about 5 minutes before removing from mold. Serve hot with whipped cream or sauce.

To steam pudding: Pour into greased mold, filling only about two-thirds full. Cover tightly with lid, aluminum foil, or several layers of waxed paper. Place a rack or inverted saucer in bottom of large heavy saucepan or Dutch oven. Add water to a depth of 2 inches. Bring water to a boil; then place tightly covered pudding on the rack. Cover. Boil gently. (Or use a steamer.) Pudding made ahead may be refrigerated or frozen. Resteam until hot, about ½ hour.

Tropical Fruit Pudding

4 to 5 servings

    1¾ cups cold milk
    1 package (4-serving size) vanilla instant pudding mix
    ½ cup cut orange sections
    ½ teaspoon grated orange rind
    ⅓ cup coconut
    1 medium banana, sliced

Pour milk into bowl. Add pudding mix and beat slowly with egg beater just until well mixed, about 1 minute. (Do not overbeat; mixture will be thin.) Quickly fold in orange sections, orange rind, coconut, and banana slices. Pour at once into sherbet glasses or a serving dish and let stand to set about 5 minutes. Chill.

LaRue's Sugarplum Pudding

2 1-quart molds or 4 1-pound cans
16 servings

    1 cup pitted dried prunes, cut up
    2 eggs, well beaten
    1 cup brown sugar, firmly packed
    1 cup flour
    ½ teaspoon baking soda
    ½ teaspoon baking powder
    1 teaspoon salt
    1 teaspoon ground allspice
    1 teaspoon cinnamon
    1 teaspoon nutmeg
    ¼ teaspoon cloves
    1 cup buttermilk
    2 cups finely ground suet
    1 cup seeded raisins (if unavailable, seedless will do)

In a small bowl, soak prunes in hot water. Drain when ready to use.

In large bowl of electric mixer, combine eggs and sugar; beat well until light and well blended. Sift together flour, soda, baking powder, salt, and spices. Add to egg mixture alternately with buttermilk. Stir in suet, prunes, and raisins. Steam for 2½ to 3 hours, or until cake tester inserted in pudding comes out clean. See Steamed Chocolate Pudding for steaming directions.

Let pudding stand a few minutes after removing from cooker. Run knife or small spatula carefully around the edge of mold. Pudding should come out easily onto serving platter.

Sugarplum Pudding Sauce

About 2½ cups

    ¼ cup butter (no substitues)
    1 cup sugar
    4 tablespoons flour
    1 to 1½ cups boiling water
    ½ pint whipping cream

Mix butter, sugar, and flour well in heavy saucepan or top of double boiler. Add boiling water; cook over medium heat, stirring often, until sauce becomes thick and transparent. Cover and let simmer about 10 minutes. Stir twice.

Whip cream until stiff, and fold into hot sauce. Keep covered until ready to serve. If it has cooled, warm slowly before serving.

Please, no vanilla or other flavoring! This is a very tasty, buttery sauce.

Banana Split Cake Dessert (p. 135)

Vanilla Pudding Sauce

1⅓ cups

¼ cup butter
2 tablespoons flour
Pinch of salt
2 tablespoons sugar
1 cup hot water
½ teaspoon vanilla
¼ cup rich cream

In top of double boiler or over low heat, melt butter. Stir in flour, salt, and sugar, and cook, stirring constantly, until thick. Gradually add hot water and cook, stirring constantly, until mixture thickens. Add vanilla and cream and continue cooking, stirring constantly until mixture is thick and smooth. Serve over hot steamed pudding.

Flan (Caramel Custard)

4 servings

¼ cup sugar
¼ teaspoon salt
½ teaspoon vanilla
1 tall can (14 ounces) evaporated milk
2 eggs, slightly beaten
¼ cup milk (optional)
4 tablespoons Caramel Sauce (below)

Prepare custard and bake in custard cups as for Creme Caramel (below). Chill. Unmold in serving dishes. This is a favorite "South of the Border" dessert.

Creme Caramel

350 degrees F.
4 to 5 servings

¼ cup sugar
½ teaspoon salt
½ teaspoon vanilla
2½ cups milk
3 eggs, slightly beaten
4 to 5 tablespoons Caramel Sauce (below)

Combine sugar, salt, vanilla, milk, and eggs. Stir well; strain. Put 1 tablespoon caramel sauce in each of four or five 6-ounce custard cups, or put 4 tablespoons sauce in a deep 1-quart baking dish. Pour custard carefully over caramel sauce. Place cups or baking dish in a pan about 2 to 2½ inches deep;

pour boiling water around cups to come almost to level of custard.

Bake 30 to 40 minutes, or until a knife inserted near center of custard comes out clean. Remove custard cups or baking dish from water at once. Chill thoroughly before unmolding. (Custard may be served warm, if you prefer, but it won't unmold unless it is chilled thoroughly.)

Custard may be baked without sauce, if preferred, with a sprinkle of nutmeg on top. For a glamorous buffet-supper dessert, bake caramel custard in a ring mold; unmold on a plate to fit the ring, and fill the center of the ring with whipped cream. Increase recipe to fit the size of mold used (for a 6-cup mold, this recipe should be doubled).

Caramel Sauce

About 1 cup

1½ cups sugar
1 cup hot water
1 tablespoon butter
⅛ teaspoon salt
½ teaspoon vanilla

Put sugar in heavy frying pan over medium heat; stir constantly until sugar is melted and becomes light brown. Remove syrup from heat and add water slowly and carefully (the syrup steams up quickly, and it is easy to get a steam burn).

Return pan to heat and boil slowly while stirring until caramel is melted and slightly thickened (238 degrees F.). Remove from heat; stir in butter, salt, and vanilla. Use immediately, or store in glass jar until ready to use. We keep this in the refrigerator for quick use. If it gets too thick, put the glass jar in a simmering pan of water until sauce melts again.

Blender Chocolate Mousse

4 to 6 servings

1 package (6 ounces) chocolate chips
2 tablespoons sugar
1 egg
Dash of salt
1 teaspoon vanilla
1 cup milk, heated to boiling
½ cup whipping cream, whipped

Put chips, sugar, egg, salt, and vanilla in blender container. Pour in boiling milk and blend for 1 minute. Pour into small, individual soufflé cups. Chill. Serve with a small dollop of whipped cream. This is a very rich, elegant dessert, and a small serving will suffice.

Banana Split Cake Dessert

9×13×2-inch pan
18 servings

    1 package (12 ounces) vanilla wafers
    ½ cup (¼ pound) butter or margarine
    4 cups powdered sugar
    1 cup (½ pound) butter or margarine
    2 eggs
    1 teaspoon vanilla
    1 can (20 ounces) crushed pineapple, well drained
    3 to 4 bananas, sliced
    Lemon juice
    2 cups frozen whipped topping
    Maraschino cherries
    Chopped nuts
    Chocolate syrup or fudge sauce

Crush vanilla wafers (about 4 cups crumbs). Melt ½ cup butter and pour over wafers; mix well. Press into pan and refrigerate 30 minutes.

Combine powdered sugar, 1 cup butter, eggs, and vanilla. Beat with electric mixer until well blended and smooth, at least five minutes. Spread over vanilla wafer crust.

Spread well-drained crushed pineapple over filling. Dip banana slices in lemon juice and place on top of crushed pineapple layer. Cover completely with whipped topping. Garnish with cherries and nuts; then drizzle chocolate syrup over entire top. Extra syrup may be drizzled over each piece as it is served.

Cherry-topped Refrigerator Cake

9×9×2-inch pan
6 to 9 servings

    14 whole graham crackers
    1 large package (5⅝ ounces) vanilla-flavor instant pudding mix
    2 cups cold milk (do not use unpasteurized milk*)
    1 cup Cool Whip, thawed
    1 can (21 ounces) cherry pie filling

Line pan with whole graham crackers, breaking crackers, if necessary, to fit. Prepare pudding mix

with milk as directed on package for pudding. Let stand 5 minutes, then blend in whipped topping. Spread half the pudding mixture over the crackers. Add another layer of crackers; top with remaining pudding mixture and remaining crackers. Spread cherry pie filling over top layer of crackers. Chill 3 hours or longer. Blueberry pie filling or 1 pint strawberry halves, brushed with currant jelly, may be used in place of cherry topping, if desired.

*Note: Raw milk contains an enzyme that reacts with this pudding mixture to produce a soapy taste.

Chocolate Soufflé

350 degrees F.
4 to 6 servings

    2 tablespoons butter
    1 tablespoon flour
    1 cup milk
    1 ounce baking chocolate, cut in pieces
    ⅓ cup sugar
    3 egg yolks
    1 teaspoon vanilla
    3 egg whites
    Whipped cream

Melt butter over medium heat and stir in the flour until well-blended. In a separate saucepan, heat but do not boil the milk, chocolate, and sugar. Add the hot milk mixture to the flour mixture, stirring constantly until well blended. Beat the egg yolks until light. Beat part of the sauce into the yolks, then add the yolk mixture to the rest of the sauce; stir the custard over low heat to thicken slightly. Add the vanilla. Cool.

Whip the egg whites until stiff but not dry. Beat one-third of the egg whites into chocolate mixture. Then fold remainder of egg whites lightly into mixture.

Use a straight-sided, 1-quart ovenproof baking dish. Grease the bottom and sides well with butter and then coat the buttered surfaces with a thorough dusting of powdered sugar. Set the soufflé dish in a pan of hot water. Pour in soufflé mixture, and bake about 20 minutes, or until firm. Serve at once with whipped cream.

This is a recipe that you put in the oven after you start to eat. Let the guests wait for the soufflé; do not try to keep soufflé waiting for guests.

Ribbon Jell-O

9×13×2-inch pan
18-24 servings

> 6 or 7 packages (3 ounces each) Jell-O in 6 or 7
>   different flavors and colors
> 1 pint sour cream
> ½ pint whipped topping

Add 1 cup boiling water to 1 package of Jell-O in a small stainless steel bowl; stir to dissolve. Pour half of Jell-O into a 9×13-inch pan and place on a level shelf in refrigerator to chill. Set the small metal bowl with the other half of the dissolved Jell-O into a larger bowl of ice. When the layer has set in the shallow pan, the gelatin over ice will be syrupy (it doesn't take long, since quantities are small). Add a heaping tablespoon of sour cream to the Jell-O in small bowl and beat until well mixed, using hand or electric beater. Pour this over the clear Jell-O in the shallow pan. Return to refrigerator; when set, repeat, using a contrasting color of Jell-O. Green (lime-flavor) is a good color for the first layer.

When the last layer has set, frost with a mixture of the remaining sour cream and the whipped topping. (Blending the two toppings gives them an excellent spreading consistency.) Keep dessert chilled. Cut in squares to serve.

Note: Each layer should be set only enough to hold the next layer. If set too hard, the layers will not bond well and may slip when served.

Molded Ambrosia

8 to 10 servings

> 1 package (3 ounces) orange-flavor gelatin
> ⅓ cup sugar
> 1 cup hot water
> 1 can (20 ounces) crushed pineapple, well drained
> 1 can (16 ounces) mandarin orange sections,
>   well drained
> 1 cup whipping cream
> 1 cup sour cream
> 1 teaspoon vanilla
> ½ cup flaked coconut

Combine gelatin and sugar, and dissolve in hot water. Chill until partially set. Add drained fruit, and return to refrigerator for a few minutes while whipping cream.

Whip cream; fold in sour cream and vanilla and

coconut. Fold whipped mixture into gelatin-fruit mixture. Pour into mold or attractive serving bowl. Chill. Garnish with a sprinkle of coconut or a few reserved orange sections, if desired.

Festive Fruit Salad Dessert

9×9×2-inch pan
9 servings

> 1 can (11 ounces) whole berry cranberry sauce
> 1 package (3 ounces) strawberry-flavor gelatin
> ½ cup boiling water
> 1 cup cold water
> 1 can (13½ ounces) pineapple tidbits
> ½ cup chopped nuts
> ½ cup diced celery
> Whipped cream (optional)

Crush cranberry sauce with fork. (Reserve a few berries for garnish.) Combine gelatin with boiling water and stir to dissolve completely. Add cold water. Add cranberry sauce and mix well. Refrigerate and allow to set until thick. Fold in pineapple, nuts, and celery; set until firm. Garnish with a dab of whipped cream and a whole cranberry, if desired.

Gourmet Fruit Delight

8 servings

> 1 can (16 ounces) pears or 1 pint home-canned pears
> 1 box (10 ounces) frozen raspberries or 1 pint box
>   (2 cups) fresh raspberries
> 2 oranges, peeled and sectioned, or 1 can (11 ounces)
>   Mandarin oranges, drained
> Grated peel from one orange (optional)
> 2 or 3 bananas, sliced
> ¼ cup brown sugar, sifted
> ½ pint sour cream

Purée pears with juice in blender, food mill, or food processor until smooth. Pour into bowl and fold in raspberries, orange sections, grated peel, and bananas. Pour into serving bowl and chill. Fold brown sugar into sour cream, or put sour cream into a small serving bowl and sift brown sugar over it. Serve fruit at the table into your prettiest sauce dishes, and pass sour cream mixture to be spooned over it as desired.

Easy Rote Grutze (Raspberry Fruit Soup)

4 to 6 servings (about 3½ cups)

    2 packages (10 ounces each) frozen red raspberries
    2 cups water
    ⅛ teaspoon salt
    1 tablespoon sugar
    1 teaspoon lemon juice
    ½ cup currant jelly
    1 small package (3 ounces) raspberry-flavor gelatin
    Cream

Simmer raspberries and water together for about 5 minutes (or until berries thaw). Press through sieve; then add salt, sugar, lemon juice, and currant jelly, and bring again to a boil. Add gelatin; stir to dissolve. Pour into serving bowl and chill about 3 hours. Serve with whipped cream, sour cream, or table cream as desired.

Orange Fruit Soup

5 or 6 servings

    2 tablespoons Minute Tapioca
    1½ cups water
    1 tablespoon sugar
    Dash of salt
    ½ cup frozen orange juice concentrate
    ½ cup diced orange sections
    1 can (8 ounces) pineapple chunks, drained
    1 medium banana, sliced
    5 or 6 fresh strawberries, sliced

Combine the tapioca and water in saucepan. Cook and stir over medium heat until mixture comes to a boil. Remove from heat. Add sugar, salt, and concentrated orange juice; stir to blend. Cool, stirring after 15 minutes. Cover and chill. Before serving, fold in orange sections, drained pineapple, and sliced banana. Garnish with the strawberries, if desired.

Heavenly Fresh Strawberry Dessert

5 or 6 servings

    1 quart fresh strawberries
    ⅔ cup sour cream
    ⅓ cup brown sugar
    Extra sour cream and brown sugar (optional)

Wash and hull strawberries. Drain thoroughly. If berries are large, slice them. Combine sour cream and brown sugar in a bowl. Add strawberries, and blend thoroughly but gently. Let stand to chill (about 1 hour). Spoon into serving dishes. If desired, top each serving with a dollop of sour cream and a sprinkle of brown sugar.

Rote Grutze (Fruit Soup)

5⅓ cups, or 10 to 12 servings

    4 cups each raspberries and red currants, or
        use any proportion of raspberries and currants
    2 cups water
    Dash of salt
    1½ cups sugar
    ½ cup Minute Tapioca
    Table cream

Wash and pick over raspberries and currants. Remove the big stems from currants. Add water, crush berries, and boil for about 10 minutes. Purée in blender or food processor. Strain to remove seeds. Put purée into a large kettle and add salt, sugar, and tapioca. Bring to a boil and cook about 5 minutes or until thick. Pour into a serving bowl and chill. Serve with cream.

Note: This is a very favorite dessert. When summer fruits are not available, it may be made with raspberry gelatin and red currant jelly. (See recipe below.) The name is German and means red fruit pudding. The red fruits—raspberries and currants—are the best combination. These fruits may also be juiced and canned together. One quart juice makes 8 to 10 servings. Keep a few quarts on hand for special occasions.

Yummy Cheesecake Pie

9×13×2-inch pan
350 degrees F.
12 to 15 servings

   ½ cup (¼ pound) butter
   1 cup flour
   2 tablespoons sugar
   ½ cup nuts, chopped fine
   1 package (8 ounces) cream cheese
   1 package (8 ounces) Cool Whip
   ½ cup powdered sugar
   1 package (3¾ ounces) vanilla pudding and
      pie filling (not instant)
   1 package (3¾ ounces) chocolate pudding and pie
      filling (not instant)
   3 cups milk (do not use unpasteurized milk*)

Cut butter into flour and sugar as for pie crust.
Add nuts. Pack and press into pan. Bake for 15 to 20
minutes. Remove from oven and cool thoroughly.

Soften cream cheese and blend well with 1 cup of
the Cool Whip and the powdered sugar. Set aside.

Combine the two puddings (chocolate lovers may
prefer to use one large package of chocolate pudding
and pie filling, omitting the vanilla pudding
entirely). Add milk and cook as package directs.
Remove from heat. Cover surface of cooked
pudding with plastic wrap to prevent a skin from
forming as pudding cools. Cool thoroughly.

To put Cheesecake Pie together: Spread cream cheese
mixture over cooled crust. On top of this, spread
cooled pudding. Top with additional Cool Whip or
whipped cream and decorate with shaved chocolate,
if desired.

*Raw milk contains an enzyme (which is inactivated when the milk is
pasteurized) that combines with the fat in non-dairy whipped topping to
produce a soapy flavor.*

Date Roll

8 servings

   ½ pound marshmallows, cut fine
   ½ pound walnuts, chopped
   ½ pound dates, cut fine
   1 tall can (14 ounces) evaporated milk
   ½ pound graham cracker meal
   1 cup cream, whipped

Combine marshmallows, walnuts, dates, and
evaporated milk; form a loaf, then roll in graham
cracker meal to completely cover loaf. Roll in heavy
waxed paper. Refrigerate overnight. Cut into slices.
Serve with whipped cream.

Broken-Glass Cake Dessert

2 9-inch pie plates, or 1 9-inch spring-form pan,
   or 3-quart mold
16 servings

   3 packages (3 ounces each) Jell-O, 3 different colors
   3 cups boiling water
   1½ cups cold water
   1 package (3 ounces) lemon-flavor Jell-O
   1 cup boiling water
   ¼ cup sugar
   ½ cup pineapple juice
   1½ cups graham cracker crumbs mixed with ⅓ cup
      melted butter, or use vanilla wafers or lady
      fingers to line pie pans
   2 cups whipping cream or 4 cups whipped
      topping, prepared according to package directions

Prepare the first three packages of Jell-O
separately, using 1 cup boiling water to dissolve
each. Add ½ cup cold water to each. Pour each
flavor into an 8-inch square pan (pie pans will do).
Chill until firm, or overnight.

Combine the lemon-flavor Jell-O and sugar; add
the remaining cup boiling water and stir until both
are dissolved. Stir in pineapple juice (apple juice is
also nice in this mixture). Chill until thickened but
not set.

In the meantime, prepare pans. If using pie pans,
line pans with broken vanilla wafers in bottom of
pan, whole wafers around edge (see photo, p. 139).
Or use lady fingers or graham cracker crumb mixture. If using spring-form pan, use the crumb mixture; line bottom and sides of pan, pressing well to
make a firm base.

Cut the firm gelatin into half-inch cubes. Blend
whipped topping (or whipped cream) with
thickened lemon Jell-O. Fold in cubed gelatin. Pour
into prepared pan. Chill at least 5 hours or overnight.

Surprise Fresh Fruit Treat

2 cups dressing (about 8 servings)

   1 carton (8 ounces) Cool Whip
   1 carton (8 ounces) raspberry yogurt
   Mixed fresh fruits, any combination desired

Blend Cool Whip with yogurt. Serve in dollops
over fresh fruit.

Broken-Glass Cake Dessert (p. 138), Ribbon Jell-O (p. 136) ▷

Warm Spicy Fruit

4 to 6 servings

12 ounces mixed dried fruits
½ cup raisins
4 cups water
2 cups orange juice or apple juice
1 tablespoon Minute Tapioca
¼ teaspoon salt
⅓ cup sugar
1 3-inch cinnamon stick
6 whole cloves

Combine all ingredients in a large saucepan. Simmer, covered, until fruits are tender (about 30 to 40 minutes). Remove cinnamon and cloves, and serve fruit hot or warm.

Canned Fruit Ambrosia

8 servings

1 can (20 ounces) pineapple tidbits or chunks
1 can (16 ounces) Mandarin orange sections
¼ cup maraschino cherries
½ cup flaked coconut

Drain all fruit. Arrange in an attractive serving bowl. Sprinkle with coconut.

Fruit Snack Squares

9×9×2-inch pan
18 servings, 1×2 inches each

½ cup butter or margarine
4 cups miniature marshmallows (32 large)
½ cup instant non-fat dry milk
¼ cup powdered orange breakfast drink (Tang)
1 cup raisins
1 cup dried apricots or peaches
4 cups oat cereal (Cheerios)

Melt butter and marshmallows over low heat. When melted, remove from heat and add dry milk and powdered orange drink. Stir in raisins, dried fruits, and cereal until all are coated with orange mixture. Press into buttered pan and cool. Cut into squares to serve.

Note: This is a tasty snack, excellent for packed or hike lunches because there is nothing to melt. For a nutritious breakfast, serve two 3-inch Fruit Snack Squares with a glass of milk.

Ruby (Raspberry) Sauce

1 cup sauce

1 package (10 ounces) frozen raspberries
2 to 4 tablespoons sugar
1 to 2 tablespoons water, if desired

Heat raspberries and sugar (use smaller amount when sauce is used with sweet fruits) in small saucepan until berries are thawed and juice flows. Purée in blender or food mill; strain to remove seeds.

Ruby Grapefruit

8 servings

4 large grapefruit
1 recipe Ruby Sauce

Peel and section grapefruit. Chill. To serve:
1. Pour undiluted Ruby Sauce over grapefruit sections in serving bowl. Serve 5 sections plus sauce in each individual serving dish.
2. Place 5 grapefruit sections in each individual serving dish. Spoon some of the sauce over each.

Ruby Strawberries

5 or 6 servings

1 quart fresh strawberries
1 recipe Ruby Sauce

Wash, hull, and drain strawberries. Depending on size, leave strawberries whole, cut them in half, or slice them into a serving bowl. (If strawberries are very tart, sprinkle with about ¼ cup sugar, or add sugar to taste.) Pour Ruby Sauce over berries, and chill. A topping of slivered almonds makes a festive addition.

Ruby Sherbet

6 servings

1 quart lemon sherbet
1 recipe Ruby Sauce

Place one large scoop lemon sherbet in each serving dish. Top with Ruby Sauce.

Peach Cardinale

8 servings

8 peach halves, fresh or canned
1 recipe Ruby Sauce
Whipped cream, if desired

To serve, place one peach half with cut side down in serving dish. Spoon on about 1 tablespoon Ruby Sauce. Garnish with a very small dollop of whipped cream or whipped topping. Puréed frozen strawberries are also very nice with peaches.

Apple Dumpling Roll

8×8×2-inch pan
375 degrees F.
6 to 9 servings

3½ cups coarsely shredded or thinly sliced
    tart apples
2 tablespoons sugar
½ cup water
¾ cup sugar
2 tablespoons lemon juice
1 tablespoon butter
1¼ cups flour
2 tablespoons sugar
3 teaspoons baking powder
¼ teaspoon salt
¼ cup shortening
1 egg, beaten
½ cup milk
½ cup brown sugar
Cinnamon

Combine apples, 2 tablespoons sugar, and ½ cup water. Boil 5 minutes. Drain apples; reserve syrup. Measure ¾ cup syrup. Add water if needed; pour syrup into baking pan. Stir in ¾ cup sugar, lemon juice, and butter. Place baking pan in preheated oven while preparing rolls.

In a large bowl, sift flour, sugar, baking powder, and salt. Cut in shortening to resemble coarse meal. Combine egg and milk. Add to flour mixture; stir with a fork. Transfer dough to a floured board, and pat or roll into 12×18-inch rectangle.

Spread dough with drained apples. Sprinkle with brown sugar and cinnamon. Roll, jelly-roll style; cut in 2-inch thick slices. Place in syrup in pan, cut side down. Bake 30 minutes, or until lightly browned. Serve warm or cold with table cream or Jiffy Lemon Sauce (below).

Jiffy Lemon Sauce

About 1¾ cups

½ cup sugar
2 tablespoons cornstarch
⅛ teaspoon salt
1 cup water
Grated rind from one lemon (about 1 teaspoon)
¼ cup lemon juice
2 tablespoons butter or margarine

Mix sugar, cornstarch, and salt in small saucepan. Add ¼ cup water and blend well. Add remaining water and bring to a boil, stirring constantly. Boil until thickened and clear. Remove from heat and add remaining ingredients. Serve warm.

Grandma's Fruit Cobbler

9×9×2-inch baking pan
400 degrees F.
9 servings

4 cups fruit, peeled, pitted, sliced
¾ to 1 cup sugar
2 to 3 tablespoons cornstarch
¼ to ½ cup water (depends on juiciness of fruit)
2 cups biscuit mix
⅔ cup milk
1 tablespoon sugar
Melted butter or margarine
Sugar
Cinnamon

Combine fruit, sugar, cornstarch, and water in saucepan. Heat to boiling and cook, stirring constantly until mixture is slightly thickened. Set aside.

Combine buscuit mix, milk, and sugar; stir to make a soft dough. Roll out on floured surface and cut into strips.

Place hot fruit mixture in baking pan. Place strips across the fruit mixture, overlapping slightly until entire surface is covered. Brush melted butter over strips; sprinkle with sugar and cinnamon. Bake 30 to 40 minutes, or until fruit is tender and crust is brown.

Suggested fruits: Peaches, apricots, cherries, nectarines, blueberries.

Baked Apples Tapioca

2-quart baking dish
375 degrees F.
6 to 8 servings

3 cups pared and sliced tart apples
2 tablespoons butter or margarine
¼ teaspoon cinnamon
⅓ cup Minute Tapioca
1 cup brown sugar, firmly packed
1 teaspoon salt
2½ cups water
1 to 2 tablespoons lemon juice

Arrange apples in greased baking dish. Dot with butter and sprinkle with cinnamon. Combine remaining ingredients in saucepan. Cook and stir over medium heat until mixture comes to a boil. Pour over apples. Cover and bake for 25 minutes, or until apples are tender. Stir. Serve warm or chilled, with cream, if desired.

Yummy Chocolate Mint

9×13×2-inch baking pan
12 servings

1 package (10 ounces) vanilla wafers, crushed
2 squares chocolate, melted
2 cups powdered sugar
½ cup (¼ pound) butter or margarine
2 eggs, separated
1 teaspoon vanilla
¼ teaspoon salt
½ cup chopped nuts
1 quart ice cream, softened

Grease baking pan; place half of the vanilla wafer crumbs in the bottom. Mix chocolate, sugar, butter, and egg yolks. Add vanilla and salt, and beat well. Beat egg whites until stiff, and fold into chocolate mixture. Spread chocolate mixture over crumbs. Cover with the chopped nuts. Spread softened ice cream on top. Sprinkle with remaining crumbs. Place in freezer. Remove from freezer 10 minutes before serving. Cut into squares to serve.

Almond Baked Peaches

325 degrees F.
6 servings

6 canned peach halves, drained (reserve syrup)
½ cup slivered toasted almonds
2 tablespoons honey
2 tablespoons lemon juice
½ teaspoon grated lemon rind
1 tablespoon butter
Whipped cream (optional)

Place peaches in baking dish, cavity side up. Sprinkle with almonds and honey. Boil peach syrup over high heat until reduced to 1 cup. Remove from heat; add lemon juice and rind. Pour syrup over peaches; dot with butter. Bake until peaches are hot and glazed. Serve hot or cold, topped with whipped cream, if desired.

Fresh Pears in Lemon-Butter Sauce

6 to 8 servings

6 to 8 fresh winter pears
½ cup sugar (scant)
1 cup water
2 tablespoons lemon juice
2 tablespoons butter

Peel, core, and cut pears in half. Make a syrup of the sugar and water. Boil 5 minutes. Add pears, lemon juice, and butter. Cover and simmer gently for 20 to 30 minutes, or until pears are translucent and fork-tender. Serve warm with the delicious juice.

Note: This recipe may be halved, doubled, or scaled up to feed a crowd.

Canned Pears in Lemon-Butter Sauce

Drain pears from any size can desired. Measure juice, and add lemon juice and butter in proportions listed above. Add pears; heat. The flavor isn't quite so good as with fresh pears, but this is an easy, change-of-pace way to serve pears.

Favorite Fruit Ice Cream

4-quart ice cream freezer
4 quarts

    3 cups sugar
    3 cups milk
    3 cups whipping cream or part whipping cream and
        part evaporated milk
    1 cup orange juice or pineapple juice
    ½ cup lemon juice
    3 mashed bananas

Dissolve sugar in milk and cream. Add fruit juices and bananas and freeze in ice cream freezer. Remove dasher and pack for easy serving. Let ripen up to 2 hours if desired.

For other fruit flavors, omit or reduce banana, then add a 16- to 20-ounce can crushed pineapple, or 3 cups apricot purée, or crushed peaches, or 2 cups crushed strawberries or raspberries. If sweetened frozen fruits are used, reduce sugar by about 1 cup (taste and adjust sweetness). If fresh fruit other than bananas is used, sprinkle half of sugar on crushed fruit first and allow to stand a few minutes before adding rest of sugar to milk-cream. (This is to avoid icy chunks of frozen fruit in the ice cream.)

Carita's Vanilla Ice Cream

4-quart freezer

    4 eggs
    2½ cups sugar
    1 pint whipping cream
    1 can (13 ounces) evaporated milk
    3 to 4 teaspoons vanilla*
    ½ teaspoon salt
    1 tablespoon flour
    Milk

In large bowl of electric mixer, beat eggs until very light and thick. Continue beating and add remaining ingredients, one at a time, except milk. Pour mixture into freezer can; then add milk up to the fill line. Assemble into freezer container; pack with ice and salt according to manufacturer's directions, and freeze.

Recipe may be halved to make 2 quarts; make 1½ times for a 6-quart freezer.

*Use vanilla to taste, but in general, the smaller amount if you use real vanilla extract, the larger amount for imitation vanilla. Don't forget that freezing dilutes the taste.

Buttermilk or Yogurt Pineapple Sherbet

8 servings

    2 cups buttermilk or plain yogurt
    ⅔ cup sugar
    1 cup crushed pineapple and juice
    1 teaspoon vanilla
    1 egg white

Mix buttermilk or yogurt, all but 2 tablespoons of the sugar, pineapple and juice, and vanilla. Partially freeze using eight parts ice to one part salt. Beat egg white until stiff; beat in remaining 2 tablespoons sugar. Add to partially frozen mixture and complete freezing.

Easy Fruit Frappé

12 to 14 servings

    1 quart vanilla ice cream
    1 quart pineapple sherbet
    1 or 2 packages (10 ounces each) frozen raspberries
    2 or 3 bananas, cut into small pieces

Soften ice cream and sherbet in refrigerator (just enough to mix; don't let them melt); mix well. Thaw raspberries just enough to separate. Fold raspberries, juice and all, and bananas into ice cream and sherbet mixture. This is best when served right after mixing, but it may be made ahead and refrozen. Bananas may darken if the mixture stands too long.

Lemon Cream Sherbet

4-quart ice cream freezer
4 quarts

    4 cups sugar
    2 quarts whole milk
    1 teaspoon lemon extract or finely grated lemon rind
    1 pint whipping cream or 1 cup whipping cream and
        1 cup evaporated milk
    1 cup lemon juice

Add sugar to milk, lemon extract, and cream. Stir until dissolved. Add lemon juice; stir. Freeze in hand-turned or electric freezer.

Ice-Box Lemon Cream Sherbet

About 1¼ quarts
6 servings

    1 cups sugar
    2 cups milk
    Grated rind from 1 lemon
    ½ cup lemon juice
    2 egg whites
    1 cup whipping cream
    Pinch of salt

Stir sugar into milk until dissolved. Add grated lemon rind and juice. Blend well. Freeze for one hour in two freezer trays (or use loaf pans or a Pyrex bowl), or until ice crystals form around edge.

Beat egg whites until stiff. Whip cream. Combine cream with egg whites; then add to frozen mixture in large bowl of electric mixer. Add salt. Beat just until the mixture is well blended. Return to freezer. Freeze for 3 hours, or until firm.

Cranberry Ice

Ice cream freezer or unsectioned refrigerator trays
8 to 9 cups

    1 pound fresh cranberries
    2 cups hot water
    2 teaspoons unflavored gelatin
    ¼ cup cold water
    2 cups sugar
    2 cups cold water
    ¼ cup lemon juice
    ½ cup orange juice (optional)
    2 teaspoons grated orange rind
    1 teaspoon grated lemon rind

Cook cranberries in 2 cups water. Press through sieve or food mill to remove skins. Sprinkle gelatin on ¼ cup cold water; let stand a few minutes; add to hot cranberry purée. Add rest of ingredients, and check for sweetness. Freeze in ice cream freezer or in refrigerator trays. When frozen in trays, turn into large bowl and beat with rotary beater until fluffy; return to trays for firming.

Candies

Caramel Corn No. 1

1½ cups sugar
1 cup brown sugar
¾ cup water
½ cup dark corn syrup
1½ cups raw peanuts
1 teaspoon salt
½ cup butter or margarine
1 teaspoon vanilla
1 teaspoon baking soda
4 quarts popped corn, warm

Combine sugars, water, and corn syrup in a large, heavy saucepan. Cook to 230 degrees F.* on candy thermometer. Then add peanuts. Cook to 280 degrees F.* Add salt and butter. Cook to 290 degrees F.* Remove from heat. Combine vanilla and baking soda and add to syrup.

Pour warm corn into a large pan, such as a dishpan. Pour syrup over corn, and stir quickly to coat all corn. Dump onto a slab and spread thin. When cool, break into pieces.

Note: Brazil nuts make a nice addition along with the peanuts.

See Index for Altitude Adjustments.

Caramel Corn No. 2

5 to 6 quarts popped corn, warm
1 cup corn syrup
¼ cup molasses
1 cup Eagle Brand sweetened condensed milk
1 tablespoon margarine
1 cup sugar
1 cup brown sugar

Place popcorn in warm oven while preparing coating. Boil all remaining ingredients to a firm soft-ball stage (about 236 degrees F.*), stirring constantly. Pour over popcorn in a large dishpan-type container. Stir to coat all kernels. Spread out on trays to cool. Break into pieces. Store in plastic bags in cool place.

See Index for Altitude Adjustments.

Easy Popcorn Balls

6 tablespoons light corn syrup
2 tablespoons butter or margarine
1 tablespoon water
½ cup miniature marshmallows
5 drops food coloring
1 cup powdered sugar
4 quarts unbuttered popcorn

Blend corn syrup, butter, and water in saucepan on medium heat. Stir until well blended. Add marshmallows; when melted, add food coloring and powdered sugar. Stir until all are dissolved and bubbling rapidly. Heat popcorn in a warm oven and place in a large dish or pan. Pour syrup slowly over popcorn, and mix with a wooden spoon until all is coated. With lightly buttered hands, shape coated popcorn into balls, if desired; or let cool and break into pieces and serve.

Peanut Brittle and Caramel Corn

Large saucepan

2 cups sugar
1 cup light corn syrup
½ cup hot water
2 to 3 cups raw Spanish peanuts
1 tablespoon butter or margarine
1 teaspoon vanilla
Pinch of salt
2 teaspoons baking soda

Heat sugar, corn syrup, and water, stirring until sugar is completely dissolved. Cook to long-thread or soft-ball stage (about 236 degrees F.*). Add peanuts. Continue cooking, stirring with long-handled wooden spoon until syrup is a light golden color and gives a hard crack test in cold water (about 290 degrees F.*). Remove from heat. Stir in butter, vanilla, and salt (candy will spatter a little). Add soda and stir quickly and well (candy will foam up). Quickly pour and spread onto a very large buttered baking sheet. When cool, turn brittle over and hit lightly with knife handle to break into pieces.

For thin brittle: spread as thin as possible when

pouring. Use 2 large baking sheets. Cool slightly. Wet hands with water, or wear clean gloves to avoid burning fingers as you stretch hot brittle to desired thinness by gingerly pulling and releasing it.

See Index for Altitude Adjustments.

Caramel Corn

    4 to 6 quarts popped corn
    Hot Peanut Brittle (above)

Heat popcorn in large roasting pan in 325 degree F. oven while brittle is cooking (peanuts in brittle recipe may be omitted or reduced, if desired). Pour hot brittle over hot popcorn, distributing brittle somewhat evenly and tossing quickly to mix. Use 2 long-handled wooden spoons for tossing. Beware of hot brittle. Drop by clusters on Formica surface or waxed paper.

Caramels

7½ × 11-inch metal pan

    2 cups sugar
    1¼ cups white corn syrup
    3 cups heavy cream, or 1 cup heavy cream and 2
        cups half and half*
    1 cup coarsely chopped nuts (pecans, walnuts, or
        whole filberts are nice), optional

Combine sugar, corn syrup, and 1 cup of cream in a heavy pan. Heat slowly and stir constantly until it starts to boil. Cook to soft-ball stage (236 degrees F.**). Add second cup of cream and cook to soft-ball stage; then add the third cup of cream and cook to firm-ball stage (248 degrees F.**). Stir just occasionally during the cooking of the first two cups of cream. With the third cup of cream, stir constantly until a firm ball is formed in cold water. Add nuts. Butter the pan, and scrape the caramel into it. When cold, cut around edges of pan to loosen caramel; then turn pan upside down and strike hard to release candy onto cutting board. Cut candy into squares, and wrap in waxed paper.

Be sure cream is fresh, or the mixture will tend to curdle.
**See Index for Altitude Adjustments.*

Rocky Road Fudge

9×9×2-inch pan
About 80 1-inch pieces

    5 to 8 large marshmallows, cut into fourths
    ¼ pound butter or margarine
    1 small package (6 ounces) chocolate chips
    2 cups sugar
    ¾ cup evaporated milk (or use small can and make
        up the measure with whole milk or light cream)
    10 large marshmallows
    1 cup nuts
    ½ teaspoon vanilla

Place cut marshmallows on a tray and freeze. In a large bowl cut the butter into the chocolate chips. Set aside. Bring to a boil in a heavy 3-quart saucepan the sugar, evaporated milk, and the 10 large marshmallows. Boil and stir rapidly (this burns easily) for 5 minutes. Pour over chocolate and butter. Stir until mixture starts to thicken. Add nuts, vanilla, and frozen cut marshmallows. Pour into buttered pan. Place in refrigerator to set. Cut into pieces and serve.

Southern-style Divinity

2-quart heavy saucepan
3 to 4 dozen pieces

    2½ cups sugar
    ½ cup light corn syrup
    ½ cup water
    ¼ teaspoon salt
    2 egg whites
    1 teaspoon vanilla
    ¼ to ½ cup chunky-style peanut butter

Heat sugar, corn syrup, water, and salt over low heat, stirring constantly until sugar dissolves. Boil to 260 degrees F.* or hard-ball stage. Pour in thin stream over stiffly beaten egg whites, beating all the time at high speed. Continue beating until mixture holds its shape when a spoonful is placed on waxed paper. Add vanilla and peanut butter; stir in gently but quickly. Drop with a swirl on waxed paper as individual candies, or pour into a lightly buttered pan. Cut pan candies into pieces. Store in a covered container.

See Index for Altitude Adjustments.

Top row: Caramel Corn No. 1 (p. 145), Honey Butter (p. 103), Molasses Refrigerator Muffins (p. 94); center row: Pulled Butter Mints (p. 148), Brownie Drops (p. 123), Snowballs (p. 127); bottom row: Orange Nut Bread (p. 93), Noels (p. 126), Fudge Nut Crunch (p. 148)

Easy Chocolate Logs or Nuggets

2 cups powdered sugar
1 can (14 ounces) sweetened condensed milk
1 package (14 ounces) flaked coconut
1 teaspoon vanilla
1 package (12 ounces) chocolate chips

Mix sugar, sweetened condensed milk, coconut, and vanilla together. Form into long rolls about the diameter of a nickel. The mixture will be sticky, so use waxed paper in forming the rolls. Freeze until firm. When ready to dip, melt the chocolate chips in a double boiler. Cut the frozen rolls into 1-inch logs or ½-inch nuggets and place on a fork. Lower the candy into the chocolate mixture and coat the entire piece. Place on a cooling rack to harden.

Variations: Vary the chocolate flavors by using semisweet chocolate chips or milk chocolate or mint-flavored chips. A nut half may be placed on the top of each log and dipped along with the candy. Finely chopped nuts or candied fruit may be added to the coconut mixture.

Fudge Nut Crunch

8×8×2-inch pan
1 pound candy

½ cup finely chopped nuts
¾ cup brown sugar, firmly packed
½ cup butter
1 package (6 ounces) chocolate chips

Sprinkle nuts over bottom of lightly greased pan. Combine sugar and butter in medium saucepan; bring to a rolling boil, stirring constantly. Continue boiling 4 to 5 minutes or to a temperature of 270 degrees F.* on candy thermometer. Pour cooked mixture over nuts in pan. Sprinkle top with chocolate chips. Cover for 2 minutes; then evenly spread chips. Chill until topping is firm. Remove from pan and break or cut into pieces.

See Index for Altitude Adjustments.

Pulled Butter Mints

3 cups sugar
1 cup water
½ cup (¼ pound) butter
Green food color
1 teaspoon Schilling's pure mint flavoring

In a heavy saucepan, combine the sugar, water, and butter; mix well. Place on medium heat; don't stir after mixture starts to heat. Cook with lid on until mixture boils. Take lid off and cook to 248 degrees F.* on candy thermometer. Wash crystals down three or four times. At 248 degrees F.* add 2 drops green color. Cook to 258 degrees F.*

Pour out candy to cool on a greased marble slab. Pour on mint flavoring. Let cool to lukewarm. Roll jelly-roll fashion. Pick up in hands and pull like taffy until desired consistency. Stretch into a rope about 1 inch in diameter onto a board covered with cornstarch. Cut immediately into 1-inch pieces (if candy gets hard, you can't cut it). Let stand on board to dry about an hour. Store in can with tight-fitting lid to ripen (about 12 to 24 hours).

Variation: Use yellow color instead of green, rum extract instead of mint.

See Index for Altitude Adjustments.

Peanut Butter Cups

3 dozen cups

3 tablespoons butter or margarine
1 cup powdered sugar
1 teaspoon vanilla
½ cup peanut butter
½ cup chopped nuts (optional)
1 cup milk chocolate morsels

Mix butter, powdered sugar, vanilla, peanut butter, and nuts together. Shape into balls, using 1½ teaspoon mixture for each. Chill for 15 minutes. Melt chocolate over hot water, stirring constantly until just melted. Using a fork or small spoon, dip each ball into the chocolate until it is coated. Set on a rack or pie plate to cool until firm.

Peanut Butter Chews

1 cup peanut butter
1 cup honey
1 cup raisins (optional)
1 to 2 cups instant nonfat dry milk

Combine peanut butter and honey and blend well. Add raisins, if desired. Add enough instant nonfat dry milk to make a consistency that will cut with a knife and hold its shape. Press into a greased cake pan or pie plate and chill. Cut into squares to serve, or cut into fancy shapes for holiday or party treats.

Apricot Peanut Granola

15×10×1-inch jelly-roll pan
300 degrees F.
7 cups

3 cups old-fashioned oats
½ cup wheat germ
1 cup flaked coconut
¼ cup oil
¼ cup honey
1 cup peanuts
1½ cups dried apricots, cut into small pieces
½ cup sunflower nuts

Combine oats, wheat germ, and coconut in a large bowl. Heat oil and honey to just below boiling point. Pour over oat mixture, tossing to coat thoroughly. Spread mixture evenly in jelly-roll pan.

Roast at 300 degrees F. for 30 minutes, stirring occasionally until mixture is lightly browned. Remove from oven; mix in with peanuts, apricots, and sunflower nuts. Cool. Store in tightly covered container.

Spiced Nuts

1 cup sugar
5 tablespoons water
1 tablespoon cinnamon
1 teaspoon vanilla
3 cups large pecan halves

Bring all ingredients, except nuts, to a boil, and cook to soft-ball stage (about 236 degrees F.*). Remove from heat, and stir in nuts. Let cool.

*See Index for Altitude Adjustments.

Canning and Preserving

Home-canned Apple Pie Filling

2 quarts or 4 pints

> 1½ cups sugar
> 2½ cups water
> 4 teaspoons commercial ascorbic or citric acid
>   mixtures (Fruit Fresh, etc.)
> 2 quarts (8 cups) sliced and peeled apples*
> 6 tablespoons cornstarch
> ¼ teaspoon salt
> ½ cup lemon juice (necessary only when using
>   Red and Yellow Delicious varieties)

Dissolve 1 cup sugar in 2 cups water by heating gently. Cool; add ascorbic or citric acid mixture.

Peel and slice apples ¼ inch thick into the sugar-water-acid solution. Gently boil the apples in the solution for 5 minutes. Remove from heat and let the apple mixture sit for 10 minutes.

Combine the remaining ½ cup sugar, cornstarch, and salt. Mix with ½ cup water until a smooth paste is formed. Slowly add this paste to the apple mixture and stir just enough to disperse the starch throughout. Stir in lemon juice, if needed.

Bring the apple filling to a boil and hold for 1 minute. Immediately put into jars. Place lids, and secure on bands firmly. Process in a boiling water bath or steam canner for 40 minutes at sea level (add 2 minutes of processing time for each 1000 feet above sea level). (Recipe courtesy of Utah State University Extension.)

Note: The initial 1 cup sugar may be increased or decreased by ¼ cup without affecting the processing time. To avoid an unsafe product, do not change the other proportions in the recipe. Do not attempt to double or triple the recipe.

Apple varieties: Jonathan, McIntosh, Granny Smith, Red Delicious, and Yellow Delicious.

Home-canned Sour Cherry Pie Filling

2 quarts

> 2 quarts (8 cups) sour pie cherries, pitted
> 2½ cups sugar
> 2½ cups water
> 6 tablespoons cornstarch
> ¼ teaspoon salt

Combine pitted cherries with 2 cups sugar and 2 cups water. Boil gently without stirring for 5 minutes, or until foaming ceases. Remove from heat. Combine remaining ½ cup water and ½ cup sugar, cornstarch, and salt. Mix until cornstarch is well dispersed. Add to the cooked cherries; stir just enough to distribute starch into cherries. Bring to a gentle boil and hold for 1 minute.

Pour while boiling into hot jars to within 1 inch of top. Place lids, and screw on bands firmly. Immediately place into a boiling water bath or steam canner and process for 30 minutes at sea level (add 2 minutes processing time for each 1000 feet above sea level). (Recipe courtesy of Utah State University Extension.)

Green Tomato Mincemeat

5 to 6 quarts

> 3 pounds green tomatoes (about 9 medium)
> 3 pounds tart apples (about 9 medium)
> 8 cups brown sugar, or use part granulated
> 2 pounds (4 cups) raisins
> 1 cup finely ground suet or ¾ cup margarine
> 2 tablespoons salt
> 2 tablespoons cinnamon
> 1 teaspoon cloves
> 1 teaspoon nutmeg
> 1 cup cider vinegar

Grind tomatoes. Drain and measure juice; add water equal to amount of juice. Set aside. Scald and drain tomatoes twice; discard water. Grind, or chop fine, the apples. Add to the tomatoes, along with reserved juice mixture, brown sugar, raisins, and suet. Cook over medium heat until clear, stirring occasionally. Add salt, spices, and vinegar. Cook to desired thickness. Pack in hot 1-quart canning jars. Place lids, and screw bands on tight. Process in water bath or steam canner for 25 minutes, making altitude adjustments as necessary. Use one quart jar for each "mince" pie.

◁ *Suet Biscuits (p. 95), Old-fashioned Tomato Preserves (p. 154)*

Maraschino Cherries

4 pints

    10 cups Royal Anne or other firm light cherries
    1 tablespoon alum
    ¼ cup salt
    7 cups sugar
    1 ounce red food color (or green, if desired)
    1 teaspoon almond extract

Wash and pit cherries. Drain before measuring. Dissolve alum and salt in 2 quarts cold water. Add cherries. Let stand about 6 hours. (If cherries float, cover with plate weighed down with a jar filled with water.) Drain and rinse cherries.

Add sugar to 2 cups fresh water; cook until sugar dissolves. Add cherries; boil 2 minutes. Remove from heat. Add food color and extract. Let stand in a cool place 18 to 24 hours. Return to heat and boil another 2 minutes. Pour, boiling hot, into hot jars. Adjust lids, and process in boiling water bath or steam canner for about 5 minutes at sea level (add one minute for each 1000 feet above sea level), to assure sterile seal.

Raspberry Jam from Green Tomatoes

6 to 8 jelly glasses or jars

    5 cups ground or finely chopped green tomatoes
    5 cups sugar
    ¼ cup lemon juice
    1 package (6 ounces) raspberry-flavor Jell-O
    1 package (10 ounces) frozen raspberries (optional)

Mix tomatoes, sugar, and lemon juice; boil 5 minutes, stirring often. Remove from heat; add Jell-O and stir until dissolved. Pour into scalded glasses or jars. Seal with melted wax or canning lids, processing about 5 minutes in boiling water bath to assure sterile seal if canning jars are used. If frozen raspberries are used, add after tomato mixture has boiled 5 minutes; then boil an additional 2 minutes. This jam seems thin as poured, but it thickens on standing. Once opened, store jam covered in refrigerator.

Pickled Beets

About 4 quarts

    4 quarts small to medium beets, tops removed and
        scrubbed well
    4 cups vinegar
    2 cups water
    2½ cups sugar
    2 teaspoons allspice
    1 3-inch stick whole cinnamon
    ½ teaspoon whole cloves
    1 to 2 teaspoons salt

Cook beets until just tender. Slip off skins. Combine vinegar, water, sugar, spices (tied in a bag), and salt. Simmer 15 minutes. Add beets and simmer 5 minutes longer. Pack beets in hot canning jars. Bring syrup to a boil; remove spice bag, then pour syrup over beets. If you run a little short of syrup, fill jar with hot vinegar. Adjust lids and seal. Process in water bath or steam canner 30 minutes. See Altitude Adjustment (Index).

Fresh-Pack Dill Pickles

7 to 8 quarts

    18 pounds 3- to 5-inch cucumbers (about)
    1½ cups salt (not iodized)
    8 quarts water
    1½ quarts white vinegar
    ¾ cup salt (not iodized)
    ¼ cup sugar (optional)
    2½ quarts water
    2 tablespoons whole pickling spice, tied loosely in
        cheesecloth bag
    Dill heads, fresh or dried
    Whole mustard seed
    1 hot red pepper

Scrub cucumbers well. Mix 1½ cups salt and 8 quarts water in a large crock or canning kettle. Stir to dissolve; then add the cucumbers and let soak overnight. Drain.

Combine vinegar, ¾ cup salt, sugar, 2½ quarts water, and pickling spice. Heat to boiling. Pack cucumbers into hot quart canning jars. To each jar add 3 dill heads (more, if desired), 2 teaspoons mustard seed, and a small piece of hot red pepper. Remove spice bag from boiling vinegar mixture, and pour syrup over cucumbers, leaving ½ inch head space. Adjust lids. Process in boiling water bath or steam canner for 20 minutes. See Altitude Adjustment (Index).

Fresh-Pack Dilly Beans

24 pints

    10 pounds beans (Blue Lake pole beans are
        especially good)
    2 large bunches dried dill
    1 large bulb of garlic
    1 hot red pepper
    3 quarts vinegar
    3 quarts water
    1 cup salt

Fill jars with straight small to medium beans. Divide dill among the jars. To each, add 1 small clove garlic and a very small piece of red pepper.

Heat vinegar and water with salt. Pour boiling liquid over beans, filling jar to ½ inch from top. Adjust lids, and process in water bath or steam canner for 10 minutes. See Altitude Adjustment (Index).

Penny's Plum or Peach Chutney

3 or 4 ½-pint jars

    ¾ cup sugar
    ¾ cup brown sugar
    ¾ cup cider vinegar
    1¼ teaspoons crushed dry red peppers
    1 teaspoon salt
    2 teaspoons mustard seed
    2 cloves garlic, thinly sliced
    1 small onion, thinly sliced
    ½ cup candied ginger, thinly sliced
    1 cup seedless white raisins (dark may be used)
    1 quart (about 2 dozen) fresh purple plums, halved
        and pitted, or 1 quart firm fresh peaches,
        peeled, pitted, and sliced

Mix sugars and vinegar in kettle and bring to a boil. Add remaining ingredients except fruit and mix well. Then stir in fruit. Simmer until slightly thickened—about 50 minutes—stirring occasionally and gently. Fill hot sterilized jars with hot chutney. Process in boiling water bath or steam canner about 5 minutes to seal. Store in cool, dark place.

Delicious Sweet Pickles

    100 small pickling cucumbers
    1 cup pickling salt (non-iodized)
    1 gallon water
    1 quart vinegar
    1 quart water
    1 tablespoon alum
    1 teaspoon turmeric
    7 cups sugar
    1½ quarts vinegar
    3 tablespoons pickling spice

Step 1: Scrub cucumbers in cool water. Put into a crock, stainless steel pan, or enamel pan (about 5-gallon size). Make a solution of the salt and 1 gallon water, and pour over cucumbers. Let stand 8 days. If cucumbers float, hold them down with a plate that fits into container and a weight (a rock or a sturdy plastic bag filled with water). Drain off salt solution. Wash cucumbers thoroughly and replace in washed crock.

Step 2: Pour over cucumbers a boiling solution of 1 quart vinegar, 1 quart water, and alum. Let stand 3 days; then drain off solution and wash again. Cut cucumbers as desired (in fourths lengthwise, or leave whole if they are small enough).

Step 3: Replace cucumbers in crock and pour over them a boiling syrup of turmeric, 5 cups of the sugar, 1½ quarts vinegar, and pickling spice. Let stand 3 days. Drain, but save the syrup and reheat. Add remaining sugar. Pour over cucumbers. Repeat the draining and reheating of syrup for 4 days. On the fourth day pack drained cucumbers into canning jars. Pour boiling syrup over them in the jars. Seal jars, and process them for 10 minutes in boiling water bath or steam canner.

If you should run short of syrup to cover cucumbers (the amount needed will vary somewhat, depending on size of cucumber), make up a bit more using same proportions of vinegar and sugar. Taste for sweetness and spice level.

Old-fashioned Tomato Preserves

3 pints, or 5 or 6 8-ounce glasses

    4 cups prepared tomatoes
    4 cups sugar
    ¼ cup lemon juice
    ½ teaspoon butter or margarine
    ½ lemon, thinly sliced, with slices halved or
        quartered (optional)
    1 pouch Certo (liquid fruit pectin)

Skin tomatoes; cut in wedges, about 8 to a tomato. Remove large seed pods and the watery juice that forms. (You can accomplish this to some extent by letting tomatoes drain in a collander as you prepare them.) Measure 4 cups into a large kettle. Add sugar, lemon juice, and butter. Bring rapidly to a boil, and boil hard for 20 to 30 minutes, or until well thickened. Add lemon slices during last few minutes of cooking. Remove from heat and add Certo. Stir well; then pack hot into canning jars. Secure lids, and process in boiling water bath or steam canner for 10 minutes, to assure sterile seal.

Garden Relish

6 pints

    4 large carrots
    8 medium onions
    2 large heads cabbage
    3 red peppers
    6 green peppers
    ½ cup salt
    3 pints (6 cups) white vinegar
    6 cups sugar
    2 tablespoons celery seed
    2 tablespoons mustard seed

Chop carrots, onions, cabbage, and peppers by putting them through the fine blade of a food chopper or using a food processor. Add salt and let stand about 3 hours. Drain thoroughly. Add remaining ingredients. Spoon into jars; cover with tight-fitting lids. Store in cool place. Relish will keep in the refrigerator for several months.

Note: This relish is a wonderful accompaniment for roast beef, ham, hamburger, or most other meats.

Easy Chili Sauce

6½ pints

    Prepared tomatoes to make 4 quarts
        (about 10 pounds)
    4 green peppers
    4 sweet red peppers
    1 hot pepper, if desired
    6 medium yellow onions
    ½ cup non-iodized salt
    1 cup brown sugar
    2 cups sugar
    3 cups cider vinegar
    ½ teaspoon each cinnamon, allspice, cloves,
        nutmeg, paprika, cayenne pepper

Scald, then peel tomatoes; cut in quarters, or eighths if tomatoes are large. (We like to remove at least part of the seeds at this point, but this is the tedious part of the preparation, and it isn't necessary.)

Remove seeds and veins from peppers and grind with onions fairly fine. Mix peppers and onions with the tomatoes in a large stainless steel or enamel bowl. (Don't use aluminum.) Sprinkle with salt. Let stand overnight or several hours. Stir well; then drain off most of the juice through a collander. Put drained tomato mixture in large preserving kettle or 6-quart Dutch oven. Add remaining ingredients.

Bring to boil over medium heat, stirring occasionally, and boil gently for about 30 minutes or to desired thickness. Stir often so that mixture won't stick and burn. Pour hot sauce into 1-pint canning jars; seal and process in boiling water bath or steam canner or steamer for 5 minutes.

Note: Eight green peppers may be used, but the color of the finished product won't be as nice as with half red peppers.

Canned Trout

Pressure canner

Skin fish; cut in pieces to fit, and pack in pint jars. To each jar add:

1 teaspoon sugar
1 teaspoon salt
1 teaspoon lemon juice
1 teaspoon vinegar
½ teaspoon liquid smoke (optional)
1 teaspoon butter
1 1-inch square bacon

Do *not* fill jars with liquid. Fit lids and seal; then follow directions for fish in pressure canner manual. Process at 12 pounds pressure for 100 minutes (1 hour 40 minutes). Canned trout may be used in the same ways as canned tuna or salmon.

Note: Be aware of your state fish and game laws before you lay in a great supply of trout. In Utah, for example, it is illegal to have more than 8 fish per license in your possession.

Meet Together Often

Large Party Meals

Whether you're preparing for a ward banquet or a picnic, a Relief Society luncheon, or a punch-and-cookies reception, cooking for a crowd almost always assumes larger-than-life proportions to the person responsible for the food to be served. How to take such an assignment in stride is the purpose of this section, which is dedicated to all who are about to plan, prepare, and serve a meal to a large group, whether Church, family, club, or other social situation.

Responsibilities of Food Chairman or Committee

1. Plan the menu.
2. Buy the food and/or arrange for it to be furnished.
3. Take care of food purchased, including cleaning and storage.
4. Schedule the jobs to be done.
5. Check the kitchen equipment.
6. Plan for table settings and decorations.
7. Plan for food service.
8. Take care of leftover food and borrowed equipment.
9. Plan for cleanup of dishes and kitchen.

Begin with the Menu

1. Keep the menu simple. Be sure you can handle it.
2. Select foods that are familiar and popular with most people, that are easy to prepare and do not require a lot of last-minute preparation, and that can be held awhile without losing their attractiveness.
3. Plan for foods that can be divided into units and assigned out for different cooks to prepare in their own homes. Then give each a well-written recipe that includes notes, descriptions, and safeguards so that results will be reasonably the same.
4. Utilize good buys and economies: fruits and vegetables in season, meat and poultry specials, home-made items rather than store-bought when possible.

Think Safety

A gala occasion that ends with food poisoning becomes an unhappy occasion indeed. It can happen so easily unless basic sanitation rules are rigidly adhered to. Food poisoning is likely to occur under three conditions:
1. Food stands too long in a warm kitchen.
2. Food goes into the refrigerator as it should, but the refrigerator is so overloaded that it can't keep the food cool, or storage containers are so large that the center never gets cold.
3. Food has not been kept at a temperature cool enough and is not then heated enough (or is heated too slowly) to destroy any bacteria that have begun to grow.

To avoid the possibility of food poisoning, adhere strictly to the following guidelines:
1. All food workers must be scrupulously clean themselves, and must adhere to cleanliness in their work habits. This means a clean, sanitary kitchen to work in, clean dishes and working tools, and scrubbed hands.
2. Refrigerator temperatures must be maintained at 40 degrees or below.
3. Perishable foods that must have careful attention are poultry, meat, fish, mayonnaise, milk, and cream, and mixtures containing any of these ingredients. None of these should be allowed to stand at room temperature.
4. Hot, soapy water should be used for washing all dishes—and scalding water for rinsing.
5. All food should be covered with plastic wrap or bags, foil, or lids.
6. Anyone with a skin infection or cold should never be allowed to handle food.

The Relief Society Luncheon

Month in and month out, for more years than most of us even remember, Relief Society sisters have socialized at this special function. Thousands of devoted women the world over have cooked delicious meals, either at home or in church kitchens, searching out special recipes that have quickly passed from one group to another.

Along with other measures to streamline the

Relief Society luncheon fare: Golden Summer Punch (p. 11), Pulled Butter Mints (p. 148), Date-Nut Pinwheel Sandwich (p. 10), Ribbon Sandwich (p. 9), fresh fruit, Brownie (p. 129)

work, economize, and keep things in proportion, fewer Relief Society luncheons are now held and they are usually much simpler. They are still important, however, not only to bring the sisters closer together, but to serve as a teaching tool for younger members who may still be learning how to plan, prepare, and serve wholesome, economical meals.

Guidelines for a Luncheon

The photo on page 156 illustrates food for a typical Relief Society social. You might be more imaginative, but this photo is meant to illustrate some basic points if you would make the food for your luncheon memorable.

1. Keep the meal service simple and attractive.

2. Make the food look attractive and dainty.

3. Present food that tantalizes rather than stuffs. Don't overload the plates. A one- or two-inch brownie square eaten in two bites will do more to satisfy than a serving that satiates.

4. A fruit salad is a popular favorite. Combine any fruits that please, and try to include at least one fresh fruit in season. Recipes for a variety of fruit salads and dressings are found in *The Mormon Family Cookbook,* or serve a plain dish of fruits or fruited gelatin. In the photo we have shown a salad made entirely of fresh fruits because the photo was taken "in the season thereof."

5. Provide something that is not sweet. We have shown two sandwiches—a Ribbon Sandwich and a Pinwheel (see Index). Small rye loaves would do well with any favorite spread, or fruit and nut loaves may be sliced thin and spread with cream cheese.

6. A tray or bowl of vegetables, cut in sticks, slices, or flowerets, is colorful and nutritious. Raw vegetables are especially popular with a variety of dips.

7. While paper service saves work, paper products are expensive. The time you save in dishwashing may be consumed in hunting for the plates in the color and quality you need to keep the luncheon service pretty and dainty. But using just any old paper plate or cup may spoil the effect you are attempting to accomplish. So if you must use paper plates and cups, try to select some that enhance the mood and decor of the luncheon.

Dividing the Work

In the next section are menu suggestions with recipes that divide well for assignment to individual committee members. Some of the menus are more elaborate for special occasions, and, of course, they would adapt well for family entertaining as well as group functions. Some are seasonal; others may be "taste-test" sessions following a food demonstration.

While each suggested menu should provide a complete, satisfying meal, if a heavier meal is desired, you may add a vegetable, salad, or beverage. Quantities of each item, determination of where and how each is to be prepared, and assignments to be made will have to be adapted to your individual situation. (See "Guide for Buying and Cooking for Large Groups.")

When working with a committee, decide whether to have a few members make up quantity recipes or many members to make up only one recipe—one cake or pie, one batch of bread, one casserole, and so on. Usually a compromise is in order. The committee may not be large enough for the one-batch approach; on the other hand, home-size equipment and utensils are generally not adequate for the recipe that makes 100 servings, so the amount must be divided up.

To illustrate, let's take a typical luncheon menu to serve 50.

> Creamed Chicken and Mushrooms
> Crispy Cornbread
> Holiday Waldorf Salad
> Fresh Pears in Lemon-Butter Sauce

The recipe for Creamed Chicken and Mushrooms (see Index) makes 6 1-cup servings, but it can easily be doubled. Four times the double recipe would stretch to make 50 servings. This would be difficult to handle in one batch under normal home-use conditions. White sauce cooked in large amounts thickens very slowly, even when the milk is scalding hot to start. If it is stirred too much, it will often thin out. Scorching is also a danger. Thus, it would be well to have four people make one double recipe each or two people make two double batches each. Rewrite the recipe, doubling all ingredients, before assigning the work; otherwise it is too easy to make mistakes.

Crispy Cornbread, with or without bacon added, makes an easy and delicious base for the creamed chicken. One recipe makes a $9 \times 13 \times 2$-inch pan of cornbread, which can be cut into 4 rows across and 6 down, for 24 servings. One person might easily make the double recipe needed, baked in two pans.

For the Waldorf Salad, one person could make the entire recipe if the apples aren't to be peeled. (Red apples with skin left on are very attractive.) For the Pears in Lemon-Butter Sauce, it would be well to have at least two persons each prepare a recipe to feed 25. Allow one small pear per person. Twenty-five pears for one person to peel is quite enough.

Menu Suggestions

Following are 14 additional menus, with recipes found in *The Mormon Family Cookbook.* Check Index for page numbers.

Menu 1

Chicken Custard Casserole
Raw Cranberry Relish
Easy Pan Rolls
Poppy Seed Cake

Menu 2

Chicken Noodle Soup
Hot Buttered Saltines
Yummy Cheesecake Pie

Menu 3

Three-Bean Salad
Bran Muffins
Apple Dumpling Roll with Lemon Sauce

Menu 4

Tomato Bouillon
Layered "Masked" Salad
Butterflake Rolls
Carrot Cake

Menu 5

Wonderful Wassail
Ham Slice
Easy Baked Beans
Arlean's Molasses Refrigerator Muffins
Easy Fruit Frappé

Menu 6

Ham and Asparagus Roll-ups
with Mustard Sauce
Golden Yam Rolls
Jellied Fruit Salad
Cherry-topped Refrigerator Cake

Menu 7

Molded Shrimp Salad
Cornmeal Refrigerator Rolls
Baked Apples Tapioca

Menu 8

Tuna-Vegetable Casserole
Cheese Straws
Rote Grutze (Fruit Soup)

Menu 9

Beef-Vegetable-Noodle Casserole
Elegant Bran Bread
Lemon Cream Sherbet

Menu 10

Salad Bar
Cheese Straws
Apple Crisp

Menu 11

French Onion Soup
with Cheese and Bread Topping
Tropical Fruit Pudding
Oatmeal Crisps

Menu 12

Yam and Sausage Skillet
Easy Pan Rolls
Molded Sour Cream and Cucumber Salad
Brownies

Menu 13

Beef Enchilada Casserole
with
Lettuce and Tomatoes
Picnic Cake

Menu 14

Turkey Pies
Pineapple-Grapefruit Salad
Applesauce Cake

Church Dinners

For a large function where upwards of several hundred are to be served, it is better to serve meat that is easy to handle, such as ham, beef, or turkey, or a portion-controlled dish, such as fried chicken or Swiss steak. For a less formal occasion, a casserole, such as lasagna, baked beans, or meatballs, would be suitable. Or you may prefer to serve a supper from the soup kettle: chili, spaghetti, soups, stews, or even beef Stroganoff.

Some of the quantity recipes in this section are adapted from a set of booklets titled *Feeding a Crowd*, published by General Foods Corporation. They were developed especially to help people who need to adapt basic cookery to feeding larger groups than they are accustomed to, but using home-size cooking utensils and equipment. All of the recipes were thoroughly tested in General Foods Kitchens; in addition, many have been use-tested by General Foods home economists in actual church, club, and social group situations. We have made recipe changes only to adapt them to our Mormon culture and have used them as the basis for our own menu suggestions.

Turkey Pies for a Crowd

75 to 100 individual pies

    1 25-pound or larger turkey
    Tart-size pie crusts
    2½ gallons turkey broth
    3 tablespoons Worcestershire sauce
    2 to 3 tablespoons Kitchen Bouquet gravy browner
    2 tablespoons rubbed sage
    6 to 8 potatoes
    10 to 12 carrots
    1 onion
    2 cups flour
    1 cup cornstarch
    1 large jar (4 ounces) pimientos, chopped
    2 large bags (32 ounces each) frozen green peas,
       cooked slightly
    Salt and pepper

Prepare turkey according to instructions on wrapper, removing giblets and neck to use later for broth. Roast turkey until done according to poultry roasting chart or according to automatic timer in turkey. While turkey is roasting, simmer the giblets and neck in two quarts of water. When turkey is done, cool and remove all meat from the bones. Cut into small bite-sized pieces. Wrap carefully and freeze or refrigerate.

Combine drippings from turkey, liquid used to simmer giblets and neck, and enough additional water to total 2½ to 3 gallons, or enough to cover turkey carcass in a very large kettle (a cold-pack canner works well). Add turkey carcass and simmer for 2 to 3 hours, until all meat has come off bones and juices are extracted from bones. Broth can then be frozen or refrigerated until pie filling is made.

Make pie crusts according to favorite pastry recipe. Cut into circles and fit into 4- or 6-inch tart pans. Bake. When cooled completely, remove from tins and freeze in a rigid container (a large plastic box does nicely). Make up one or two additional recipes of pastry; cut into fancy shapes with cookie cutters and bake to use for pie tops. About an hour before you are ready to assemble the turkey pies, remove pie shells from freezer and allow to warm to room temperature.

To make filling: Remove turkey from freezer and thaw completely. Combine turkey broth, Worcestershire sauce, Kitchen Bouquet, and sage; heat to boiling. Add potatoes, carrots, and onion, and cook until tender. Remove; cool and chop vegetables. Cover and set aside. Combine flour and cornstarch with enough water to make a paste, and add slowly to boiling stock; cook until thickened, stirring often. When thickened, gently stir in chopped vegetables, pimientos, peas, and turkey. Add salt and pepper to taste. Cover and keep hot until pies are assembled.

To assemble pies for serving: Place a pie shell on individual plate. Fill with ½ cup of hot pie filling. Top each with a pastry shape and garnish with a sprig of parsley, if desired. The pies should be assembled on the plate they are to be served on, as they are not in their pie tins, and they will be too fragile to handle once they are filled. Serve immediately.

Guide for Buying and Cooking for Large Groups

	Serving size per person	Servings per pound	Amount to buy for 25	Amount to buy for 50
Meats				
Bacon	2 slices	about 8-10	3 pounds	6 pounds
Beef rib roast, bone in, then boned and rolled	7 ounces raw	2¼	12-15 pounds	25-30 pounds
Beef pot roast, boneless	5½ ounces raw	3	9 pounds	17 pounds
Beef, ground	4-5 ounces raw	3-4	6-8 pounds	12-15 pounds
Ham, canned	4½ ounces	3¾	7 pounds	14 pounds
Ham, bone in	5½ ounces	3	9 pounds	17 pounds
Lamb leg roast	7-8 ounces raw	2-2½	11-13 pounds	22-25 pounds
Pork loin roast, bone in	8 ounces raw	2	13 pounds	25 pounds
Poultry (dressed, ready-to-cook)				
Chicken roaster or fryer	10-12 ounces raw	1½ +	15-19 pounds	31-38 pounds
Chicken for pie, salad, creamed dishes, etc.	6-8 ounces raw	2-2½	10-12 pounds	20-25 pounds
Turkey to roast	8-10 ounces raw	2	12-15 pounds	25-30 pounds
Turkey for pie, salad, creamed dishes, etc.	5-6 ounces raw	3	7-10 pounds	15-20 pounds
Salads and Relishes				
Cranberry sauce	2 ounces	8	3 1-pound cans	6 1-pound cans
French dressing	2 tablespoons	8 per cup	3 cups	1½ quarts
Mayonnaise	1⅓ Tb	12 per cup	2 cups	1 quart
Olives or pickles	⅛ cup	6 per cup	1 quart	2 quarts
Lettuce	1 cup	6 cups pieces 7½ cups shredded	3-5 pounds	6-9 pounds
Vegetables				
Frozen peas, green beans, corn	⅓-½ cup	5-6	5 pounds or 4-5 20-ounce packages	11 pounds
Frozen carrots	⅓-½ cup	7	4 20-ounce packages	8 or 9 20-ounce packages
Potatoes	⅔-1 cup	2-3	7-12 pounds	15-25 pounds
Cabbage, raw, shredded	½ cup	5½-6	4-5 pounds	8-10 pounds
Yams or sweet potatoes	½ cup	4	6 pounds	12 pounds
Pasta (serving size varies greatly, usually 1 to 2 ounces dry weight per person)				
Noodles	1 cup cooked	8	3 pounds	6 pounds
Spaghetti	1 cup cooked	7	3½ pounds	7 pounds
Macaroni	1 cup cooked	10	2½ pounds	5 pounds
Rice (serving size varies greatly, usually 1 to 2 ounces raw per person)*				
1 ounce raw	⅝ cup cooked	16	1½ pounds	3-3¼ pounds
2 ounces raw	1¼ cup cooked	8	3 pounds	6-6½ pounds
Dry beans (1 cup raw swells to 2½ to 3 cups cooked)				
Great Northern, Pinto, or small white	1 cup cooked	6½	4 pounds	8 pounds
Bread	1 slice	16	1½-2 pounds	3-4 pounds
Butter	1-2 pats	72	½ pound	1-1½ pounds

*1 cup raw rice swells to about 3 cups cooked.

Roast Beef

Shallow roasting pan with rack
350 degrees F.
20 to 24 servings, about 4 ounces each

8 pounds boneless top round of beef, rolled and tied
½ cup flour
1 teaspoon salt
⅛ teaspoon pepper

Dredge meat with mixture of flour, salt, and pepper (this helps brown the meat). Place meat on rack in pan, fat side up. Roast, uncovered, to desired degree of doneness—2 hours and 15 minutes for rare, 2 hours and 30 minutes for medium, and 3 hours for well-done. A meat thermometer inserted so bulb is near center of meat helps identify doneness. Turn meat once or twice to roast evenly. Remove from oven when meat reaches desired doneness. Place meat on warm platter or shallow pan; let stand at least 20 minutes before slicing. Make gravy.

Brown Gravy

16 to 20 servings, 3 or 4 tablespoons each

½ cup fat from drippings of roast
  (or stock and fat plus liquid)
4 cups liquid (use stock, drippings, vegetable
  cooking water, milk, etc.)
½ cup flour

After cooking meat, pour drippings or stock into a cup or bowl; let stand a few minutes. Then skim off fat from top; measure ½ cup for recipe. Loosen any meat bits left in cooking pan by adding a small amount of hot water and stirring and scraping. Add to remaining drippings or stock; measure 4 cups, adding broth, bouillon, vegetable cooking water, or milk, if needed.

Heat fat in saucepan; blend in flour; cook and stir until frothy, a few minutes. Remove from heat. Add liquid all at once, stirring constantly. Return to heat, and cook and stir until mixture comes to a boil. Simmer 3 minutes, stirring frequently. Season to taste. Strain, if desired.

If darker color is desired, increase flour to ½ cup plus 2 tablespoons. Heat flour in dry pan over medium heat, stirring, until lightly browned. Add fat and proceed as above. Or use a commercial gravy browner (Kitchen Bouquet) according to instructions on bottle.

Beef-Vegetable-Noodle Casserole

9×13×2-inch pan
350 degrees F.
15 to 20 servings

1 pound medium noodles
1 tablespoon oil
1 large onion, chopped
1 large green pepper, stemmed, deveined, and
  chopped
1 pound lean ground beef
4 teaspoons salt (or to taste)
1 teaspoon chili powder
1 can (16 ounces) cream-style corn
1 quart tomatoes, or 2 cans (16 ounces each)
1 can (16 ounces) pitted ripe olives, halved
  lengthwise
1 can (8 ounces) tomato sauce
¾ to 1 cup shredded cheese

Cook noodles according to package directions, adding oil to cooking water. Add onion and pepper to meat in frying pan. Cook and stir until meat is slightly browned. Add remaining ingredients except cheese. Blend well. Taste and adjust seasonings. Pour into baking pan. Sprinkle with cheese. Bake for about 1 hour, or until hot and thickened.

Beef Stew

50 ¾-cup servings (2½ gallons)

2½ cups chopped onions
½ cup shortening or oil
10 pounds stew beef, trimmed and cut in pieces
3 quarts water
Salt
Pepper
3 to 4 pounds potatoes (2½ quarts diced in large
  pieces)
3 to 4 pounds carrots (2½ quarts diced)
1¼ cups flour
2½ cups liquid (water and/or potato and carrot
  cooking liquid)

Brown onions in shortening slowly until browned. Add meat, water, salt, and pepper. Cook 1½ hours, or until meat is tender. Cook potatoes and carrots in salted water until tender. Drain and add to meat. Shake flour and 2½ cups liquid in glass jar. Add to stew and cook to desired consistency. Correct seasoning, if needed.

Lasagna

2 9×13×2-inch baking pans
375 degrees F.
30 servings

Lasagna Sauce

1 pound Italian sausage, casing removed
1 pound ground beef
1 large onion, chopped
1 clove garlic, minced
1 tablespoon basil
2 teaspoons fennel seeds
2 teaspoons salt
1 can (29 ounces) tomatoes
3 cans (6 ounces each) tomato paste
1 cup water

In large frying pan, brown sausage and ground beef slowly. Add onion and garlic, and cook 5 more minutes. Add remaining ingredients; simmer for 1 hour.

Lasagna Filling

1 package (16 ounces) lasagna noodles
1 tablespoon salt
1 tablespoon oil
1 carton (16 ounces) ricotta cheese
1 pint cottage cheese
½ cup grated Parmesan cheese
3 eggs
2 tablespoons parsley flakes, or ¼ cup fresh parsley
1 teaspoon salt
1 pound Mozzarella cheese, thinly sliced

Cook noodles in boiling water to which salt and oil have been added. Drain. Combine first three cheeses, eggs, parsley, and 1 teaspoon salt. Beat together until well mixed.

To assemble: Line baking pan with single layer of noodles. Spread with Lasagna Filling (cheese-egg mixture) and then with Lasagna Sauce (meat mixture). Next add a layer of Mozzarella cheese. Repeat with another layer of each until all noodles are used. Top with sauce and dot with Mozzarella cheese. Lasagna can be frozen or refrigerated at this point. When ready to bake, remove from freezer or refrigerator, and allow to warm for 30 minutes. Bake uncovered for 45 minutes, or until cheese is melted and mixture is bubbling all over. This will take 20 to 30 minutes, or longer if lasagna has been frozen.

Spaghetti, Macaroni, or Other Pastas

24 ⅓-cup servings

18 quarts water
⅓ cup oil
⅓ cup salt
3 pounds spaghetti, macaroni or other pastas

Bring water to full boil in very large kettle. Add oil and salt. Gradually add pasta so that it does not stick together or to bottom of pan. Return to a boil and boil 10 to 12 minutes, stirring occasionally, until desired tenderness. Drain. Adjust seasoning. Serve with butter, grated cheese, or a sauce.

Note: If holding pasta 30 minutes or so before serving, drain, then rinse with cold water. Before serving, place in a colander over a pot containing 2 inches of boiling water, below pasta level. Cover and heat with the steam.

Potato Salad for a Crowd

6½ quarts (about 50 servings)

15 pounds potatoes
2 cups Italian-style dressing (seasoned oil and vinegar)
1½ tablespoons salt
½ cup vinegar
12 hard-cooked eggs, chopped
4 cups (about 1 pound) celery, chopped
1 large onion, chopped
2 cups mayonnaise (or as desired)
¾ cup chopped parsley

Red or white potatoes are especially good for potato salad. Scrub, then cook them with skins on until just tender. Cool slightly; remove skins. Cube or slice potatoes. Or use old potatoes from storage; pare, then cook until tender. Slice.

Combine dressing, salt, and vinegar. Pour over warm potatoes. Mix gently, then let stand until cold. Add remaining ingredients; mix gently. Chill at least an hour (overnight is better), then serve.

Potatoes au Gratin

375 degrees F.

	30 ½-cup servings 2 9 × 13 × 2-inch pans	60 ½-cup servings 4 9 × 13 × 2-inch pans
Potatoes	8 pounds as purchased 4 quarts cooked, diced	15 pounds as purchased 7½ quarts cooked, diced
Butter or margarine	¾ cup	1½ cups
Flour	⅞ cup	1¾ cups
Salt	1 tablespoon	2 tablespoons
Pepper	¾ teaspoon	1½ teaspoons
Milk, hot	2¼ quarts	4½ quarts
Cheese, processed Cheddar, finely cut	1¼ quarts (1 lb. 4 oz.)	2½ quarts (2 lb. 8 oz.)
Cheese, shredded	2 cups (8 oz.)	1 quart (1 lb.)

Boil potatoes, either in jackets or peeled, until just tender. Remove skins; cube or slice potatoes. Combine butter, flour, salt, pepper. Add milk gradually, stirring constantly. Cook while stirring until thickened. Add finely cut cheese and stir until cheese is melted. Add potatoes and additional salt, if needed. Pour into buttered baking pans. Sprinkle with grated cheese. Bake 15 to 20 minutes, or until cheese is lightly browned.

Fruit and Chicken Salad

24 servings

- 8 chicken half-breasts, about 4½ pounds, or use 6 cups cooked, cubed chicken meat
- 1 stalk celery, washed and trimmed (use entire stalk)
- 2 large cans (20 ounces each) pineapple tidbits or chunks, drained and juice reserved
- 2 large cans (16 ounces each) Mandarin oranges, drained (save juice for other use)
- 2 large apples
- 1 tablespoon lemon juice
- 1 cup sour cream
- 1½ cups Miracle Whip or mayonnaise
- 3 tablespoons juice from canned pineapple
- 3 tablespoons orange juice
- 1 cup nuts, coarsely chopped (optional)
- 1 large head lettuce (red lettuce is especially nice)

Slice celery into bite-size pieces. Pare apple, if desired, although unpared apples add color to the salad. Cut apple into bite-size pieces; place in a small bowl and pour on lemon juice. Toss to coat each piece.

Combine all fruits with chicken pieces in a large bowl. Blend sour cream and salad dressing; add pineapple and orange juice and mix well. Pour the dressing over the fruit mixture and toss gently to thoroughly coat. Carefully fold in nuts. Serve on lettuce leaves. This recipe can be doubled or halved easily.

Other dressing: Honey Fruit Dressing or Poppy Seed Dressing (see Index).

Waldorf Salad

	25 ⅓-cup servings (2½ quarts)	50 ⅓-cup servings (5 quarts)
Mayonnaise	1 cup	2 cups
Whipped cream	½ cup	1 cup
Apples, tart	4 pounds	8 pounds
Celery, chopped	1 pound	2 pounds
Salt	1 teaspoon	2 teaspoons
Sugar (optional)	2 tablespoons	¼ cup
Marshmallows, cut (optional)	4 ounces	8 ounces
Walnuts, chopped	4 ounces	8 ounces

Blend mayonnaise and whipped cream. Core and chop apples, adding to dressing immediately. Add other ingredients except walnuts; mix lightly. Salad can be chilled before serving. Add walnuts just before serving.

Cabbage Salad

25 ⅓-cup servings (4½ quarts)

- 4 pounds cabbage, shredded
- 2 cups sour cream or 1 cup each sour cream and mayonnaise
- ¼ cup sugar
- ¼ cup vinegar
- 1 teaspoon salt

Place shredded cabbage in large container. Add a mixture of the sour cream, sugar, vinegar, and salt until of desired consistency. Chill.

Variations: Substitute chopped apples or grated carrots for about half the cabbage. Or reduce cabbage to 3 pounds and add 2 cans (16 ounces each) crushed pineapple and ½ pound cut marshmallows.

Salad Bar

Whenever you are feeding a crowd, or even a small group, a salad bar can take the pressure off the cook and satisfy even finicky guests. Let each person build a salad, large or small, to suit himself. Provide at least two popular dressings, including a seasoned oil-and-vinegar type and one with a mayonnaise or salad dressing base. Thousand Island and Blue Cheese dressings are generally the most popular. You don't have to make your own, as very good commercial products are available.

Basic Items for 50 Servings

5 1-pound heads iceberg lettuce, torn into bite-size pieces
2 cans (16 ounces each) red kidney beans, drained
1 to 2 cans (16 ounces each) sliced beets (pickled, if desired)
2 cans (16 ounces each) Garbanzo beans
1 pound cherry tomatoes
1 bunch green onions, sliced
Fresh sliced cucumber
Fresh sliced mushrooms

Additional Items for Salad Bar

Alfalfa sprouts
Bean sprouts
Cauliflowerettes
Broccoli florets
Shredded carrots
Sliced zucchini
Fresh green peas
Sunflower seeds
Sesame seeds
Pumpkin seeds
Seasoned toast cubes or croutons
Halved ripe olives
Grated cheese
Seedless grapes
Melon chunks
Fresh strawberry halves

Puff Pudding

3 8×8-inch or 9×9-inch square pans
350 degrees F.
27 to 30 servings, about ⅔ cup each

1½ cups (3 sticks) butter or margarine
2 tablespoons grated lemon rind
3 cups sugar
12 egg yolks
1 cup lemon juice
1½ cups Grape-Nuts cereal
¾ cup flour
6 cups milk
12 egg whites

To butter and grated lemon rind in large mixing bowl, gradually add sugar, creaming well after each addition. When light and fluffy, add yolks; beat well. Stir in lemon juice. Add cereal, flour, and milk, and mix well. (This may look curdled but it smooths out in baking.) Beat whites until soft round peaks form; then fold gently into first mixture. Pour into buttered baking pans. Place each in a larger baking pan containing hot water. Bake 1 hour. Cool at least 30 minutes before serving.

Fruit Coffee Cake

2 10×15-inch jelly-roll pans or 2 9×13×2-inch pans
425 degrees F.
40 servings

8 cups biscuit mix
1½ cups sugar
2 eggs
2 cups milk
3 cans (20 ounces each) sliced apples (about 1½ quarts), unsweetened, or sliced peaches or halved plums
1 to 2 cups sugar (use less if sweetened fruit is used)
¼ cup flour
2 teaspoons cinnamon
1 teaspoon salt
½ cup butter, softened

Combine biscuit mix and 1½ cups sugar in large bowl; mix well. In medium bowl beat eggs; stir in milk. Add to dry ingredients, and stir until well blended. Pour into two buttered pans.

Drain fruit well; arrange evenly on top of batter. Combine 2 cups sugar, flour, cinnamon, and salt; then blend or cut in butter. Sprinkle mixture over apples. Bake 20 minutes. Serve warm.

Buttermilk Brownies (Cake Type)

400 degrees F.

	9 × 9 × 2-inch baking pan 16 2-inch squares	11 × 17 × 2-inch pan 32 to 40 squares
Flour	1 cup	2 cups
Sugar	1¼ cups	2½ cups
Baking soda	½ teaspoon	1 teaspoon
Salt	Dash	⅛ teaspoon
Water	½ cup	1 cup
Butter or margarine	½ cup (1 stick)	1 cup (2 sticks)
Cocoa	2 tablespoons	¼ cup
Buttermilk	¼ cup	½ cup
Eggs, beaten	1	2
Vanilla	½ teaspoon	1 teaspoon
Nuts, chopped	½ cup	1 cup

Sift dry ingredients together. Bring water to a boil; add butter and cocoa; add to dry ingredients. Add buttermilk, eggs, vanilla, and nuts. Mix well. Pour into buttered pans and bake 15 minutes or until set. Cool in pan; frost.

Frosting

Butter	¼ cup	¼ pound
Buttermilk	3 tablespoons	6 tablespoons
Cocoa	2 tablespoons	4 tablespoons
Powdered sugar	½ pound (about)	1 pound (about)
Vanilla	½ teaspoon	1 teaspoon

Combine butter, buttermilk, and cocoa in a saucepan; bring to a boil. Remove from heat and stir in powdered sugar to a soft spreading consistency. Stir in vanilla. Spread on brownies before cutting.

Apple Crisp

400 degrees F.

	9 × 10-inch shallow pan or casserole 6 to 8 portions	3 or 4 9 × 13 × 2-inch baking pans 50 to 60 portions
Apples, peeled and sliced	1 quart (about)	8 quarts (about)
Lemon juice	1 tablespoon (about)	¼ cup (about)
Cinnamon	1 teaspoon	2 tablespoons
Butter or margarine	½ cup (1 stick)	2½ cups (5 sticks)
Flour	¾ cup	2½ cups
Sugar	⅓ cup	3½ cups
Brown sugar	½ cup	4 cups
Nutmeg	½ teaspoon (optional)	2 teaspoons (optional)
Cream or ice cream		

Arrange apples in shallow pans, filling pans almost full. Sprinkle apples with a little lemon juice unless they are tart. Sprinkle with cinnamon. Mix together butter, flour, sugar, brown sugar, and nutmeg until mixture is well blended and crumbly. Distribute sugar mixture over apples in a thick layer, packing it down over them. Bake for 30 to 40 minutes, or until apples are tender and crust is lightly browned and crisp. Serve warm with cream or ice cream.

Applesauce Cake

2 9×13×2-inch baking pans
375 degrees F.
40 servings

  4 eggs
  ¾ cup water
  7½ cups biscuit mix
  3 cups sugar
  1 teaspoon baking soda
  1 tablespoon cinnamon
  1 teaspoon cloves
  1 teaspoon nutmeg
  4 cups thick applesauce
  2¼ cups raisins
  1 cup walnuts, chopped

In medium-size bowl beat eggs; add water. In large mixer bowl combine biscuit mix, sugar, soda, and spices. Add egg mixture and half of applesauce; beat at low speed of mixer or by hand until blended, about 2 minutes. Add remaining applesauce; beat until blended, about 2 minutes. Stir in raisins and nuts. Pour into pans lined with wax paper, pushing batter well into corners. Bake 50 to 55 minutes, or until cake tester inserted in center comes out clean. Cool in pans 10 minutes; turn out onto racks and remove paper.

At altitudes less than 3,000 feet, use a 350-degree F. oven and add ⅓ cup sugar. Bake 55 to 60 minutes.

Rosy Baked Apples

2 9×13×2-inch baking pans
400 degrees F.
24 servings

  24 large baking apples (Rome Beauties preferred)
  2 packages (6 ounces each) red fruit-flavored gelatin
  4 cups sugar
  1 teaspoon salt
  3 quarts boiling water

Wash and core apples. Peel a 1-inch circular strip from stem end of each. Dissolve gelatin, sugar, and salt in boiling water in baking pans. Place apples, peeled ends down, in liquid. Bake about 20 minutes; then turn apples, peeled end up, and continue baking, basting frequently, until tender, about 1 hour. Cool, basting occasionally. Serve with cream, ice cream, or whipped topping, if desired.

Ice Cream Dreamy Delight

9×13×2-inch baking pan
350 degrees F.
24 servings

  2 cups flour
  ½ cup quick-cooking oatmeal
  ½ cup brown sugar, packed
  1 cup (2 sticks) butter or margarine
  1 cup chopped nuts
  2 jars (10 ounces each) caramel or butterscotch
    ice cream topping
  ½ gallon vanilla ice cream
  ½ cup chopped nuts
  1 jar (4 ounces) maraschino cherries, halved

Combine flour, oatmeal, and brown sugar. Blend well. Cut in butter until mixture is about the size of peas. Stir in 1 cup nuts. Spread the mixture on a cookie sheet or baking pan, and bake for 10 to 15 minutes, or until lightly browned, stirring occasionally. Remove from oven and, while hot, crumble half of mixture evenly into baking pan.

Drizzle one jar of the ice cream topping over crumbs in pan. Soften ice cream slightly and spread evenly over crumb-topping mixture. Sprinkle remaining half of crumb mixture over ice cream layer, then drizzle second jar of ice cream topping over this. Garnish with remaining nuts. Freeze for several hours, until firm. Remove from freezer about 15 minutes before serving. Cut into 2-inch squares, and garnish each serving with a maraschino cherry half.

Helpful Hints and Special Instructions

Definitions of Terms

In this book, when a recipe calls for these items, we mean:

Eggs: large.

Flour: all-purpose enriched white. Whole wheat flour may be substituted in many recipes with a slight reduction in amount.

Sifted flour: flour that has been freshly sifted before being spooned into the measuring cup and then leveled off without packing.

Baking powder: double-acting.

Butter or margarine: either, though in some recipes butter adds a special flavor. Butter is better where its hardening properties at cold temperatures are important, as in graham cracker crusts. Sometimes other fats, such as bacon or ham drippings, chicken fat, or oils, can be substituted.

Milk: fresh or reconstituted from evaporated or dried. In most recipes whole, 2 percent, or skim milk may be used, though texture and flavor (as well as calories) will not be the same.

Taste to adjust seasonings: adapt to your preferences. You may wish to use more or less salt, sugar, spices, and herbs. With powerful seasonings, such as curry or chili pepper, add only part before tasting and adjusting.

Servings: appetite, age, activity, general health, and other factors affect what an individual considers as a serving. What constitutes a large serving for one person may be totally inadequate for another. In general, a serving of vegetables measures about ½ cup; of meat, 3 to 4 ounces; of a casserole main dish or soup, at least 1 cup. Some portion sizes are self-limiting, such as a chicken breast or individual steak. We have often tried to help you judge by giving quantity as well as number of servings.

Measuring

Dry ingredients: scoop measure full and level off with a straight edge, without packing.

Brown sugar: Pack well into cup to get a full measure.

Liquids: Use a glass measuring cup with extra space at the top, to provide a better view of the liquid level

and facilitate carrying liquid to the area where it will be used.

Fats: A stick (¼ pound) of butter or margarine equals ½ cup. Portions of the stick can be cut fairly accurately.

Weighing is fast and easy if an accurate scale is available.

Boil-overs

Pastas, rice, split peas, and other foods that foam up and over are less of a problem if you add 1 to 2 tablespoons oil or butter to the boiling water.

Heat milk in a double boiler or in a saucepan, uncovered, over low heat to prevent boil-overs. Watch it and stir occasionally.

Energy Savers

In cooking vegetables, soups, and meats, once the pot is boiling, turn the heat low enough to barely keep boiling. Rapidly boiling water cooks no faster than water that boils slowly, but water is lost through evaporation faster. A tight-fitting lid reduces the amount of heat needed to keep the pot boiling and speeds its arrival at the boiling point.

Choose pans to fit the heating unit and appropriate for the amount of food to be heated.

In baking, use the oven more efficiently by:

1. Filling the oven at each baking (leave space for heat circulation).

2. Baking a series of foods, beginning with those needing the highest temperature and ending with those needing the lowest temperature.

3. Many items, such as potatoes and casseroles, may be put in the oven during the preheat period, thus shortening heating time.

4. Turn the oven off for the last minutes of cooking.

Chill hot foods by surrounding the pan with cold water. This is faster than chilling in the refrigerator, and it takes less fuel energy. Change the water and stir occasionally.

In the refrigerator and freezer, keep all foods properly covered to reduce drying, flavor exchanges, and excess energy use.

Using Frozen Meats

When cooking meat that is still frozen, increase the cooking time. Large roasts need approximately one-half more cooking time; small roasts need proportionately less additional time.

For steaks and chops, increase the time by one-fourth to one-half. If broiling, place chops or steaks at least four inches from the heat so exterior surfaces do not become too brown before the interior is heated. In pan broiling, have the pan hot enough to brown the meat quickly before it thaws and "waters" in the pan; then lower the heat to cook the meat slowly. Ground meat need not be thawed unless it requires shaping into loaves or patties; however, the cooking time must be increased for frozen meat.

Altitude Adjustments

Adjustments may need to be made for changes in altitude in the following areas of food preparation:

Boiling in Water

Water boils at lower temperatures as elevation increases above sea level. Potatoes may need 15 minutes to cook in San Francisco, 30 minutes in Salt Lake City, and 45 minutes at Utah's ski resorts. If boiled in Death Valley, which is below sea level, they will cook even faster than at sea level because water is hotter when it boils. A Fahrenheit thermometer should register 212 degrees at sea level but only 203 degrees at 4,500 feet. To adjust cooking time for vegetables, fruits, meats, water-bath canning, or pressure canning:

1. Allow more time at higher elevations for cooking foods in boiling water.

2. Increase processing time in boiling water-bath canning by 2 minutes for each 1,000 feet above sea level if 20 minutes or more are called for; otherwise increase only 1 minute per 1,000 feet.

3. Increase pressure in pressure-canner canning by ½ pound for each 1,000 feet above sea level.

4. Expect foods to dry out faster at higher elevations, especially if humidity is low. Make bread dough as soft as possible, and store bread, cakes, and cookies well covered to keep moist.

Candies

Recipes for candies should always be written for sea level, as are ours, but check your other recipes to be sure, since friends, newspapers, and other sources may have made the adjustments already—and you may not know for what altitude the adjustments were made. Use these steps in adjusting temperatures for our sugar mixtures and all others written for sea level.

1. Hold your thermometer in a pan of boiling water for a few minutes, being careful to keep the bulb below water level but not touching the sides or bottom of the pan. Record the temperature (for example, 203 degrees F. in Salt Lake City).

2. Subtract this reading from the boiling point of water at sea level, or 212 degrees F. Thus 212 degrees (sea level) minus 203 degrees (your elevation reading) equals 9 degrees difference between the sea-level boiling point and the boiling point in your kitchen.

3. Subtract this difference from any candy recipe temperature to give you the new and corrected temperature for your elevation. For example, if the temperature given in the recipe is 234 degrees, subtract 9 degrees (your correction); the result is 225 degrees, the corrected temperature for this recipe.

4. Since all sugar solutions boil at temperatures above the boiling point of water, this adjustment must be made for each recipe.

Many cooks make this check (thermometer in boiling water) every time they make a batch of candy because this corrects for barometric pressure changes; however, such small changes are usually not that important. Another benefit from testing your thermometer in boiling water is that this makes corrections for errors in your thermometer scale. Another thermometer in the same pan of water may read 202 or 204, for example, so their corrections will be 10 and 8 degrees based on our example above.

Cakes

At higher elevations, less air pressure is pushing down on the batter in a cake pan, so the cake can rise faster and higher than it would at a lower elevation. The batter may rise so high that it goes over the pan sides and may even drop onto the oven bottom. Some cake recipes are so delicately balanced that they collapse from this strain, leaving a sway-back center, shiny and coarse crust, low volume, and coarse texture. Suggested solutions, which are generally done in the order listed (all three may be needed), include the following:

1. Increase the pan size (i.e., from an 8-inch round to a 9-inch round or 8-inch square pan).

2. Increase the oven temperature (i.e., from 350 degrees F. to 375 degrees F.) so the cake sets sooner and therefore does not get too light; and decrease the baking time.

3. Decrease the amount of baking powder used. For 5,000 feet above sea level, decrease the amount by one-eighth (i.e., from 2 teaspoons to 1¾ teaspoons); at 7,500 feet and up, decrease the amount by one-fourth (from 2 teaspoons to 1½ teaspoons).

For a cake mix, follow 1 and 2, but since the baking powder is already included in the mix, increase the batter's "resistance" (heaviness or toughness) by adding additional flour, usually 2 to 3 tablespoons plus about the same increase in liquid. Most commercial mixes have adjustments printed on the package.

Our recipes for cakes have been tested and adjusted for 4,500 feet (Salt Lake City). Make adjustments if your elevation differs greatly.

Substitutions for Wine and Liquor in Cooking

No recipes in this book call for alcoholic beverages to season either cooked or uncooked foods. Alcohol does dissipate with heat, but many cooks prefer not to use it in their cooking. Sometimes the alcoholic ingredient can be omitted; often a substitution can be made. Here are a few general rules to consider when adapting a recipe that calls for an alcoholic beverage:

1. If the ingredient is used only for seasoning, simply omit it and taste to adjust seasonings, adding herbs, spices, or any other "pick-up" desired. Seasonings can be potent, so add cautiously.

2. A quantity of an alcoholic beverage will require replacement by an equal quantity of liquid. For a main course dish, use clear soup; for a dessert, use fruit juice. Sometimes milk or water will work well.

3. When the recipe calls for rum, use rum extract with juice, water, or milk. A syrup of butter, sugar, and water with rum extract serves very well as a sauce for mince pie, for example.

4. To flame, you must have alcohol. A small amount of lemon extract poured on sugar cubes will provide a colorful flame. To prevent a strong flavor, avoid contact of cube with the food.

Can Sizes

8-ounce (buffet size) = 1 cup
10½-ounce (picnic or soup) = 1¼ cups
12-ounce (vacuum) = 1½ cups
14- to 16-ounce (no. 300) = 1¾ cups
16- to 17-ounce (no. 303) = 2 cups
20-ounce (no. 2) = 2½ cups
29-ounce (no. 2½) = 3½ cups
46 fluid ounces (no. 3 cylinder) = 5¾ cups
6 pounds 8 ounces to 7 pounds 5 ounces (no. 10) = 12 to 13 cups (equals 7 no. 303 cans or 5 no. 2 cans)

Weights and Measures

3 teaspoons = 1 tablespoon
4 tablespoons = ¼ cup
5⅓ tablespoons = ⅓ cup
8 tablespoons = ½ cup
10⅔ tablespoons = ⅔ cup
12 tablespoons = ¾ cup
16 tablespoons = 1 cup
1 ounce = 30 grams (28.35)
1 pound = 454 grams (0.45 kilograms)
1 quart = 0.95 liters

Substitutions and Equivalents

When the recipe calls for:	You may substitute:
1 ounce (1 square) baking chocolate	3 tablespoons cocoa or carob powder plus 1 tablespoon fat
1 tablespoon flour for thickening	½ tablespoon cornstarch, potato starch, rice, or arrowroot starch; or 1 tablespoon quick-cooking tapioca; or 1 egg or 2 yolks; or 2 tablespoons granular cereal, such as cornmeal
1 egg	2 yolks; or 3⅓ tablespoons fresh or frozen egg; or 2½ tablespoons dry whole egg powder plus 2½ tablespoons water
1 cup corn syrup	1 cup sugar plus ¼ cup liquid
1 cup honey	1¼ cups sugar plus ¼ cup liquid
1 cup brown sugar, packed	1 cup granular white sugar plus 1 tablespoon molasses
1 package dry yeast	Scant tablespoon dry yeast or 1 cake fresh yeast
1 teaspoon baking powder	¼ teaspoon baking soda plus any one of the following acids: ⅝ teaspoon cream of tartar ½ cup sour milk, buttermilk, or yogurt ½ tablespoon vinegar or lemon juice ¼ to ½ cup molasses ½ cup applesauce or mashed ripe banana
1 cup self-rising flour	1 cup flour plus 1½ teaspoons baking powder plus ½ teaspoon salt
1 cup cake flour, sifted	⅞ cup sifted all-purpose flour
1 cup sifted all-purpose flour	⅞ cup unsifted all-purpose flour; or 1½ cups dry bread crumbs
1 cup dry bread crumbs	3 slices bread, dried
1 cup soft bread crumbs	1½ slices bread, fresh
1 3-ounce package gelatin dessert powder	1 tablespoon unflavored gelatin plus flavorings to set 2 cups liquid
1 cup milk	½ cup evaporated milk plus ½ cup water; or ⅓ cup instant nonfat dry milk plus water to make 1 cup; or ¼ cup (or 3 tablespoons) powdered nonfat milk plus water to make 1 cup; or 2½ teaspoons butter or margarine added to nonfat milk to equal whole milk
1 cup buttermilk, yogurt, or sour milk	1 cup milk plus 1 tablespoon vinegar or lemon juice; or 1 cup milk plus 1¼ teaspoons cream of tartar
1 cup table cream (about 20% butterfat)	1 cup milk plus 3 tablespoons butter or margarine
1 cup half-and-half (about 10% butterfat)	¾ cup skim or whole milk plus ¼ cup whipping cream
1 cup whipping cream (about 30 to 40% butterfat, store type)	¾ cup milk plus ⅓ cup butter or margarine (this will not whip)
1 cup butter or margarine	½ teaspoon salt added to ⅞ cup oil or lard or 1½ cups suet chopped fine or ⅞ to 1 cup hydrogenated vegetable fat
1 tablespoon instant dry onion	1 small fresh onion
1 clove garlic	1 teaspoon garlic salt; or ⅛ teaspoon garlic powder
1 teaspoon dry mustard	1 tablespoon prepared mustard
1 tablespoon fresh herbs	1 teaspoon dry herbs (approximately)
1 cup tomato juice	½ cup tomato sauce plus ½ cup water
1 cup orange juice	¼ cup frozen orange concentrate plus ¾ cup water
1 pound fresh mushrooms	3 cans (4 ounces each) canned-in-butter mushrooms

Index

Afton's fresh peach pie, 107
All-purpose marinade, 29
All-purpose sauce for vegetables, 89
Almond
    baked peaches, 142
    -chicken casserole, 71
    rice, 72
Althea's tacos, 52
Altitude adjustments, 169-70
Ambrosia
    canned fruit, 140
    molded, 136
Angel pie
    berry, 112
    lemon, 112
"Any old fruit" loaves, 119
Appetizers
    cheese ball, easy, 5
    cheese ball, olive-nut, 5
    cheese ball, shrimp, 5
    cheese balls to go, 5
    cheese krispies, 10
    chicken liver paté, 8
    crab meat appetizer, hot, 9
    crab rolls, 9
    curry vegetable dip, 6
    date-nut pinwheel sandwiches, 10
    egg dip, 6
    gold bricks, 10
    green chilies dip, 6
    jalapeno jelly, 8
    Mediterranean butter, 8
    Mexican butter, 8
    Mexican platter dip, 6
    pecan spread, 8
    ribbon sandwiches, 9
    shrimp rolls, 8
    vegetable dip, 6
Apple
    bread, 92
    crisp (quantity recipe), 166
    dumpling roll, 141
    -maple flan, 108
    pie, 107
    pie, quick cookie, 108
    pie filling, home-canned, 151
Apples
    glazed, 84
    rosy, baked (quantity recipe), 167
    tapioca, baked, 142
Applesauce cake, 113;
    quantity recipe, 167
Apricot
    bars, 128
    cookie rolls, 129
    peanut granola, 149

Arlean's molasses refrigerator
    muffins, 94
Armenian pilaf, 88
Artichoke heart-spinach casserole, 41
Asparagus (see Casserole)
Aunt Molly's delicious French
    dressing, 29
Avocado strawberry ring, 20

Baked almond chicken casserole, 71
Baked apples
    rosy (quantity recipe), 167
    tapioca, 142
Baked beans
    calico, 33
    classic, 34
    country-style, 33
    easy, 33
    Swedish, 33
Baked broccoli or spinach, 35
Baked chilies relleno, 79
Baked fish with cheese, 59
Baked lentils, 37
Baked stuffed tomatoes, 41
Baked summer squash, 41
Baklava, 112
Banana
    bread, 91
    cream pie, 107
    orange refresher, 11
    split cake dessert, 135
Barbecue sauce
    Texas-style, 82
    firehouse, 82
    lemon, 82
Barbecued meats
    brisket of beef, 47
    oven-barbecued pork roast, 54
    oven-barbecued spareribs, 54
    oven-barbecued turkey, 74
Barbecued zucchini and onions, 42
Basic cream pie filling, 106
Basic fresh fruit pie, 110
Basic pastry, 106
Basic sweet dough, 100
Beaten batter coffee cake or rolls, 101
Bean(s)
    baked, 33-34
    green, Floy's, 34
    green, Orientale, 34
    salted, 34
    pasta with, 34
    salad, three, 30
    soup, famous senate, 14
Beef
    brisket, barbecued, 47

brisket, fresh, 46
burgoo, 50
celebration hamburger steaks, 50
Danish chop suey, 51
enchilada casserole, 53
eye-of-round fillet, 47
fillet, with mushroom sauce, 46
flank steak, 48
flank steak, hickory smoked, 48
goulash, quick, 48
roast, Cinderella, 142
roast (quantity recipe), 162
stew, fireside, 50
stew (quantity recipe), 162
stroganoff, 50
sweet and sour meatballs, 51
-vegetable-noodle casserole
    (quantity recipe), 162
Beets, pickled, 152
Berry angel pie, 112
Best-ever meat loaf, 52
Beverages
    banana orange refresher, 11
    eggnog, 95
    golden summer punch, 11
    grape juice punch, 12
    hot tomato zip, 12
    orange Julia, 11
    pineapple eggnog punch, 10
    sassy slush, 11
    three-fruit slush, 11
    tomato bouillon, 12
    tropical cooler, 10
    wonderful wassail, 12
Bishop's bread, 91
Black and white pie, 107
Black forest cake, 116
Blender chocolate mousse, 134
Blender pancakes, 96
Blender quiche, 78
Boiling in water, altitude adjustments
    for, 69
Boil-overs, 168
Bonanza bread, 92
Borscht, creamy, Hotel Utah style, 18
Bran bread, 91
Bran muffins, 94
Bread
    apple, 92
    banana, 91
    bishop's, 91
    bonanza 92
    bran, elegant, 91
    corn, crispy, 93
    corn, dried, 93
    corn, fresh, 93

Danish nut loaf, 92
dilly, 97
garlic, 101
Irish soda, 93
orange nut, 93
whole wheat, Phyllis's, 97
Bread pudding, 131
Breakfast cookies, 125
Brisket of beef, 46; barbecued, 47
Broccoli
casserole, 35
baked, 35
soup, cream of, 15
Broken-glass cake dessert, 138
Brown sugar pecan peach shortcake, 118
Brownie(s)
basic, 123
buttermilk (quantity recipe), 166
drops, 123
waffle-iron, 130
Brussels sprouts supreme, 35
Bubble wreath, 100
Buffet salad, 25
Bulgur, 88
Buns, thirty-minute hamburger, 99
Burgers
lentil, 36
pizza, 53
Burgoo, 51
Butter
Honey or maple, 103
Mediterranean, 8
Mexican, 8
Butter cream frosting, 121
Butter fingers
baking powder, 95
yeast, 95
Butterflake rolls, Farol's, 97
Buttermilk brownies (quantity recipe), 166
Buttermilk or yogurt pineapple sherbert, 143
Butternut squash soup, 15
Butterscotch pecan toasts, 101
Butterscotch pie, 108
Buying and cooking for large groups, 161

Cabbage
savory, 35
salad (quantity recipe), 164
Cake
applesauce, 113
black forest, 116
carob, 119
carrot, 114
cherry nut, 113
chocolate rocky road, 115
hummingbird, 115
picnic, 114

pineapple carrot, 113
pioneer, 114
poppy seed, 116
poundcake, old-time, 116
pudding, fruit cocktail, 115
Spanish, 118
strawberry, 118
(see also Shortcake)
Cake dessert
banana split, 135
broken-glass, 138
Cake doughnuts, Grandma Grover's, 120
Cakes, altitude adjustments for, 169-70
Calico bean bake, 33
Campfire potatoes and onions, 39
Can sizes, 170
Candied yams and apples, 39
Candies, altitude adjustments for, 169
Canned fruit ambrosia, 140
Canned trout, 155
Canning and preserving, 151-55
Cantaloupe salad, 21
Caramel
corn no. 1, 145
corn no. 2, 145
corn and peanut brittle, 145-47
custard (flan), 135
frosting, quick, 122
Caramels, 147
Carita's vanilla ice cream, 143
Carob cake and frosting, 119
Carrot
cake, 114
cake, pineapple, 113
salad, marinated, 29
Carrots
honeyed, 36
in onion sauce, 36
Casseroles
baked almond chicken, 71
baked bean, 33-34
beef enchilada, 53
beef-vegetable-noodle (quantity recipe), 162
chicken and rice, 70
chicken breasts in vegetable creme, 70
chicken custard, 73
chicken salad, 73
chicken supreme, 69
company brunch, 80
dried corn, 36
enchilada, 77
ham and asparagus roll-ups, 56
ham, egg, and asparagus, 56
ham loaf, 56
layered spinach and noodle, 40
lentil, 37

Orleans rice and vegetable bake, 44
shrimp and cheese, 63
shrimp, easy, 62
shrimp, party, 63
Spanish chicken, 72
spinach-artichoke heart, 40
tuna-vegetable, 63
zucchini, 43
zucchini and green chili, 42
zucchini layers, 42
Celebration hamburger steaks, 50
Cheese
ball, easy, 5
ball, olive-nut, 5
ball, shrimp, 5
balls to go, 5
grits, 87
Krispies, 10
puff or strata, 79
sausage fondue, 78
-spinach soufflé, 78
straws, 102
Cheesecake pie, 138
Cherries, maraschino, 152
Cherry nut cake, 113
Cherry pie filling, home canned, 151
Cherry-topped refrigerator cake, 135
Chess pie, lemon, 109
Chewy oatmeal cookies, 124
Chicken
à la king, 70
-almond casserole, 71
and fruit salad (quantity recipe), 164
and mushrooms, creamed, 70
and rice casserole, 70
baked in casserole, 66
baked in foil, 66
breasts in caper sauce, 69
breasts in vegetable creme, 70
curried, with coconut, 71
curried, with dumplings, 72
curry salad with fruit, 27
custard casserole, 73
enchilada, 76
fruit salad plate, 26
in gelatin salad, 26
liver paté, 8
marinated, tangy garlic and sour cream, 71
meat, preparing, 66
noodle soup, 16
orange, delicious, 72
rolls, crescent, 73
salad casserole, 73
salad exotic, 25
sandwiches, 76
simmered, 66
Spanish, casserole, 72
stock for soup, 16

stretch the, 65
supreme, 69
Chili sauce, 154
Chili supper in a hurry, 53
Chilies relleno, baked, 69
Chilled cucumber cream soup, 17
Chocolate
    butter cream frosting, 122
    butter frosting, fluffy, 122
    cream cheese frosting, 122
    cream pie, 107
    creme, French, 112
    frosting, 122
    fudge nut crunch, 148
    log (dessert), 120
    logs or nuggets (candies), 148
    mint dessert, 142
    mint ice cream pie, 110
    mousse, blender, 134
    pudding, steamed, 133
    rocky road cake, 115
    rocky road frosting, 115
    rocky road fudge, 147
    soufflé, 135
Chop suey, Danish, 51
Chowder
    clam, 16
    clam, hurry-up, 16
    corn, quick, 15
    fish, 16
Christmas kisses, 127
Christmas pudding, old-time, 131
Church dinners, 160
Chutney, plum or peach, 153
Cinderella roast beef, 46
Cinnamon bread (variation of
    Beaten batter coffee cake), 101
Cinnamon sour cream coffee cake,
    102
Cinnamon bars, glazed, 129
Clam
    chowder, 16
    chowder, hurry-up, 16
    sauce, white, with spaghetti, 64
Classic baked beans, 34
Cobbler, Grandma's fruit, 141
Coconut cream pie, 107
Coconut-pecan bars, 130
Coffee cake
    beaten batter, 101
    cinnamon sour cream, 102
Cole slaw, seven-day, 25
Company brunch casserole, 80
Cookies
    apricot bars, 128
    apricot rolls, 129
    breakfast, 125
    brownie drops, 123
    brownies, 129
    brownies, waffle-iron, 130
    Christmas kisses, 127

cinnamon bars, glazed, 129
    coconut-pecan bars, 130
    ginger, soft, 125
    jam, 125
    Joan's lemonade, 125
    lemon-prune bars, 128
    lemon sponge squares, 128
    linzer, 127
    noels, 126
    oatmeal, 124
    oatmeal, chewy, 124
    oatmeal crisps, 124
    oatmeal, krispie, 124
    oatmeal, waffle-iron, 130
    pecan pie, 128
    raisin, jumbo, 126
    raisin-filled, 126
    snowballs, 127
    surprise balls, 127
Cooking and buying for large groups
    (chart), 161
Coquilles Saint-Jacques, 64
Corn
    bread, dried, 93
    cakes, summer, 96
    chowder, quick, 15
    pudding, dried, 36
    relish, confetti, 86
    squaw, 36
Cornbread
    crispy, 93
    fresh corn, 93
Cornmeal refrigerator rolls, 98
Cottage cheese pancakes, 96
Cottage-fried tomatoes, 41
Cottage potatoes, 38
Country-style baked beans, 33
Crab
    and avocado salad, 27
    appetizer, 9
    rolls, 9
    salad casserole, 63
Cracked wheat salad (tabouli), 28
Crackers
    graham, 103
    wheat thins, 101
Cranberry
    cream roll, 120
    ice, 144
    pork and pears, 54
    relish, raw, 96
Cream cheese
    chocolate frosting, 122
    filling, 120
    frosting, 114
    orange frosting, 113
Cream of broccoli soup, 15
Cream of tomato soup, 14
Cream pie filling, basic, 106
Cream puff pie, glazed, 110
Creamy borscht, Hotel Utah style, 18

Creamy dressing for fruit salad, 29
Creamy lemon dressing, 29
Creamy romaine salad, 23
Creamed chicken and mushrooms, 70
Creme caramel, 134
Crescent chicken rolls, 73
Crispy cornbread, 93
Crumb crust, basic, 106
Crusty French bread pizza, 102
Cucumber cream soup, chilled, 17
Cucumber slices, gingered, 86
Cupcakes, raisin, 119
Curried baked chicken with coconut,
    71
Curried chicken with dumplings, 72
Curried fruit, 86
Curry, shrimp, 62
Curry sauce, 71
Curry vegetable dip, 8
Custard-type Yorkshire pudding, 81

Danish chop suey, 51
Danish nut loaf, 92
Date roll, 138
Delicate dessert pancakes, 97
Delicious sweet pickles, 153
Deluxe brown rice, 88
Dill pickles, fresh-pack, 152
Dilly beans, fresh-pack, 153
Dilly bread, 98
Dips
    curry vegetable, 6
    egg, tasty, 6
    fresh vegetable, 6
    green chilies, 6
    Mexican platter, 6
Divinity, southern-style, 147
Doughnuts, cake, Grandma
    Grover's, 120
Dried corn bread, 93
Dried corn pudding, 36
Dressing (stuffing)
    baked pineapple, 82
    mushroom bread, 82
Dressings, salad. See Salad dressings
Dumplings
    curried chicken with, 72
    for stew, 81

Easy recipes
    baked beans, 33
    brioche, 100
    broccoli casserole, 35
    cheese ball, 5
    chocolate frosting, 122
    chocolate log, 120
    chocolate logs or nuggets, 148
    fruit frappé, 143
    pan rolls, 97
    popcorn balls, 145
    raisin-filled cookies, 126
    shrimp casserole, 62

Egg and olive sauce, 84
Egg dip, tasty, 8
Egg main dishes
    baked chilies relleno, 79
    blender quiche, 68
    cheese omelet, 77
    cheese puff or strata, 79
    cheese-spinach soufflé roll, 78
    company brunch casserole, 79
    fluffy omelet, 77
    quiche Lorraine, 78
    sausage fondue
Egg-fried zucchini crisps, 42
Egg noodles, 87
Eggnog gems, 95
Elegant bran bread, 91
Elegant dishes, recipe suggestions
    for, 4
Enchilada
    casserole, 77
    chicken or turkey, 76
Energy-saving ideas, 168
Equivalents and substitutions, list
    of, 171
Ever-ready vegetable combo, 45
Exotic oven rice, 87
Eye-of-round fillet of beef, 47

Family home evening, recipes for, 1
Famous senate bean soup, 14
Far East rice, 88
Farol's butterflake rolls, 97
Farol's golden potato bake, 38
Favorite fruit ice cream, 143
Festive fruit salad dessert, 136
Fireside stew, 50
Fish
    clam chowder, 16
    clam chowder, hurry-up, 16
    clam sauce, spaghetti with, 64
    coquilles Saint-Jacques (scallops),
        64
    crab appetizer, hot, 9
    crab and avocado salad, 27
    crab rolls, 9
    crab salad casserole, 63
    fish baked with cheese, 49
    fish chowder, 16
    fish cooked the Canadian method,
        57
    fish fillets in sour cream, 59
    fish loaf with dill sauce, 62
    halibut, smothered, 58
    salmon bake, golden, 61
    salmon loaf, 59
    salmon pie, 61
    salmon salad, 27
    salmon steaks with mustard-dill
        sauce, 59
    shrimp and cheese casserole, 63

shrimp balls, hot, 9
shrimp casserole, easy, 62
shrimp casserole, party, 63
shrimp cheese ball, 5
shrimp curry, 63
shrimp, pan-fried, Grand Central
    Oyster Bar style, 64
shrimp salad, New Orleans, 27
shrimp soup, super, 16
scallops (Coquilles Saint-Jacques),
    64
sole marinade, 59
swordfish steak meuniere, 58
trout almondine, 58
trout, canned, 155
tuna-vegetable casserole, 63
Flan (caramel custard), 134
Flan, maple-apple, 108
Flank steak, 48
Fluffy butter cream frosting, 121;
    chocolate butter cream frosting,
    121
Fluffy omelet, 77
Fluffy seven-minute frosting, 122
Foil dinners, 57
Frappé, easy fruit, 143
French chocolate cream for meringue
    shells, 112
French onion soup, 14
Fresh fruit pie, basic, 110
Fresh-pack dill pickles, 152
Fresh-pack dilly beans, 153
Frosting
    broiled topping, 118
    butter cream, 121
    caramel, quick, 112
    carob, 119
    chocolate, 122
    chocolate butter, fluffy, 121
    chocolate cream cheese, 122
    cream cheese, 114
    fluffy butter, 121
    fluffy seven-minute, 122
    for eggnog gems, 95
    fudge, and sauce, 123
    glossy powdered sugar glaze, 121
    instructions for making, 121
    lemon, 128
    orange cream cheese, 113
    peanut butter fudge, Marilyn's,
        123
    praline, 128
    rocky road, 115
    sea foam, 123
    strawberry, 118
    sugarplum, 123
Frozen meats, how to cook, 169
Fruit
    ambrosia, canned, 140
    and chicken salad (quantity
        recipe), 164

cobbler, Grandma's, 141
cocktail pudding cake, 115
coffee cake (quantity recipe), 165
curried, 86
delight, gourmet, 136
frappé, 143
ice cream, 143
in easy puff shell, 111
loaves, "any old," 119
nut bread (variation of Beaten
    batter coffee cake), 101
pie, fresh, 110
pudding, tropical, 133
punch, 111
salad dessert, festive, 136
shortcake, 116
snack squares, 140
soup (rote grutze), 137
soup, raspberry (easy rote
    grutze), 137
soup, orange, 137
tart, 110
-topped bread (see Beaten batter
    coffee cake), 101
treat, surprise, 138
Fudge
    nut crunch, 148
    rocky road, 147
    sauce and frosting, 123

Garden lettuce salad with cream and
    sugar, 23
Garden relish, 154
Garlic bread, 101
Gelatin salads, instructions for, 19
Ginger cookies, soft, 125
Gingered cucumber slices, 86
Glaze, glossy powdered sugar, 121
Glazed apples, 84
Glazed cinnamon bars, 129
Glazed cream puff pie, 110
Glossy powdered sugar glaze, 121
Gold bricks, 10
Golden salmon bake, 61
Golden summer punch, 11
Goulash, quick beef, 48
Gourmet fruit delight, 136
Gourmet shrimp and cheese
    casserole, 63
Graham crackers, 103
Grandma Grover's cake doughnuts,
    120
Grandma's fruit cobbler, 141
Granola, apricot peanut, 149
Grape juice punch, 12
Grapefruit, ruby, 140
Gravy
    brown, 162
    milk, 84
Green and gold vegetable ring, 44
Green and yellow rice, 88

Green beans
  Floy's, 34
  Orientale, 34
  salted, 34
Green chilies dip, 6
Green goddess salad dressing, 28
Green rice, 89
Green tomato mincemeat, 151
Green tomatoes, raspberry jam from, 152
Greens, wilted, 23
Grits, cheese, 87
Guides for buying and cooking for large groups, 161

Halibut, smothered, 58
Ham
  and asparagus roll-ups, 56
  and potato casserole, 55
  and turkey tetrazzini, 75
  and vegetable medley, 56
  egg, and asparagus casserole, 56
  loaf, 56
  stretch the, 55
Hamburger buns, 99
Hamburger steaks, 50
Heavenly fresh strawberry dessert, 137
Hellberg's zuchini goop, 42
Herb bread (variation of Beaten batter coffee cake), 101
Hickory smoked flank steak, 48
Holiday Waldorf salad, 21
Hollandaise sauce, 85; mock, 85
Home-canned apple pie filling, 151
Home-canned sour cherry pie filling, 151
Honey dressing for fruit salad, 28
Honey or maple butter, 103
Honeyed carrots, 36
Hong Kong pork chops, 54
Hot crabmeat appetizer, 9
Hot crab rolls, 9
Hot rolls, Marj's, 98
Hot shrimp rolls, 9
Hot tomato zip, 12
Hummingbird cake, 115
"Hurry-up" meals, 4

Ice-box lemon cream sherbet, 144
Ice cream
  dreamy delight (quantity recipe), 167
  fruit, 143
  pie, chocolate mint, 110
  vanilla, Carita's, 143
Ice, cranberry, 144
"In the season thereof" recipes, 3
Irish soda bread, 93

Jam cookies, 125
Jellied fruit salad, 21
Jell-O, ribbon, 136
Jiffy lemon sauce, 141
Joan's lemonade cookies, 125
Jumbo raisin cookies, 126

Korean vegetable salad, 24
Krispie oatmeal cookies, 124

Large groups, cooking and buying for, 161
Large party meals, instructions for, 157
LaRue's sugarplum pudding, 133
LaRue's Yorkshire pudding, 81
Lasagna (quantity recipe), 162
Layered "masked" salad, 24
Layered spinach and noodle casserole, 40
Lettuce salad, garden, with cream and sugar, 23
Lemon
  angel pie, 112
  butter cream frosting, 121
  chess pie, 109
  cream sherbet, 143 ·
  cream sherbet, ice-box, 144
  frosting, 128
  meringue party pie, 109
  meringue pie, 109
  -prune bars, 128
  pudding, Pearl's, 131
  sauce, jiffy, 141
  sponge squares, 129
Lemonade cookies, Joan's, 125
Lentil(s)
  baked, 37
  burgers, 36
  casserole, 37
Liquor in cooking, substitutions for, 170
Lima bean marinade, 30
Linzer cookies, 127
"Love thy neighbor" recipes, 1
Low-cal French fries, 38
"Low-energy" cooked wheat, 87
Luncheons, Relief Society, 157-59

Macaroni (quantity recipe), 162
Main meal vegetable soup, 13
Maple-apple flan, 108
Maple butter, 103
Maraschino cherries, 152
Marinade
  all-purpose, 29
  lima bean, 30
  sole, 59
  West Coast, for beef, 83
Marinated vegetables, 29
  carrot salad, 29

lima bean marinade, 30
  vegetables, pickled, 30
  vegetables, super-deluxe, 30
Mary Lou's easy sticky ring, 100
Measuring, 168
Meatballs
  Middle East pilaf with, 52
  in mushroom sauce, 52
  sweet and sour, 51
Meatloaf, best-ever, 52
"Meet together often" recipes, 1-2
Menu suggestions for Relief Society luncheons, 159-60
Meringue
  cookies, 111
  French chocolate, 112
  pie, lemon, 107
  shells, 111
Meuniere sauce, 58
Mexican platter dip, 6
Mexican skillet, 54
Middle East pilaf with meatballs, 52
Mincemeat, green tomato, 151
Minestrone, quick, 15
Mints, pulled butter, 148
Mock sour cream, 86
Molded ambrosia, 136
Molded salads
  avocado strawberry ring, 20
  chicken in gelatin, 26
  cranberry and turkey ring, 26
  jellied fruit, 21
  orange pecan, 20
  pineapple cottage cheese, 20
  pineapple-grapefruit, 20
  shrimp, 21
  sour cream and cucumber, 20
  spinach-cottage cheese, 19
Mousse, blender chocolate, 134
Muffins
  Arlean's molasses refrigerator, 94
  bran, 94
  eggnog gems, 95
  wheat, 94
Mushrooms
  noodles with, 37
  peas à la, 38
  stuffed, 37
Mustard
  -dill sauce, 59
  ring, 83
  sauce for beef, 83
  sauce, whipped cream, 83

Never-fail pie crust, 106
New Orleans shrimp salad, 27
Noels, 126
Noodle-beef-vegetable casserole (quantity recipe), 162
Noodles: egg, 87
  with mushrooms, 37

Nut bread, orange, 93
Nut loaf, Danish, 92
Nuts, spiced, 149

Oatmeal
    cookies, 124
    cookies, chewy, 124
    cookies, krispie, 124
    cookies, waffle-iron, 130
    crisps, 124
Old-fashioned cooked potato salad
    dressing, 24
Old-fashioned rice pudding, 131
Old-fashioned tomato preserves, 154
Old-time Christmas pudding, 131
Old-time poundcake, 116
Olive-nut cheese ball, 5
Omelet
    fluffy, 77
    cheese, 77
Onion soup, French, 14
Onions
    and zucchini, peas with, 38
    and potatoes, campfire, 39
Orange
    bread (variation of Beaten batter
        coffee cake), 101
    chicken delicious, 72
    cream cheese frosting, 113
    fruit soup, 137
    Julia, 11
    nut bread, 93
    pecan salad, 20
Orleans rice and vegetable bake, 44
Oven-barbecued pork roast, 54
Oven-barbecued spareribs, 54
Oven-barbecued turkey, 74
Oyster pan roast, 64

Pancakes
    blender, 96
    cottage cheese, 96
    delicate dessert, 96
    summer corn cakes, 96
Party meals, instructions for, 157
Party shrimp casserole, 63
Pasta with beans, 34
Pastas (quantity recipe), 162
Pastry
    basic, directions for making, 105
    basic, 106
    never-fail, 106
Paté, chicken liver, 8
Peach(es)
    almond-baked, 142
    cardinale, 141
    chutney, quick, 85
    or plum chutney, 153
    pie, Afton's fresh, 107
    quick spiced, 86

Peanut brittle and caramel corn, 145
Peanut butter chews, 149
Peanut butter cups, 148
Peanut butter fudge frosting,
    Marilyn's, 123
Pearl's lemon pudding, 131
Peas à la mushrooms, 38
Peas with onions and zucchini, 38
Pears in lemon-butter sauce, 142
Pecan
    -coconut bars, 130
    filling, 128
    peach shortcake, brown sugar, 118
    pie cookies, 128
    pie, southern, 107
    spread, 8
Pepper steak with rice, 50
Phyllis's whole wheat bread, 97
Pickled beets, 152
Pickles
    delicious sweet, 153
    dill, fresh-pack, 152
    dilly beans, fresh-pack, 153
Picnic cake, 114
Picnic potato salad, 24
Pie crust. See Pastry
Pie filling, home-canned
    apple, 151
    sour cherry, 151
Pie, salmon, 61
Pies (dessert)
    apple, 107
    apple, quick cookie, 108
    basic cream, 106
    basic fresh fruit, 110
    berry angel, 112
    butterscotch, 108
    cheesecake, 138
    chocolate mint ice cream, 110
    cream puff, glazed, 111
    lemon angel, 112
    lemon chess, 109
    lemon meringue, 109
    lemon meringue party, 109
    lime meringue, 109
    peach, Afton's, 107
    rhubarb surprise, 107
    southern pecan, 107
Pies for a crowd, turkey, 160
Pilaf with meatballs, Middle East, 52
Pilaf, Armenian, 88
Pineapple
    carrot cake, 113
    cottage cheese salad, 20
    eggnog punch, 10
    -grapefruit salad, 20
Piquant zucchini or summer squash,
    43
Pioneer cake, 114
Pioneer recipes, 4
Pioneer scalloped potatoes, 39

Pizza burgers, 53
Pizza, crusty French bread, 102
Plum or peach chutney, 153
Popcorn balls, 145
Popovers, 96
Poppy seed cake, 116
Pork
    and pears, cranberry, 54
    burgoo, 51
    chops, Hong Kong, 54
    chops over rice, 54
    Mexican skillet, 54
    roast, oven-barbecued, 54
    sausage fondue, 78
    spareribs, oven-barbecued, 54
    See also Ham
Potato
    bake, Farol's golden, 8
    salad for a crowd, 163
    salad, picnic, 24
    soup (poor man's soup), 13
Potatoes
    and onions, campfire, 39
    au gratin (quantity recipe), 164
    cottage, 38
    low-cal French fries, 38
    scalloped, pioneer, 39
    twice-baked, 39
Poundcake, old-time, 116
Powdered sugar glaze, glossy, 121
Praline frosting, 123
Preserves, old-fashioned tomato, 154
Puddings
    bread, 131
    cake, fruit cocktail, 115
    lemon, Pearl's, 131
    old-fashioned rice, 131
    old-time Christmas, 131
    puff (quantity recipe), 165
    sauce, vanilla, 134
    steamed, chocolate, 133
    sugar plum, LaRue's, 133
    tropical fruit, 133
Puff pie shell, 111
Puff pudding (quantity recipe), 165
Pulled butter mints, 148
Punch. See Beverages

Quantity cooking, 157-67
Quantity recipes
    apple crisp, 166
    applesauce cake, 167
    beef, roast, with brown gravy, 162
    beef stew, 162
    beef-vegetable-noodle casserole,
        162
    buttermilk brownies, 166
    cabbage salad, 164
    fruit and chicken salad, 164
    fruit coffee cake, 165
    ice cream dreamy delight, 167

lasagna, 163
potato salad for a crowd, 163
potatoes au gratin, 164
puff pudding, 165
rosy baked apples, 167
spaghetti, macaroni, other pastas, 163
salad bar, 165
turkey pies for a crowd, 160
Waldorf salad, 164
Quiche
blender, 78
Lorraine, 78
Quick recipes
beef goulash, 48
blue cheese dressing, 28
caramel frosting, 122
cookie apple pie, 108
corn chowder, 15
Italian hot rolls, 98
minestrone, 15
peach chutney, 85
sauerbraten, 47
spiced peaches, 86
vegetable medley, 44

Raisin cookies, jumbo, 126
Raisin cupcakes, 119
Raisin-filled cookies, easy, 126
Raspberry
fruit soup, 137
jam from green tomatoes, 152
peach cardinale, 140
ruby grapefruit, 140
ruby sauce, 140
ruby strawberries, 140
ruby sherbet, 140
Raw cranberry relish, 86
Refrigerator cake, cherry-topped, 135
Refrigerator rolls, cornmeal, 98
Relief Society luncheons, 157-59
Relish
confetti corn, 86
fresh vegetable, 31
garden, 154
raw cranberry, 86
Rhubarb surprise pie, 108
Ribbon Jell-O, 136
Ribbon sandwiches, 9
Rice
almond, 72
and vegetable bake, Orleans, 44
deluxe brown, 88
exotic oven, 87
Far East, 88
green, 89
green and yellow, 88
Roast beef with brown gravy (quantity recipe), 162
Rock Cornish hens, 74; broiled, 74
Rocky Road cake, chocolate, 115

Rocky Road frosting, 115
Rocky Road fudge, 147
Rolls, dinner
cornmeal refrigerator, 98
Farol's butterflake, 97
golden yam, 99
Marj's hot, 98
pan, easy, 97
quick Italian, 98
Viola's sour cream twists, 99
Rolls, sweet
basic sweet dough, 100
beaten batter, 101
bubble wreath, 100
easy brioche, 100
Mary Lou's easy sticky ring, 100
Romaine salad
creamy, 23
supreme, 23
Rosy baked apples (quantity recipe), 167
Rote grutze (fruit soup), 137; easy (raspberry), 137
Roux (variation of White sauce), 85
Ruby grapefruit, 140
Ruby peach cardinale, 141
Ruby (raspberry) sauce, 140
Ruby sherbet, 140
Ruby strawberries, 140

Salad bar (quantity recipe), 165
Salad dressings
blue cheese, quick, 28
cole slaw, 25
creamy, for fruit salad, 29
French, Aunt Molly's delicious, 29
French, for fruit salad, 21
green goddess, 28
honey, for fruit salad, 28
lemon, creamy, 29
Louis, 28
old-fashioned cooked (for potato salad), 24
Salad sandwiches, 28
Salads
buffet, 25
cabbage (quantity recipe), 164
cantaloupe, 21
carrot, marinated, 29
chicken, exotic, 25
chicken curry, with fruit, 27
chicken fruit, 26
chicken in gelatin, 26
crab and avocado, 27
cranberry and turkey, ring, 26
fruit and chicken (quantity recipe), 164
garden lettuce with cream and sugar, 21
gelatin, instructions for preparing, 19

jellied fruit, 21
Korean vegetable, 24
layered "masked," 24
lima bean marinade, 30
marinated vegetables, 29, 30
orange pecan, 20
pickled marinated vegetables, 30
pineapple cottage cheese, 20
pineapple-grapefruit, 20
potato, for a crowd, 163
potato, picnic, 24
Romaine, creamy, 23
romaine supreme, 23
salmon, 27
shrimp, molded, 21
shrimp, New Orleans, 27
slaw, seven-day, 25
spinach, with mandarin oranges, 23
spinach-cottage cheese, molded, 19
sweet-sour, 25
tabouli (cracked wheat), 28
three-bean, 30
turkey, and green grape, 27
turkey supreme, 26
vegetable relish, fresh, 31
Waldorf (quantity recipe), 164
Waldorf, holiday, 21
wilted greens, 23
Salmon
bake, golden, 61
loaf, 61
pie, 61
salad, 27
soup, 16
steaks in mustard-dill sauce, 58
Sandwiches
pinwheel, date-nut, 10
ribbon, 9
salad, 28
turkey or chicken, 76
Sassy slush, 11
Sour cream
mock, 86
twists, Viola's, 99
Sour cherry pie filling, home-canned, 151
Southern pecan pie, 107
Southern-style divinity, 147
Spaghetti
primavera, 44
quantity recipe, 162
speedy, 53
squash, 40
with white clam sauce, 64
Spanish cake, 118
Spanish chicken casserole, 72
Spanish sauce, 83
Spanish wheat, 87
Speedy spaghetti, 53

Spiced nuts, 149
Spiced peaches, quick, 86
Spicy fruit, warm, 140
Spinach
    and noodle casserole, layered, 40
    baked, 35
    salad with mandarin oranges, 23
Split pea soup, 13
Squash
    baked summer, 41
    piquant summer, 43
    soup, butternut, 15
    spaghetti, 40
Squaw corn, 36
Steamed chocolate pudding, 133
Stew, beef (quantity recipe), 162
Stick ring, Mary Lou's, 100
Stir-fry dinner, 45
Storage foods, recipe suggestions
    for using, 3
Strawberries, ruby, 140
Strawberry cake with strawberry
    frosting, 118
Strawberry dessert, heavenly fresh,
    137
Stretch the chicken, 65
Stretch the ham, 55
Stretch the turkey, 66-68
"Strictly elegant" recipes, 4
Stuffed mushrooms, 37
Substitutions and equivalents, 171
Sugarplum frosting, 123
Sugarplum pudding, LaRue's, 133
Summer corn cakes, 96
Surprise balls, 127
Surprise fresh fruit treat, 138
Swedish baked beans, 33
Sweet and sour meatballs, 51
Sweet and sour salad, 25
Sweet and sour turkey wings, 75
Sweet pickles, 153
Sweet potatoes and apples, 40
Swiss steak, 47
Swordfish steak meuniere, 58

Tabouli (cracked wheat) salad, 28
Tacos, Althea's, 52
Tangy garlic and sour cream
    marinated chicken, 71
Tapioca, baked apples, 142
Tart, fresh fruit, 110
Tasty egg dip, 6

Terms, definitions of, 168
Three-bean salad, 30
Three-fruit slush, 11
Thirty-minute hamburger buns, 99
Toasts, butterscotch pecan, 101
Tomato
    bouillon, 12
    mincemeat, green, 151
    preserves, old-fashioned, 154
    soup, cream of, 15
    soup, fresh, 14
    zip, hot, 12
Tomatoes
    baked stuffed, 41
    cottage-fried, 41
    green, raspberry jam from, 152
Tropical cooler, 10
Tropical fruit pudding, 133
Trout, canned, 155
Trout almondine, 58
Tuna-vegetable casserole, 63
Turkey
    and dressing, scalloped, 74
    and green grape salad, 26
    and ham tetrazzini, 75
    biscuit roll, 76
    creole, 75
    enchilada, 76
    for many meals, 68
    good-bye, 76
    oven-barbecued, 74
    pies for a crowd, 160
    sandwich fillings, 76
    soup, 17
    stretch the, 66-68
    turnovers, 77
    wings, sweet and sour, 75
Twice-baked potatoes, 39

Vanilla ice cream, Carita's, 143
Vanilla pudding sauce, 134
Vegetable(s)
    all purpose sauce for, 89
    combo, ever-ready, 45
    dip, curry, 6
    dip, fresh, 6
    marinated, 29-30
    medley, ham and, 56
    medley, quick, 44
    medleys, 43
    -noodle-beef casserole (quantity
        recipe), 162

relish or salad, fresh, 31
    ring, green and gold, 44
    salads, 23-25, 31
    soup, 13
    stir-fry dinner, 45
    See also individual vegetables
Viola's sour cream twists, 99

Waffle-iron brownies, 130
Waffle-iron oatmeal cookies, 130
Waldorf salad
    holiday, 21
    quantity recipe, 164
Warm spicy fruit, 140
Wassail, wonderful, 12
Water, boiling in, altitude
    adjustments for, 169
Weights and measures, 170
Wheat
    cracked, salad (tabouli), 28
    "low-energy" cooked, 87
    muffins, 94
    Spanish, 87
    thins, 101
Whipped cream mustard sauce, 83
White sauce, 85
Wilted greens, 23
Wine in cooking, substitutions for,
    170
Wonderful wassail, 12

Yam and sausage casserole, 57
Yam rolls, golden, 99
Yams, candied, and apples, 39
Yams in orange sauce, 40
Year's supply, recipe suggestions for
    using, 3
Yorkshire pudding, 81
    custard type, 81
    LaRue's, 81
Yummy cheesecake pie, 138
Yummy chocolate mint, 142

Zucchini
    and green chili casserole, 42
    and onions, barbecued, 42
    bread, 92
    casserole, 43
    crisps, egg-fried, 42
    goop, Hellberg's, 42
    layers, 43
    peas with onions and, 38
    piquant, 43